Dearest Beatie My Darling Jack

Dearest Beatie My Darling Jack

A VICTORIAN COUPLE'S LOVE LETTERS

WILLOW BOOKS
COLLINS
8 Grafton Street
London
1983

TO ALL THOSE WHO CAN'T EVER THROW ANYTHING OUT

Willow Books
William Collins Sons & Co Ltd
London · Glasgow · Sydney
Auckland · Toronto · Johannesburg

First published in Great Britain 1983

© Elizabeth Anne Power/Rosalie Vicars-Harris/David Fordham 1983

Conceived, edited & designed by
Rosalie Vicars-Harris & David Fordham
New Media Publishing Ltd, 38 Bourne Street, London, SW1W 8JA

Dearest Beatie – My Darling Jack
1. Great Britain – Social life & customs – 19th century
I. Vicars-Harris, Rosalie
941.081   DA560

ISBN 0 00 218015 4

Filmset by SX Composing Ltd, Rayleigh, Essex
Printed in Great Britain by William Collins Sons & Co Ltd, Glasgow

Editor's Note:
In attempting to retain the charm and authenticity of the original letters, with their idiosyncrasies and inconsistencies, it has meant that certain oddities of language, punctuation and spelling have been retained. It was typical of Beatrice that she considered Sunday the only day of the week to warrant a capital letter and that, despite many letters from her friend signed Aimée, Beatrice consistently used a grave accent, as did the engraver of her silver charm. Some letters from the collection have been excluded but where these and short passages from within the letters have been cut, the content, where relevant, has been incorporated in a caption.

The editor and designer would like to thank the many relations and friends of Jack and Beatrice who have kindly helped in the search for photographs and information, in particular Anne Power and Peter Hughes. Despite numerous enquiries, however, sadly, perhaps the most important photograph of all is still to be found – the photograph taken by Mr. Pym, the Streatham photographer, of Jack and Beatrice's wedding. Perhaps it will now come to light.

The photograph on the previous page shows some of the main characters in Jack and Beatrice's story at a happier and more settled time in their lives. It was taken on Visitor's Day at the annual camp of the Warwickshire Yeomanry, to which Jack's brother Joe, standing centre, belonged. The visitors, seated from left to right, were Phelps and Ida, Jack and Beatrice. (T)

Contents

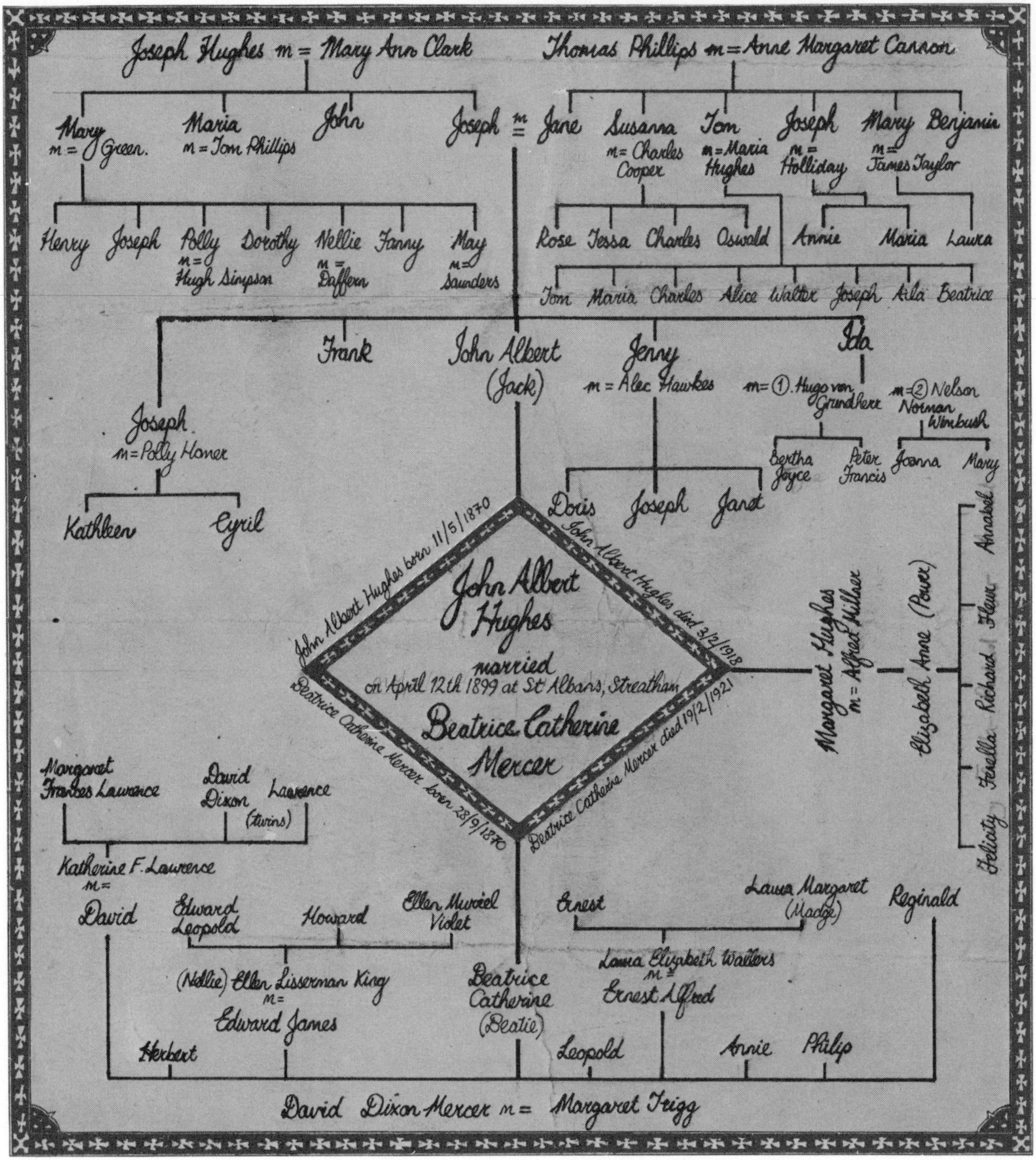
Joseph Hughes m = Mary Ann Clark
Thomas Phillips m = Anne Margaret Cannon
Mary m = Green.
Maria m = Tom Phillips
John
Joseph m = Jane
Susanna m = Charles Cooper
Tom m = Maria Hughes
Joseph m = Holliday
Mary m = James Taylor
Benjamin
Henry
Joseph
Polly m = Hugh Simpson
Dorothy
Nellie m = Daffern
Fanny
May m = Saunders
Rose
Tessa
Charles
Oswald
Annie
Maria
Laura
Tom
Maria
Charles
Alice
Walter
Joseph
Aila
Beatrice
Frank
John Albert (Jack)
Jenny m = Alec Hawkes
Ida
m = (1) Hugo von Grundherr
m = (2) Nelson Norman Wimbush
Joseph m = Polly Honer
Bertha Joyce
Peter Francis
Joanna
Mary
Kathleen
Cyril
Doris
Joseph
Janet
John Albert Hughes born 11/5/1870
John Albert Hughes died 3/2/1918
John Albert Hughes
married
on April 12th 1899 at St Albans, Streatham
Beatrice Catherine Mercer
Beatrice Catherine Mercer born 28/9/1870
Beatrice Catherine Mercer died 19/2/1921
Margaret Hughes m = Alfred Millner
Elizabeth Anne (Power)
Annabel
Fleur
Richard
Fenella
Felicity
Margaret Frances Lawrence
David Dixon
Lawrence
(twins)
Katherine F. Lawrence m =
David
Edward Leopold
Howard
Ellen Muriel Violet
Ernest
Laura Margaret (Madge)
Reginald
(Nellie) Ellen Lisserman King m =
Edward James
Beatrice Catherine (Beatie)
Laura Elizabeth Walters m =
Ernest Alfred
Herbert
Leopold
Annie
Philip
David Dixon Mercer m = Margaret Trigg

Introduction

TO JACK HUGHES & BEATRICE MERCER

John Albert Hughes (Jack) was born in Castle Bromwich, near Birmingham, in 1870, the youngest son of Joseph Hughes who died when Jack was aged eighteen. Jack therefore became a junior partner in the family metal business, also run by Jack's widowed mother, his Uncle John and brother Joe. Jack also had another brother, Frank, with an 'affliction', and two sisters, Jennie married to Alec, and schoolgirl sister Ida. The Hughes family were living at Linwood Lodge by 1898. This was a large detached house in Gravelly Hill, north Birmingham.

Beatrice Mercer was born the same year as Jack – in suburban London. Beatrice led the life of a genteel young woman, the only daughter of David Dixon Mercer whose family has been associated with the Royal Navy and with Rothschild's banking firm for generations. Beatrice had two elder brothers, David with the Royal Marines, and Ted, married to Nellie. Her younger brothers, Ernie and Reg, lived at home at 'Roselea', Thrale Road, Streatham Park. Granny, Mrs. Mercer's mother, also lived with the family.

A photograph of Jack's grandfather, founder of the Albion Metal Works in 1830. He began the business as a brass caster in Potter Street, then became a brass and iron caster and moved to Aston Street with his two sons. Joe and John moved the business to Woodcock Street after his death in 1880. (V)

Marriage Certificate.

EDGBASTON, IN THE COUNTY OF WARWICK.

Joseph Hughes   of *this* Parish,
Bachelor

and   *Mary Ann Clark*   of *this* Parish,
Spinster

were married in this Church by *Banns* this *twentieth* Day of *July* in the Year one thousand eight hundred and *thirty-four*

By me, *Charles Pixell Vicar*

This Marriage was solemnized between us {*Joseph Hughes* / *Mary Ann Clark*}

In the presence of {*Elizabeth Hodson's + mark* / *James Hodson + mark*}

No. *127*

I certify, that the above is a true extract from the Register of the Parish of Edgbaston, in the County of Warwick, taken this *20th* day of *July* 18 *34*

Charles Pixell Vicar

The marriage certificate of Jack's grandfather, Joseph Hughes. The story that has been handed down in the family that he started his own business as a result of getting the sack for taking the day off to get married, is refuted by the evidence of this, dated 1834. (A)

The silver match box case, engraved with Jack's initials which Beatrice sent to Jack "as a token of my appreciation of your many kindnesses to me", and to mark the occasion of his twenty-eighth birthday. By this time they had corresponded only occasionally and had stayed with each other's families once. (A)

Jack and Beatrice's correspondence began in March 1898 and Beatrice's letter of March 28th was the first Jack decided to keep. It referred to Jack's coming visit to 'Roselea' at Easter and Beatrice politely thanked him for his "kindness to me during my stay with your Mother" and for Jack looking after her so well. Little did she know then that would be the last time she would be invited to Linwood Lodge, Jack's home.

Linwood Lodge, May 12th 1898

My dear Beat

When I got up on Tuesday morning to a dull wet morning, and an almost empty house, I thought, well, this is a nice birthday. I got through the day without anyone wishing me the old stereotyped "Many happy returns", and naturally came to the conclusion that I was the only one aware of the fact of it being the anniversary of my natal day. But, when I got home in the evening, and saw the little packet from you I found there was someone as aware of the occasion as myself. When I opened it and read your letter and saw the present, I felt quite pleased that it was my birthday.

Well Beat, you are a little Brick, excuse the term.

I like the Box very much, pray accept my best thanks.

I shall value it much, and whenever I take it out to light the fragrant weed always think of the giver. I suppose your Ma is now at home, and "Roselea" has assumed its usual aspect. I trust she is strong and well now. Joe went up to Warwick for training, yesterday; so I am having a busy time this and next week.

However, as "all work and no play makes Jack a dull boy" I am taking a little relaxation tomorrow night in the way of a visit to The Empire. Gus Elen is there this week. I am glad to know your bike is approaching completion. We have not had much cycling the last fortnight, but weather permitting a select party is going to Stratford-on-Avon on Saturday, returning via Warwick and Kenilworth on Sunday. It is a lovely little trip, about 55 miles round, and most beautiful country. I wish you were coming. Well, Beat for the present, Au revoir and again many thanks. With best love to yourself and all

Yours very sincerely

Jack

I have already used the box several times.

Conscious that she barely knew Jack, Beatrice asked him to "Excuse my little lecture", fully expecting him to think "what cheek", but that her reason for it was that she "felt sorry that a good fellow was being spoilt", by playing billiards on a Sunday.

Just prior to Jack's birthday Beatrice had written to Jack: "I don't see that a friend who would ask you to play billiards on a Sunday is any good for you, and I cannot understand you doing it Jack. Don't do it, you are too good for that sort of thing, for you do know better, leave it to the poor creatures who do not know right from wrong." Even so, she admitted missing Jack a great deal, but still signed her letters, "Yours sincerely, Beat."

Beatie Disappointed By Jack's Mother
JUNE & JULY

The first of many family problems caused by Jack's mother on the occasion of their otherwise idyllically happy engagement. The circumstances surrounding the cause for the torn up letter do nothing to ease Beatrice's feelings at not being welcomed into Jack's family. Beatrice's love for Jack, despite everything, continues to be unshaken . . .

Linwood Lodge, June 3rd 1898

My own Dear Beat

Of course you heard this morning of my safe arrival in B'ham last night, but I do hope you didn't mind the card, but I sent that because you would get it earlier than I could wire. Well dear, I came home on the 10.30 train last night, and to my surprise Mother came by it too. As we walked up from the station it was a lovely evening, so quiet, and not a person about. I kissed her and told her of our engagement. She did not appear to be very much surprised to hear of it, and after we had talked for a few moments could not but say that I had won a good girl and that she was pleased. She will be more than pleased though for she will be proud of you, proud as I shall love. In fact, they all will. Joe congratulated me and so did poor old Frank, poor chap you know how strange he is. I have seen Ida today and she is pleased. Nin does not know yet, but Ida will be telling her tonight. It does seem, hard that I should have to leave you so soon, in fact almost the moment our engagement is settled, but never mind love I am looking forward to the 17th when I shall be with you again. I placed your photo in my room last night and kissed it before going to bed, it was the first thing for me to see when I woke this morning, and I kissed it again. But dear I must say that I would have given anything to have kissed your sweet self instead of the Photo.

I have got a nice frame for it today. I was the first in the house to get up this morning, and you cannot know how bright I felt as I went to business. Everyone at the Works was pleased to see me this morning, and one or two remarked that they were afraid something had happened as I was away so long. They little dream what has happened, but my dear I am sure it is the best thing I have done in my life. I have been a better man for knowing you. A man is a poor thing alone, but under the influence of a good woman any good qualities he may have are developed. Beat I know you have given yourself to me and I shall now have no thought but for you. Your happiness will be mine. Kiss dear Laura for me, she is a little woman, and I can never forget the part she has played between us. God knows but for her I may have lost you, but now I have

The charming wooden oval frame which Jack chose still holds Beatrice's same picture today – his one precious reminder of her over the months of their separation. Jack had not been engaged before and had shown few signs of ever marrying. (A)

Beatrice was twenty-seven when she became engaged to Jack. It was her second engagement and was considered much more suitable than the previous one.

Ted was Beatrice's elder brother Edward, married four years previously, to Nellie. Laura was Beatrice's younger brother Ernest's sweetheart whose large family, the Wallers, lived in Barry Road, Dulwich, where the Mercers lived before moving to Streatham Park.

won you. I shall be glad when I come to you on the 17th and bring you the ring dear, and how happy we shall be together when we meet all your friends the next day. I asked mother to write you a nice letter Beatie, and she promised me she would. Perhaps you will get it the same post as this.

What do Ted and Nellie think of it all. I suppose they know by this (time). I met two Hooligans this morning and the first thing they asked was whether I was engaged. I told them, yes, to the best little woman in the World. There is a Hooligan Ride tomorrow, of course love you will not mind me going will you. I know you won't, for I feel that you have the utmost confidence in me. When you come down to B'ham you can come to a Hooligan's Bicycle ride and shew them how to ride, and when I am introducing you to all my friends as the Mrs. Jack of the near future it will be indeed a happy time.

I am writing your Ma tonight but really don't know how to thank her dear self and your good Pa for their ready consent which they gave. Well dear I know you will be glad to know how my Mother received the news. I shall think especially of you on Sunday and look out for your sweet letter Monday morning. With fondest love to your dear self and Laura

Yours ever
Jack

Margaret Mercer, Beatrice's mother, was adored by the family and each of her children named one of their own daughters after her. She suffered a weak heart and her hair turned grey early in life – perhaps not surprisingly as she had given birth to nine children, four of whom died in infancy, mostly from jaundice or heart trouble. Beatrice was her only surviving daughter. (A)

"Roselea", Streatham Park. June 4th 1898

Dearest Jack

I was delighted to get your kind letter.

I must confess I was taken very much by surprise when you asked for Beatie: as I had always regarded Joe, and yourself as staunch old Bachelors, proof against the charms of any girl.

I could not but admire the manly straight forward way you approached Pa and myself on the subject. And my heart went out to you at once. I felt you were twin souls, meant for each other.

I am certain if you are both spared: you have a *very very* happy future before you. How differently I feel towards you than I did on a former occasion when I was asked to give my consent which I did *most* reluctantly.

My heart went up in profound thankfulness, that this time the man of her choice was one I could both respect, and love, and I shall not be afraid to trust our dear girl to the keeping of such a man good, and true altho' of course I am selfish enough to hope the day is far distant when you will claim your Bride.

I was very glad to hear the engagement met with your mother's approval. That was my only objection, in case she should not be pleased but that being removed I shall look upon you as our own dear Son and I hope you will spare a little corner in your heart for me.

We shall look forward to welcome you on the 17th and hope to spend a happy time together. With fondest love. Believe me

Lovingly Yours
M. Mercer

"Roselea", June 5th 1898

My own darling Jack

I received your letter card and dear letter, on friday morning and saturday morning. Please do not apologise for the card, I was only too delighted to know you arrived safely Jack dear, it seems months instead of days, since we parted. I have so wished you were here, I feel as if I could scarcely bear it. Of course as you may imagine I am delighted to hear that your Mother approves of me, for her future daughter in law, and I hope we shall always be the best of friends. I don't think she will have cause to find fault with me, as regards my duty and love to you, for I do love you dear most devotedly and you know it, don't you? I am simply longing for the 17th but it does seem such a fearful time to look forward to and I don't know how I shall let you leave me again, it will be agony.

Ted and Nellie are delighted and wish me to tell you so, they are here today and little Leo said to me, "Where's Uncle Jack" and "me going to hold Arnie's puff puff"! Nellie had told him I was going to marry you and that Leo was to be my train bearer, isn't he a funny little thing. What a lovely day you had for your parade, I hope you got on alright. I should have liked to have been there, to have seen you. I have had three such nice letters of congratulation. I must shew them to you when you come. I am proud of you Jack, and I think I am a very lucky girl to have got such a good kind and true lover as I know you will be. I hope Jennie is pleased, did you go there today? If you can try and write to me often, it will give me such joy for I do feel so lonely without you dear. I hope your mother will write to me, I have not heard yet.

Well dear I must close now, or I shall go on filling reams of paper telling you how much I love you and how proud I am of such a dear good fellow as you are, and that might make you vain, and I don't want to do that. Heaps of my dearest love and a sweet good night kiss.

Yours devotedly Beatie

Linwood Lodge, June 7th 1898

My own Dearest Beatie

I was so glad to receive your letter yesterday. It was a real treat and I have read and re-read it, in fact I read it until I could fancy that you were speaking the words to me. It is very hard that we should be so far from each other, dear, and I like yourself feel that it is ages since we parted. But never mind love we will see each other as often as possible, and when we cannot do that we will write to each other, I quite feel with what joy you would always receive a letter from me, and you cannot overestimate the comfort which your letters will bring to me, dear.

It will not be long to the 17th now Beatie. I have made arrangements about the ring. I have said I want a good one with five diamonds in, graduated, and in claw setting, I am going to bring several up with me for you to choose from.

There was no reason why Jack's mother should not approve of Beatrice's social standing. Beatrice was presented at court as a debutante in the 1880s. She wore a gown with a court train and ostrich feathers in her hair.

Fine Brilliant Half-Hoop Ring
18-carat Gold Mount, £33 15s.

Beatrice's diamonds are still in the family today but the five large stones have been split up to make several rings. (B)

Jack was just twenty-nine when he became engaged. He was the youngest surviving son, his mother having borne twelve children, seven of whom died young, mostly from an hereditary disease. (A)

I know dear that when you say my Mother will never have cause to find fault with you, that you are right. My dear Beatie, I know you love me and will be a good wife to me, if I did not know that I would never had told you of my love. But we do love each other Beatie, and have given ourselves to each other, and shall live for each other and who shall be happier than we. I am so glad to know that Ted and Nellie are pleased to hear of our engagement. I had a nice letter from Nellie this morning. She says you "are a girl in ten thousand", but Beatie that is putting it too mildly you are the best girl in the World.

Jennie and Alec are pleased with the news, and told me they hope we shall be as happy as they. I feel we shall be that Beatie. It is a funny thing do you know, darling, that I had never thought of getting married, until some considerable time after Nin and Alec were settled down, and then I used to feel when I went to see them, like a fish out of water. Here, I used to think, are a couple as happy as possible, and was afraid that such happiness could never be for me. But thank goodness I was mistaken, for Beatie you have come into my life like a star and made me the happiest man alive, and now I look upon ourselves as soon to be as happy a couple as those I often envied.

You are right dear we did have a lovely day on Sunday for the Parade, but it was almost too lovely. It was very hot indeed, and I have been far from well since last Friday, and the heat and the 3 mile march each way rather upset me. However, I am feeling better just now. My comrades little think that that was the last occasion on which I shall march to Church with them, but never mind that Beatie, you are my comrade now and I am looking forward to the time when there will be a special service for us.

I had a nice letter from your Ma on Sunday morning. She is too good though, for I don't think I am half as good as she says. But dearest, I had a good Father. I am sure there never could be a more upright man, and he set us all an example which I have ever done my best to follow. How far I have succeeded, well that is for others to say. Joe went to Manchester early this morning, and if he can get back in time would like to come up to "Roselea" on Thursday evening.

I am afraid Beatie, that he has given your Pa a lot of trouble over his tickets, but then that is characteristic of Joe.

Well darling thank your Ma for her kind letter, and with all my love and a sweet kiss. Believe me

Yours ever

Jack

❖❖❖❖❖❖

"Roselea", June 8th 1898

My own dear Jack

I feel I must have a chat with you on paper, for I feel so put out and miserable, because your Mother has not written to me and Ma says she cannot allow me to enter a family that would not receive me kindly. I felt sure your Mother would not like it, although she has always been most kind to me. I do hope she will write it would make such a difference to my feelings. I feel so dreadfully miserable I do wish you were here to soothe me. How are you dear? I hope better, mind you must take great care of yourself now, for you are not your own, but *mine*. I do love to think of the jolly times we shall have and

Beatrice did, however, receive a congratulatory letter from Jennie, 'Nin', Jack's married sister. She "had begun to think that the boys would settle down into old bachelors (usually disagreeable kind of creatures)" and was very glad that Beatrice was "going to save him from that fate".

I picture all sorts of things for the future. I only wish we were nearer, it is hard to only be able to see you occasionally. I am simply longing for the 17th, but after then I dare not think about, for I shall not know when I shall see you again. When do you start for Camp? It is exceedingly good of you to give me such a lovely ring, as I know it will be, but don't bother to bring several, I should like it much better to be your choice, I am bound to like it and I am longing to get it. I hope I am not answering this too soon, but it is a little comfort to me so I feel sure you will not mind. We went to the Albert Hall yesterday to the Masonic boys' prize giving, we were quite close to the Prince and Princess and heard every word that the Prince said. The Princess looked so sweet and so young and she has got such a pretty figure. I am going round to Nellie's this afternoon to see the children, I am glad she wrote to you, but I am afraid she said too much, I am not worthy of so much praise. I have had such nice letters from my friends, I am keeping them for you to read, in fact I intend keeping them always. You say it was seeing Alec and Jennie settled that made you think of marriage, I shall always be grateful to them and especially that I am the girl of your choice. Only wait, we will shew people what a happy couple are like, won't we dear. I hope we shan't have to wait long, don't think me forward for saying so, but I mean, so that I shall always be with you, and be yours wholly for ever.

Just fancy my bike was only geared 4–3 – no wonder I did the hills better, and he is also going to re-enamel it again for me, so that is very fair of him, don't you think so? You must try and write as often as you can, I really can't bear to wait for so long for a letter, as we arranged, I shall always answer your letters as soon as I can, so as to get back an answer, all the sooner. Well my dearie I think I must be off, if only you were with me, I do wish you were, we could have a lovely embrace and I do need comforting. Au revoir, darling

Yours most devotedly Beatie

What do your friends think about your engagement, weren't they surprised, especially the Harrops.

◇◇◇◇◇◇◇

Linwood Lodge, June 9th 1898

My own darling Beatie

It has grieved me very much that my Mother has not written to you long before this, and I can quite understand your feelings on the matter, also your Ma's, for of course she must feel most anxiously.

I have asked Mother every day if she had written to you, dearest, and she has said "No, not yet, but I will do so." Do you know, Beatie, the very first night I came home, the last thing I did was to ask Mother to write you a nice letter, and she promised she would, and yet all this time has gone by without you receiving a line from her. Really, it is anything but proper. But, Beatie, I have asked again today, and she promised to write tonight, so I suppose, and sincerely hope, that you will hear tomorrow morning, same time as this arrives. Still although she has not written, earlier, I am sure you need not fear but that my Mother entertains the best affections towards your dear self. I do hope Beatie you will hear in the morning, as promised, and that your Ma and your sweet

The masonic boys' prize giving that Beatrice attended at the Albert Hall was for the sons of freemasons who were deceased or had fallen on hard times. The Prince of Wales, to whom Beatrice sat so close, was Grand Patron of the Royal Masonic Institution for Boys. In 1902, following the death of Victoria the previous year, he was crowned Edward VII. The Princess with the "pretty figure" was Princess Alexandra. Both Beatrice's family and Jack's were notable freemasons.

One of the many congratulatory letters Beatrice did receive on her engagement. This one was from her cousin Frank, who warned her not to be nervous and ends his letter, "No kisses allowed to be sent now I guess." The Harrop family were Jack's best friends and Jack's engagement would have caused them much excitement. (A)

The Banquet Jack referred to was the Centenary Festival for the Royal Masonic Institution for Boys, in the presence of the Prince of Wales. The school needed to raise funds for new school buildings. An announcement made at the banquet revealed that a record £133,000 in total had been subscribed.

self will feel more comfortable, for I cannot bear to hear of your being otherwise.

Thank Goodness, I am feeling A.1. now, as regards myself. I will take your advice, dear, about the ring and instead of bringing several, will choose *the* one myself. I am glad you can place such reliance on my choice. Fancy still a week to the 17th. Our Brigade will go into Camp the first week in August this year, as usual. I suppose I must go, in fact at present I don't see how I can very well get out of it, but we can talk all about that dear when I come up next week. I am glad you enjoyed your visit to The Albert Hall. I suppose you are not taking a seat to view the Banquet though tomorrow evening dear. I am glad dearest to know that you are receiving such nice letters from your friends respecting our engagement, and it will be a real pleasure for me to read them when I come up.

You are right, Beatie, we will show people what a happy couple are like. I do assure you, sweetest one, there shall be nothing wanting so far as I am concerned. We can pull together, Beatie, I am sure, and I am quite as anxious for the time when we shall be always together as you can be. I am going to make a confession now Beatie. I was not at home to receive your letter this morning, as I was out all night. How badly it sounds, doesn't it but I stayed with Jack Harrop last night. It is their night at home on Wednesdays, and you know they like me to go, and would rather have me stay than come away same night, as the trains are so early. The Harrop boys are quite sincere in their congratulations, but the girls seem to take it rather coolly. They are all, however, very anxious to see you at Wylde Green when next you come to B'ham, and no one will be more proud than I when that happens. Please don't mind me going there Beatie, you have no cause to I am sure. I suppose Joe arrived at "Roselea" tonight, but it was very remiss of him, not to have written your Ma, on Wednesday night. Well, dearest, I suppose we ought not to wish the time to fly, but still I sigh roll on 17th. For the present Au Revoir, with all my fondest love.

I do hope you will feel better, sweetest, in the morning.

Yours for ever
Jack

Jack's brother Joe, the eldest surviving son aged thirty-two at this time, was also a partner in the family business. He was unmarried, though he had been engaged for a while ten years previously, and lived at home at Linwood Lodge. (T)

Does your Uncle know of our engagement?

"Roselea", June 10th 1898

My own dearest Jack

I half expected a letter from you this morning, and as you know I was not disappointed. Well dear, no letter from your Mother again but so long as it will not alter your feelings towards me, I am not going to care, although I must say, I think it most unkind of her. I suppose she thinks I am not good enough and I know I am not but if you think so that is all I care about. Jack dear don't think for one moment that I mind you going to Harrops, for I should be sorry if you did not. I can quite understand the girls not feeling very sweet towards me, for I expect they feel what a splendid fellow they have lost. I did once meet them all at New St. refreshment room, your Mother did not introduce me to the girls only to Jack and I must say I did not think much of them, but they may be alright. I am afraid I take dislike to some people when I ought not to. No I have not got a ticket to see the lion's feed tonight. I wish I had, for I am sure it will be a grand night. I had a very nice letter from Jennie yesterday and I appreciated it doubly being the first from your people. Pa is awfully excited about the affair tonight, he has not gone to business this morning.

I am glad you have decided to choose the ring, I shall like it ever so much better being your choice. It seems ages to look forward to the 17th, but thank goodness, only a week now. I shall be longing for the days to rush on. I am going to be very busy and so try to make the time go quicker. I am going out with Nellie this afternoon to the tailors. She is having a coat and skirt made at the same place, that I had mine made. Mrs. Morris was telling me the other afternoon how much she liked you, and took such a fancy to you, and she thought it so nice of you to kiss her as you did. Jack my darling I know everybody will like you of my friends they cannot help it. I know, you are my own Jack and I am so proud of your love. You will never have cause to regret it, and I know we shall be perfectly happy together but I don't see there is any prospect of my visiting your Mother again, when she does not approve of me. I don't know how we shall manage. You will have to get all ready by yourself.

Both of our servants are going, but we have been very lucky in getting Mrs. Atkins' cook and housemaid, and they are splendid girls, so that is allright. Mr. and Mrs. Morris and Nellie Morris are coming over tomorrow if fine for tennis, we started last saturday. Well my darling Jack I hope this is not too much of an epistle for you but accept all my love and many kisses

your most devoted
Beatie

The menu card and wine list for the Banquet. Beatrice was probably very wise to stay away from the Banquet, 'the lion's feed', at the Albert Hall, despite the grandeur of the Royal occasion, as she would only have been able to observe along with the other ladies. Some 5,000 people were present "including many ladies, who, however, did not dine with the brethren but occupied the gallery and tier of boxes below it". (C)

Linwood Lodge, Gravelly Hill. June 13th 1898

My own darling Beatie

Your dear letter came to hand on Saturday morning. I was delighted to hear from you again so soon, but still there was the same old annoyance, that you had not heard from my Mother. It was late on Friday night when I got home, and every one had gone off to bed. You know that oftentimes little notes are left for me, when they go to bed before I get home, and there was one that night. It was a sweet welcome one to me, dear, one from Mother, and it said "I have written to Beatie" and of course I understood from that, that you would receive a letter on Saturday morning. I trust that your Ma will now feel more comfortable, and I know dearest that you must feel so. But, how much nicer it would have been had you heard earlier, for you must then have appreciated it more, as being one's feelings expressed at the moment. I shall be most anxious Beatie to know how my Mother wrote to you, and what she had to say. My Mother is sometimes very funny I know, and it is certainly strange she did not write earlier. But still she is not half bad, in fact I can see almost every day evidence of some good she is doing. She has been very busy lately. I daresay Beatie you have seen old lady Chellingworth, some time when at B'ham, well, she has been very ill and my Mother has been going to see her, and now she is better and Mother had her at Linwood Lodge for a change for

Jack's mother, aged fifty-two by this time, had lost her husband ten years earlier. Her marriage had been a very happy and devoted one. Having had to bring up five children on her own as well as help run the family business she had become a forceful and 'difficult' woman to deal with.

Following the death of Jack's father, his Uncle John continued to be an influential senior partner in the Albion Metal Works alongside Jack's mother. He was a somewhat mysterious and quarrelsome old bachelor and was to become one of Jack and Beatrice's only allies – to be handled with extreme care.

the whole of last week. Then there is our poor cousin at Dodford, she has been ailing again and Mother has been over to comfort her a little, so she has been quite busy Beatie. I don't see any cause to think that my Mother could fancy you not good enough for me, and I trust her letter to you has dispelled any such idea, if you thought so. I know she cannot help but approve of you, dearest. But still whether she did or not, you are good enough for me Beatie, aye too good, and if you are satisfied with me then we are allright, altho' of course it is so much nicer when every one is agreeable, but I am sure my Mother will not be in the way at all. I have not yet told Uncle John of our engagement, but I have no doubt he knows all about it, but you see I have not had any conversation with him for so long a time, that I scarcely have known how to start on him. However, Beatie, for your sake, it must be done. I shall not let him know that you are aware that our relationship is so strained, but shall tell him that I wish him to meet us both on cordial terms, and to welcome you as my future wife, when you come down to B'ham and that I am ready to forget what has happened between us in the past. We have both been foolish, I have no doubt, but still I think he has been old enough to know himself better.

At last I have got the ring, dearest. I think you will like it. I have had it made specially and like it very much myself, but of course if it is not just what you would like we are not obliged to keep it but can have another made up. But I think you will like this one. The ring which you gave me for the size, I am having cleaned up. It will look like a new one. The weather from last Wednesday to Saturday was glorious here, but it was very dull all yesterday, and has been dull and quite cold today.

I went cycling Saturday and yesterday and thought of you many times. I fancied you at tennis on Saturday. I do hope you had a fine day and enjoyed it. Fancy me out cycling yesterday. Never mind, dearest, you shall take me to church next Sunday, or rather I will take you.

I am glad Mrs. Morris approves of me for I am sure she would feel anxiously about you, having been such a close friend. Shall we see her at the Pic Nic? I hope so.

News does travel Beatie. I have been congratulated by several people who have met you at the Yeomanry Balls here, and they think I am very fortunate.

Do let me know dearest what my Mother had to say to you. I am most anxious. I am so glad Nin wrote to you. She is a dear soul, and I know she loves you Beatie. For the present Au Revoir, only four days now until I come to you darling. For the meantime accept my whole love and a sweet kiss from

Yours ever

Jack

Jack's father, Joseph Hughes, died in 1888 at the age of forty-five from a weak heart. He was a much respected member of the local community, a freemason and a churchgoer. (T)

Linwood Lodge, Gravelly Hill. June 10th 1898

My Dear Beatie

I know you will think it strange that I have not answered your last letter sooner but I'll tell you how it was. I burnt it as soon as I had read it because of one or two little things it contained and then I got rather mixed up, as to what it really was, and almost forgot its contents. This week my time has been absorbed in entertaining a very old friend who has been staying the week with me and she has been very poorly for some time, and I tell her I shall have to blame her for causing me to neglect my letters. You must please excuse the delay. I promised Jack I would write at once to you, but my dear Beatie you must really excuse my not being able to do so earlier. You know I must be candid, and it took me quite by surprise because I never observed any particular intimacy between you and although I cannot deny that I felt some pleasure there was still a rather painful feeling as to whether you both had been too hasty in the giving to, and receiving from each other, such a promise as may involve the happiness of a whole life and I sincerely hope you are not mistaking momentary impulses for permanent impressions.

I pray it may be allright, and all end happily. I can't express to you now dear all I feel but hope to do so later on. So excuse more now. With love to Ma and Pa and trusting all are well. With fondest love, I am

Affectionately Yours
L'Epine Hughes

It seems that Jack's mother had tremendous difficulty expressing her feelings towards Beatrice. This was not the last time a letter to her was to be torn up and burnt. (T)

"Roselea", June 15th 1898

My own dearest Jack

I must say I was awfully disappointed not receiving a letter from you on monday morning and when I found on getting down that there was not one, presumed you had been cycling and so could not find time, however I was delighted to get one on tuesday morning. I suppose it was my mistake in writing too often but I won't do it again. I received your Mother's letter on saturday evening. I must say, I did not like the letter, there was not a particle of warmth in it, and she gave me clearly to understand that she was not over pleased, it made me so miserable when I read it, but I am not going to think any more about it, so long as you always love me, as I believe you will, I don't care for anyone else, they must make the best of it. Your Mother thinks we have been too hasty and that our promise to each other was given under a momentary impulse, isn't that nasty? but it was not so, was it Jack dear? I am going out this afternoon to tea to a friend's, with the idea of going for a ride tonight, but I have not got my machine home yet, and shall not get it until saturday. Isn't this weather awful, fancy us all on saturday, sitting huddled together in rugs and furs on the river, imagine it. We are glad of our winter coats and furs when we go out now and we are thinking of having a fire again. Be sure and bring your overcoat with you, for you will want it. I hope you will be able to stop some time with us, Joe won't mind.

It is rather funny but I quite intended when writing to you again to ask you to be friends with your Uncle, it seems such a pity and he feels it very much Joe said and another thing it would be very awkward for me, as your wife, wouldn't it dear. Fancy you a married man, it hardly seems possible, for I never dreamed you were a marrying sort and to think that I should be the girl of your choice. I am sure I shall like my ring if you do dear and it is most kind of you to have taken so much trouble. We were so surprised that Joe went home on saturday, we asked the Morris' over for tennis on his account and then he would not stay.

Jack's highly principled and intense nature, combined with his propensity to speak his mind, created many situations which Beatrice was to find she would have to help him smooth over.

This view of Streatham Hill in 1900 shows the station on the left which became such an important rendezvous for Jack and Beatrice. To meet Jack there meant quite a long walk from 'Roselea' for Beatrice. (D)

This was also Royal Ascot week and, typically, the weather reports in the newspaper were that "the wind was chilly, if not to say cold" and rain threatened – no more suitable for a race meeting than for a picnic on the river. Hardly the weather to be hoped for in 'flaming June'.

Mr. and Mrs. Morris will both be at the picnic. Kate Hogan has arranged for a carriage to be reserved for us at Clapham Junction, the train starts from Vauxhall. There will be nine going from Streatham. I do hope it will be a little warmer. I shall be at Streatham Hill on friday at 7.16, suppose you intend coming by that train. Well dear lots of love and heaps of embraces

Yours most devotedly Beatie

Linwood Lodge, June 17th 1898

My own darling Beatie

I am most pleased on arriving home just now to find your sweet letter. I was most anxious to learn in what strain my Mother had written you and am most grieved to find that she has written you so coolly. I am sure you can believe me Beatie, when I tell you, as I told you at first that I am distinctly *not* acting under any such thing as a momentary impulse. I cannot say that I have loved you from the first time that I saw you, for I have not. But this I do truthfully vow, dear, that I had liked you from the first and that liking for you has gradually grown into love as I have known you better. You know I told you that I had thought of telling you of my love for you when I came up at Easter. What I went through during that visit I can never explain. But I did not wish to say anything to you until I was quite certain that my mind was fully made up. Well, dear, it went on until Whitsuntide and I am sure my mind was made up then. You are the only girl for me, Beatie, and come what may we will stand together.

Sorry to say I have not yet made it up with Uncle John but I think I can do so tomorrow before coming away. I should not care to think of the present feeling existing between us when you come down dear.

Little did Jack realize that it was to be a long time before Beatrice was to visit Birmingham.

I take your ring and look at it several times a day Beatie, for it gives me some satisfaction, but oh tomorrow evening, we shall be able to have a sweet embrace, fancy the first for a fortnight. Really it seems like months, I have felt quite out of my calculations this week. I have been thinking each morning when I woke that it was Friday, but never mind next time I wake, it will be Friday.

I really thought Joe would have spent Sunday with you, but he is always anxious to get home again somehow.

Pray, excuse this scribble but my hand is rather shaky for I have just scorched up from town on my machine.

I am going now for an evening ride to Lichfield with Joe Brettell and the two Harrop boys. We are having a little supper together at Lichfield and arrive back about 11.30pm. Ida is having a machine, she expects it tomorrow.

Well darling tomorrow I shall be with you and we shall have a most delightful time. I do hope it will be fine and warm on Saturday. I shall be proud then. Well dearest I won't say any more now, but will leave it until tomorrow. Don't forget 7.16 Beatie, Streatham Hill. Heaps of love and a sweet kiss

*Yours ever
Jack*

Jack and Beatrice were to have to get used to much longer partings than a fortnight, and to have to rely on letters much more. They were to see each other once a month for a short weekend together at 'Roselea'.

Lichfield was a distance of some 12 miles from Linwood Lodge – no mean distance for "an evening ride" after a day's work.

Linwood Lodge, June 21st 1898

My own darling Beatie

I arrived safely in B'ham last night at 9.35. Two friends met me in, and we went up on the 10.30, and strange to say my Mother was on the same. She asked how were all at Streatham, and I said very well and all sent their love to her. I also gave your love to her altho' she did not ask after you personally. How strange she seems. What a cruel thing it seems for us to be so far from each other, dear. Fancy separated again, and for a whole month. But; darling, I suppose we must be patient. What a lovely time we had together, Beatie, but somehow I cannot fancy that I was with you for three whole days. We were so happy together that it seemed but hours instead of days. It will seem much harder to you dear than to me I am afraid, this continual parting, for of course every day brings more change to me.

I was thinking of you dear the whole journey in the train and the time seemed to pass so that we were in B'ham in no time. How I missed your sweet kiss last night, darling I cannot tell. Some kisses are as nothing, but, when they tell such love darling what a pity it is that we cannot be together to exchange them.

I suppose you are busy each day with your work. You know what I mean don't you dear. B'ham is full of people this week on account of the Royal Agricultural Show. The Prince is coming tomorrow.

It was so nice to me Beatie to read all those letters you had received from your friends. I do hope my Mother will soon shew a warmer feeling towards you darling, for then we might hope to have a lot more of each others company. But whether she does or not dear, that will make no difference to my love for you. We are meant for each other I am sure, and the love which we have for

IN THE TUNNEL.

Jack would have had plenty of time to dream about Beatrice on his long train journeys back to Birmingham after leaving her. So many kisses in their love affair had to be imagined. (E)

A photograph of the entrance hall at the Royal Agricultural Show the day Jack visited it in 1898. The show, which was held in the Park of Four Oaks Hall, was a major Midlands event for a family outing, but it was reported that "fine weather was somewhat lacking". (F)

Jack must have felt that his own family and friends were very cold and even hostile compared with Beatrice's, which must have made his parting from Beatrice and return to Birmingham even harder.

each other is of no common kind. I have felt a regard for people before now, but Beatie until I loved you I never knew what love was. Now I do. It is very happiness to me to think of you, and darling I picture ourselves together, in our little home and know that no one will be more happy than we. I have not yet been able to put things right with Uncle John, but hope that when next I write shall be able to tell you that I have, for this state of things seems truly awful.

It did seem so nice to me dear to have such a good reception all round from your friends whom I have met. I hope the weather is a little cooler with you, for I am afraid you will be melted away. Think it was hot yesterday afternoon? How I wish we could have a cuddle like we had then, eh, dear. Well darling give my love to your Pa and Ma, they are dears, also to poor dear Grandma. I am afraid you will begin to think after all these instructions for love giving that there cannot be any left for your dear self. But, Beatie accept my whole love and a sweet good night kiss and believe me

Yours for ever

Jack.

◇◇◇◇◇◇

"Roselea", June 22nd 1898

My own darling Jack

Thank you dear for your nice letter. I was so eagerly looking out for it. I feel as if this separation is more than I can bear, Jack dear, it is awful. I don't know how I shall wait a whole month.

I do wish your Mother would get alright and then perhaps she might ask me for a time, as when you do come, you are no sooner here than you have gone

Beatrice's anguish about Mrs. Hughes' rejection of her contributed greatly to the awfulness of their separation. There was certainly no chance of her being invited to stay at Linwood Lodge at this time.

again. Do let me know if she makes any more remarks about us, won't you dear, as I should like to know all.

Don't be cross with me writing so soon but I feel I must to relieve my mind a bit, for I do feel so lonely without you my darling.

Ma and Susie got home on monday about 11 o'clock, they said they had not had it a bit hot, rather different to us wasn't it dear? but nevertheless I wish I was as hot this afternoon from the same cause, I would gladly put up with it. Susie and I went to Nellie's to tea yesterday and this morning the three of us have been to Clapham Junction to the tailors, it was lovely on top of the bus, quite a nice breeze. Oh by the way I asked Nellie what they spent on their home, she said about £500, now I have no idea, whether that is a lot or not for furnishing, what do you think dear, tell me honestly. I have had another letter of congratulations from an Aunt of mine, such a funny one, finishes with a pathetic verse of poetry.

I hope you have made it alright with your Uncle. You will tell me won't you? Do write soon again darling. I shall be longing to hear from you again.

Susie is going home on friday, she thanks you for your kind message and wishes me to remember her to you. Give my love to Ida and your Mother, if she cares to have a message from me and my whole and true love for your dear self.

Yours most devotedly Beatie

One of the first steam omnibuses which began to replace the horse-drawn buses in 1897. These were not in general use until 1905. (B)

Linwood Lodge, Gravelly Hill. June 24th 1898

My own darling Beatie

Thanks for your sweet letter. My mother has not had anything further to say at present; but rest assured I shall let you now all, dear. I could not feel cross with you darling for writing so soon, rather I feel glad for you cannot tell what joy a letter from your dear self brings to me. I was glad to know they had a good day at Brighton on Monday. You know dear when I was with you, I wished to explain my position to you, (financially I mean) but you did not then care to know, but you know darling in this life we have to treat with things as they are, and not as we should like them to be, and I honestly tell you that an outlay of £500 would be altogether out of my range, and I also think, unnecessary. Don't feel hurt darling, with me for putting it so plainly, I wish I were near to comfort you.

Well darling I have put matters right between Uncle and myself, and he is as nice as possible. I have not yet told him of our engagement, altho' I expect he knows all about it; but I shall tell him between now and Monday. He is going over to the Isle of Man on Monday for about a fortnight I think. Fancy it has been over two years now since we were on friendly terms.

There is yet something else to tell dear. There was great consternation at the Drill Hall last night for Jack Hughes handed in his resignation, to take effect at once. Everybody was simply scared. My Captain told me all sorts of things, and promised to do anything and everything for me if I would continue. He said he did not think I could have taken sufficient time to think the matter over

Jack had wanted to join the Warwickshire Yeomanry also, but Joe said that there was only room for one member of the family in it, and so Jack had joined a Volunteer Artillery Regiment instead.

This was a time for Jack to put 'matters right', speak plainly and make important decisions about quite a number of different issues, Beatrice having changed his life significantly.

and I had better let it rest for a few days, but I told him my mind was quite made up, and I had not done it because I wanted making a fuss of, but because I wished him to accept it. It was a matter, he said, too important for him to deal with, and he must hand it on to the Major, and that I shall hear in the course of a few days.

I could not possibly think of going to Camp, darling this year and spending a week there which I might pass in your dear company. They will miss me sorely I know, but then their loss will be our gain won't it.

Well darling I am having a half day holiday, something unusual and am going up to the Royal Show. I do wish you were with me. But never mind let us hope things may run smoothly and then dear perhaps I may soon bring you down to B'ham.

Please forgive me for not writing last night but I was so busy with going to put in my resignation. Accept my whole love and a fond kiss from

Yours ever
Jack

"Roselea", June 26th 1898

My own darling Jack

I was so glad to receive your dear letter and was exceedingly surprised to find you had sent in your resignation. Now Jack dear, I feel awfully proud to think you have given up Camp for me, but dear, I am so afraid you will miss it so and find that my company won't make up for it, but I cannot help saying, how glad I am to think I shall have you for a whole fortnight. Now dear I must tell you that we are thinking of going to Folkestone the last week in July for a month. Mrs. Morris and Nellie for a fortnight. Pa, Ma and I, we are going to stay at the Pier Hotel (not at all expensive) so if you care to come with us during that time for your holiday you know how delighted I shall be. Ma and Mrs. Morris are going down one day to choose our bed rooms, if you think of going with us, and you like, Ma will look out a nice room for you, but let me know.

Young Leo is standing by me and he wants to know who I am writing to? I told him Uncle Jack. Everybody has admired my ring and dear, it is a lovely one, and I am very, very proud of it. I have so longed for you all day. I have not been at all well, I did not get up until dinner time. I was riding on the wet grass yesterday evening and had a side slip and had a nasty fall. I fell on top of a rose tree and the machine on top of me. I have hurt my hand and arm and it rather shook me up and I feel awfully shaky today, and the thorns have all got embedded in my skin, so I am going to poultice it, as it is so painful. I hope you didn't mind me telling you about Ted's cost of his furniture I didn't mean to hurt your feelings, only I told you I would ask Nellie. Of course I know he spent a lot and that included all he spent on decorating his drawing room, which was quite unnecessary and also a 3rd sitting room which we shall not want.

I was so glad you had made it alright with your Uncle and hope he won't mind me. Wouldn't it be nice, if your Mother would forgive me and come down to Folkestone with us. Of course you know nothing would please me

Beatrice never became quite such a keen bicycler as Jack – and indeed at first, experienced some difficulties with her new machine – and took some uncomfortable falls. (G)

better than to come down to Birmingham but please don't mention it to your Mother, unless she comes round, for I do not want to come if it would not be agreeable to her and I am sure it would not be just yet to her.

Be sure and write soon and let me know about Folkestone.

All send their love and how I wish I could wish you a proper good night darling. Never mind I will make up for it when we meet.

Yours most devotedly Beatie

While writing this letter, Beatrice was blissfully unaware of events at Linwood Lodge at that moment – events that made her hopes for a family reunion, and acceptance of her into Jack's family, even less likely.

◆◆◆◆◆◆◆

Linwood Lodge, June 28th 1898

My own darling Beatie

I received your dear letter when I got home last evening, and cannot tell you how pleased I was, for it brought such comfort to me. I was sorry though to hear you had been upset from your bicycle and trust by this time you are quite recovered.

Well darling, I have been upset very much, but not from a bicycle. You know I told you I had made friends with Uncle John, last Thursday, well, on Saturday morning Mother received a notice from his Solicitor, of his intention to retire from the business. He has given six months notice, and given power of attorney to an accountant, and cleared off on a Tour himself. Isn't he a nice *man*. It is most unpleasant for us, as we have to do everything under supervision; and God knows, we have never wronged him of a farthing. I think it is a great pity he cannot trust us another six months as he had trusted us so long.

Of course this business upset my Mother, and she has been anything but amiable. I went to Church on Sunday morning with Joe, and thought of you dear; of course I pictured you in Church also, and am sorry you could not be there. I remained at home the rest of the day, and we were very quiet and comfortable. Nin and Alec were over. After tea Mother wrote a letter to you and put it on the Mantel-piece, for me to post next morning. All went well until after supper, and then there was a conversation on business matters, and before very long there was a regular "bust up", excuse the term, but I can't think of a better.

One of two oil paintings of Jack's grandfather, Joseph Hughes. Both paintings are still owned by members of the Hughes family, four generations later. (A)

Jack's grandfather, Joseph Hughes, founded the Albion Metal Works in 1830 and Jack's father continued the business until his early death in 1888, after which time his widow controlled his shares. Uncle John's threats of withdrawal from the partnership and Jack's quarrel with his mother and precarious relationship with his Uncle John, made his own position in the business very insecure. (A)

She said she had done with me and mine for ever, and would destroy the letter she had written to you. The letter which she said was to put everything right. Well dear, she destroyed it, what it contained I don't know. Pardon me Beatie, for troubling you with all this, but the fact is I seem to be under a cloud at present, and seem hardly to be able to know who are my friends, but I feel confident that Joe is alright and the thing for us to do is to pull together and we shall pull through the cloud into sunshine. Of course I feel I must tell you all that is happening, but after all I don't think but that my Mother will regret what she has said, for Joe and I will work together and of course if she does not have us to work for her, we should be working against her. It seems truly awful that things should come to such a pass, but still I think I can see that when the matter is settled, we shall really be better off, for so long as Uncle John was to be in this business there could never be any peace for any of us. My Mother is very impetuous, and I expect she will be coming round shortly, and write you again. I am not going to let her see that her carryings on troubles me, and then I think she will be different.

I knew you would be surprised to hear of my resignation, everybody is, but then I could not think of going to Camp darling while I might be with you. I am sure I shall not miss the Camp, when I am with you dear. It seems an awful long time darling since I left you, but on thinking I find it is only a week, but I shall be so glad when it is time to come and see you again. We shall be able to have quite a nice time at Folkestone, but Beatie I cannot say definitely about that just at present. I mean the length of time I can come for, but shall let you know as early as possible.

I shall let you know how these business matters go on, and any developments that take place. But, after all darling although things look so black at present, I feel sure that it will be one of the best things that has ever happened to us. What you will think of this letter darling I don't know, but I must be candid and tell you what I know and what I feel. Well dearest accept my whole love, which nothing can alter, and a fond kiss, from

Yours ever
Jack

I do hope you have got over your tumble. Don't think too much of this business affair, but I feel I must tell you.

⬦⬦⬦⬦⬦⬦

"Roselea", June 29th 1898

Jack darling

Cheer up dearie. I am more than sorry to hear you have had an upset with your Mother again. It makes me so awfully miserable for I know it is all through me. I think it is so unkind of her to take such an objection to me, simply because I have won your dear love, but I feel Jack, that if I am always going to be the cause of all these petty annoyances it would be better if you forgot me. I don't know how she can be so horrid, she ought to be glad that you and I are so happy with our love and not always try to be marring our happiness. Of course I know, she must be worried about your Uncle John (the old beast) but I cannot see why I should suffer for him. How petty to destroy

Jack's mother was proving an impossible personality for Beatrice to get to know as her future mother-in-law. This letter was the second to Beatrice that she was to tear up before sending, following a bitter and angry row with Jack. Jack rescued the letter from the fire. (A)

The half burnt and torn up letter has been preserved to this day and by carefully piecing it together most of it can be deciphered. It tells of Jack's mother's worries about Uncle John's retirement from the business and makes excuses for her not having written to Beatrice before this. There is very little indication of any expression of feelings about the engagement however, even though the letter was meant "to put everything right"!

Beatrice does now have genuine cause for fear about the kind of life she is going to have before her if she moves to Birmingham to a family which is not only hostile to her, but also in such conflict with itself.

Beatrice's visit to the Royal Academy was to the Summer Exhibition, at which this picture, 'Love Triumphant' by G.F. Watts R.A., was one of the 1,900 exhibits. The Morris family, great friends from the days the Mercers lived in Dulwich, were still close friends. Mrs. Morris was clearly a lively and energetic woman and it was she, rather than Beatrice's mother, who frequently chaperoned Beatrice on shopping expeditions and to art galleries and the theatre in London's West End. (B)

my letter. I only hope she will come round soon and write to me again, I should so have appreciated it.

We have been wondering whether we would go to Jersey for a fortnight and then to Folkestone for a fortnight, but nothing is definitely settled yet. I don't want to go to Jersey, for it is so hot, and people say who have been that the air always makes you feel sleepy and tired and all you want to do is to lie down, now that is not my idea of a holiday and Folkestone air is so bracing and nice. I am sure you will like that and there are such delightful walks and nooks, dear I will show you round. You had better not make any arrangements until they have quite settled what they are going to do, for I am sure, I don't think they know themselves yet. I am going to spend the day with Aimée tomorrow, then I am going to spend the night at Morris' and Mrs. Morris and I are going up West on friday and to the Academy. Probably I shall then know what they have decided about their holiday. I am feeling quite alright now dear, thank you, but you see I did not come down very lightly and so shook myself muchly. I was so glad you went to Church last Sunday. I hope to go next Sunday. May and Jim are coming saturday for Sunday. The following saturday we have a tennis party and the next following, I hope to see my darling – what an age it seems to wait for. Yes dear, tell me all, I would rather know and I think it very honorable of you to tell me.

I had such a nice letter from Aunt Parker, this morning. She so wants to see you, so when we are at Folkestone I must take you over there, it is not far from there. She has also promised us ½ doz silver tea spoons, isn't she good. I know you will like her, she is such a dear old thing and so is Uncle. They are a regular old "Darby and Joan" and so happy like we shall be darling, when we get old like that.

I should think really you will be much happier and things go smoother when you are without your Uncle although it is worrying now, but I do hope your Mother will be alright to you even if she is not to me. She cannot mean what she says, but you will always have your little "girlie" to stand by you and you know it, don't you Jack dear? Well darling, be sure to write soon and tell me all. Heaps of hugs and kisses and my most devoted love,

Yours for ever
Beatie

❖❖❖❖❖

Linwood Lodge, Gravelly Hill. June 30th 1898

My own darling Beatie

I was so glad to receive your dear letter this morning, especially under the circumstances, for if possible it was more welcome than ever. You have no idea darling how depressed I have been in the last few days on account of all this miserable business; but things have now reached a crisis and when it is passed I really believe we shall feel much happier than ever we have before. I am afraid Beatie I have been rather inclined to take too gloomy a view of the affair, but still I felt I must tell you all that was happening, but I hope you have not been worrying yourself too much on my account. As regards my Mother, I know when she sees that her carryings on do not alter our love

At a time which should be one of the happiest in his life, with a holiday in Folkestone with Beatrice to look forward to, poor Jack was depressed and despondent.

for each other, that she will come to. But why she should keep so cool towards you dear, and throw such obstacles in the way I can't conceive. She ought to be proud of you darling for you are good and true; but never mind you know the old saying about "The course of true love" which is said never to run smoothly. I suppose that love without trials would not count for much, in fact there must be trials to prove that there is love. Beatie we love each other devotedly, don't we, so come what may and whatever any one else may say or do, we can stand by each other, and come out alright at the end. I am so glad to know you received a nice letter from your Aunt Parker, she must be deeply interested in you of course and anxious to see what I am like. I shall be most happy to be trotted over by you my darling and hope she will be pleased with me. It is nice to see an old couple so happy together, and I am sure dear if we are spared we shall be another regular old "Darby and Joan".

How happy we shall be together dear, on our Holiday we shall have such a nice long time together, but I do hope all these troublesome affairs will soon be settled, so that we can also get settled and be always together. I am glad you are feeling alright again after your tumble, of course I understand you would not come down very lightly.

I don't know what I am writing, an organ is just dinning "The white silk dress" in my ears. The Hooligans are having a ride on Saturday to Whittington, postponed from last Saturday on account of the thunderstorms which we had, preventing the run being carried out then. I shall go myself, but Ida will not, she does not seem to care about it somehow. There is to be a special "Hooligan" run when you come darling, and oh how I wish I felt it would be soon. I see you are getting about a bit this week, but never mind dear we shall

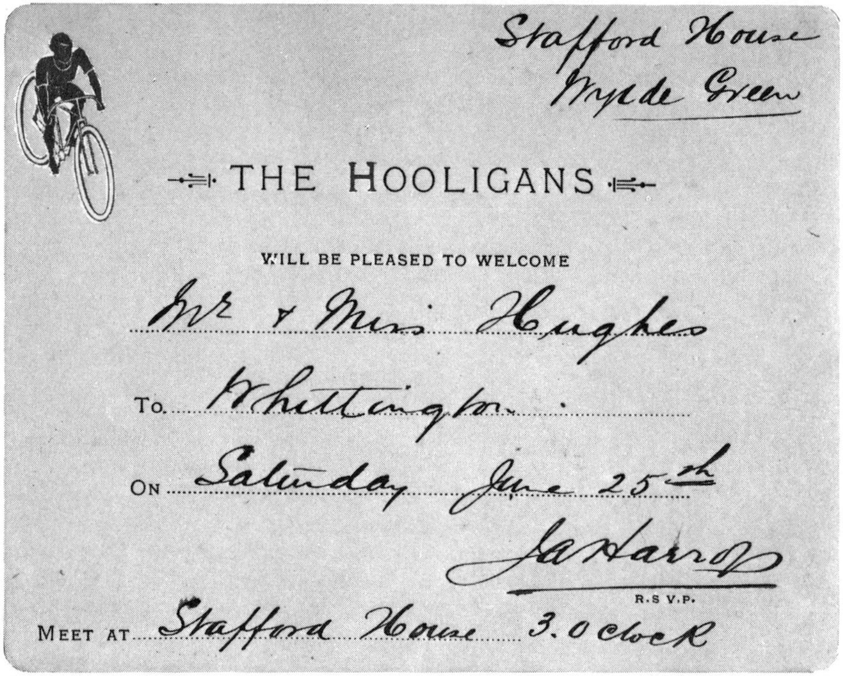

Jack's anticipation of a long and happy life with Beatrice into old age in the image of 'Darby and Joan', was of course dependent on them both "being spared" to live to old age together, a relatively unusual situation in Victorian times.

Stafford House
Wylde Green

THE HOOLIGANS

WILL BE PLEASED TO WELCOME

Mr & Mrs Hughes

To Whittington

On Saturday June 25th

Jas Harrop

R.S.V.P.

MEET AT Stafford House 3. 0 clock

This was the great era of the bicycle and the Harrops of Wylde Green were Jack's bicycling chums, responsible for organizing some of the events of The Hooligans Cycling Club. This card was an invitation for Jack and Ida. (A)

So much had to be "in imagination" in Jack and Beatrice's love affair, the development of their relationship being almost entirely dependent on the 'penny post'.

never be any younger shall we.

I do wish the time would go that I could come and see you, but for the present I give you all my love, and heaps of kisses (the latter in imagination) and am

Yours ever
Jack

<><><><><><>

"Roselea", July 2nd 1898

My own darling Jack

It was good of you to write so that I got the letter at Mrs. Morris'.

I was delighted for I do loving receiving letters from you. I am sorry, I did not write to you yesterday, but really I could not find time, for we started out soon after breakfast and had all day until 7 o'clock looking at the shops etc, I felt dead tired for I have not been feeling at all well, I think it is the weather. Mrs. Morris drove me home, I got here about 9 o'clock.

You don't tell me if your Mother is alright with you, do tell me, it does worry me so, I try not to, but I cannot help it, it makes me feel so miserable but of course, you know dear nothing will alter my great love for you and I console myself, thinking of the time when as you say we shall be settled, and always together, oh, Jack it is too lovely, we shall have some happy times. We have made up our minds not to go to Jersey, but to spend the month at Folkestone but it will be time enough to arrange when you can come when you come up. I spent the day with Aimèe on thursday, poor girl she is so wretched, she has written to Cape Town to say she shall not come out now, it appears his last excuse is that he has speculated with the money he meant to send her for her passage and so will have to wait a few weeks. What do you think of that? the beast, he ought to be kicked, but for all that I am very glad Aimèe is not going, and I feel sorry for her, especially that I am so happy in your dear love. I have asked her to come over for next week and bring her bike and Laura will be here so we shall get some jolly rides, do you know, I have only used my machine twice. Ma says she does not see the good of me having one at all. I don't know whether to take it away with me or not, I think it will be so knocked about and I could always hire, if I wanted to ride. Won't it be lovely being together at Folkestone, is your Mother going away at all, now if she had been alright, it would have been nice for her to come with us. I hope you will have a jolly run today with the Hooligans, it looks like rain here. Really it is horrid weather. I do hope we have it fine for our holidays.

I suppose when your Uncle retires from the business, it will be your Mother's solely. I pray and hope you will get along alright with her, it would be a dreadful thing to split up after all these years and it would be awful for me, for I should feel it was all on my account. Well darling, write soon and cheer your little girlie up, she does so wish you were here, it would be hot though wouldn't it dear?

ever yours wholly
Beatie

A silver charm given to Beatrice by Aimèe, Beatrice's bosom friend. She was evidently more patient than Beatrice was prepared to be as she had waited eight years to marry her fiancé in Cape Town, only to be jilted finally. (A)

Without Uncle John as an ally, Beatrice was quite right to fear for Jack's position in the business.

Linwood Lodge, July 4th 1898

My own darling Beatie

Pray forgive me for not writing to you yesterday. You will think dear, that surely I could find time on Sunday, but yesterday I was very busy indeed for a Sunday, had quite a big day. I went to Church in the morning, in fact we all went Mother and Ida, Joe and I, and I should think the Parson will think something is going to happen after all that. It is a very funny thing they have all got it about Erdington, that I am about to marry a Widow from St. Thomas' Parish B'ham, as the Banns have been put up for some one named Hughes a, "Bachelor of this Parish". I have not been congratulated personally, but have received congratulations second-hand from several people. What a joke, eh. Fancy this boy marrying a Widow. Well when I got home from Church I changed into cycling attire, and after dinner rode to Bromsgrove 17 miles, had tea there with an old chum of the Artillery, whom I met on the way (my fellow Sec for the Artillery Ball last season) and then we rode back through Dodford and calling on my cousins there had some most delicious strawberries. They were a real treat. I have arranged for them to send some on to you, for I know you will all enjoy them.

Don't trouble yourself darling, on account of my Mother, she is coming round slowly but surely. I am treating her very coolly, but as she sees she does not upset me, she will be alright.

It must indeed be a sad disappointment for Miss Aimée Tory, but who knows, maybe it is for the best. You must try and soothe her if you can, and I know you can if you try dear. But Goodness knows she has not been very charitable, in her remarks about you. Still do your part as a friend, dear.

We had an enjoyable ride on Saturday, only 9 turned out. But it was a lovely afternoon, and better I think for not having a crowd. I do hope you are feeling better now, darling, but I suppose when you were out the other day you were so anxious to see everything and knocked yourself up. I know Mrs. Morris must be very energetic, but still you must look after your dear little self you know, for me.

Fancy darling only a fortnight gone since we were together, it seems like months, but never mind let us get over another fortnight and we shall be together again. We are so happy together aren't we dear. I do miss your sweet kiss at night. But we must try and make up for lost time when we meet. What hugs and fond embraces we shall have dear, and the season getting warmer. I am thinking we shall find it rather hot. Mother will be going away for a Holiday, with Ida, when she breaks up from School; about the last week in July, but I don't think she has decided where to go yet. I have not yet told her of my intention of joining you at Folkestone, but of course she will have a pretty good idea on account of my having decided not to go to Camp this year.

Well dearest for the present "Au revoir", with my whole sincere love and heaps of fond kisses

Yours ever

Jack

By the way you really must do a little more cycling or you will get quite out of form.

Although Jack attended church regularly it was not always as often as Beatrice would have liked. In the summer months particularly he found the prospect of a cycle ride more attractive. (B)

Ida was Jack's fourteen-year-old sister and the youngest in the family, a girl with striking looks and a strong spirit. She was the only one of Mrs. Hughes' children still at school, being fourteen years younger than Jack. As the boys were too old to join on a family holiday and their father was no longer alive, Jack's mother and Ida often joined Jennie and Alec for a holiday together.

"Roselea", July 5th 1898

My own dearest Jack

Of course as you know, I was delighted to get your dear letter and to know that you are getting on alright with your Mother, and more than pleasant to know you went to Church. What a joke, the people thinking you were going to marry a widow. Were the banns published at your Church? Now dear Ma and Mrs. Morris went down to Folkestone yesterday to look at the rooms at the Pier Hotel, but Ma did not like the rooms, but she says she has got very nice ones for us at the 'Royal Victoria Hotel'. She mentioned about a room for you, they are very moderate in their charges, a single room being 2 guineas a week inclusive, but they want to know when you are thinking of going as they are booking the rooms fast. Could you come down on sat. July 30th that would be before the Bank Holiday and I thought perhaps you might get that thrown in and your fortnight start from the tuesday.

Aimèe and Laura are staying with me, and last night, we all went for a lovely ride 14½ miles and my machine runs beautifully and I managed all the hills, so, I am getting on, aren't I dear. I enclose you the latest style of hair dressing in the Park and hope you will endeavour to train yours in so fashion for the Leas at Folkestone. We so much admire it, don't you? I thought you would prefer the one coming to a point, warranted to keep the collar clean. We are having quite a crowd on saturday for tennis I think about 16, so I shall be kept busy, as you may imagine. There will be quite a party of us at Folkestone for the Ware's are going for a month, they will be in apartments and the Lewcocks are already there for a month. I went to Church alone on Sunday, May

wouldn't go, and Miss Challoner's banns were published. You remember the girl I told you about who is only 18 and going to marry a widower with 4 children, darling I couldn't help wishing they were ours, would you not be glad? I shall look forward for the strawberries, as I know the flavour will be lovely and I am so fond of them it is very kind of you to send them, for I know Jack you are spoiling me.

Be sure and let me know, when you think of coming to Folkestone so that Ma can write and engage the room for you.

Why don't you propose for your Mother and Ida to come too, but I suppose she wouldn't deign to. I enclose your tariff and you can see the picture of the house. Lots of hugs dear and oceans of kisses when we meet

Yours ever
Beatie

The fresh strawberries would have made their way to Beatrice by train for which Jack would have had to pay two shillings 'if packed in a tub' or five shillings if not, irrespective of distance.

Linwood Lodge, July 7th 1898

My own darling Beatie

I was so glad to get your dear letter, but do please forgive me for not writing you last night, but the fact is altho' I got home early last night and in good time for writing, I had had such a harassing day and felt so distracted that I could not settle down in the house to write but went and sat in the garden alone smoking until ever so late. How selfish you will say of me. You will forgive me, won't you darling? I am glad to know your Ma has settled on the diggings at Folkestone, and it is kind of her to arrange for me. Now my Holidays will be the first two weeks in August, and I shall be due back at business on Monday Aug the 15th, and I must be back, under any circumstances, then. I should much like to cycle down to Folkestone Beatie, that is if you don't mind. Of course though if I did you would not see me until the Monday evening as I should ride down on the Sunday and Monday. I have not yet looked out the route, nor shall I until I know what you think of it, dear. You might ask your Ma to kindly book me a room for the fortnight. It is just a matter whether I arrive on the Saturday preceding Bank Holiday, or on the Bank Holiday evening, that is for you to say darling. I see the G.W.R. are now running through carriages daily from B'ham to the Harbour Stn, Folkestone, arriving about 4.30 I think. I am looking forward anxiously, as yourself dear for the 16th, and when it does come how happy we will be together, for a time. I am glad you are having a nice time with Aimèe and Laura, and doing a little cycling. I went for a little run on Tuesday night about 16 miles, started at eight o'clock, and it was very enjoyable. I am glad you sent me the latest fashion plate in hair dressing, but I think it would take me a long while to grow so much on the back as is depicted in the sketch. But if I could it would no doubt be useful, as you say, in keeping down the laundry bills.

I shall be thinking of you darling on Saturday with your Tennis Party. I do hope you will have a fine day. You will of course be very busy, and I wish I could be near to help you, never mind I will do that the following Saturday. It is of course nice to have some friends that you know near when away on Holidays, but I don't think we shall feel the need of them very much personally

A timetable for 1898 for the Great Western Railway. Industrial Birmingham benefited tremendously from the construction of the national railway networks as it was situated at the centre of a large number of radiating lines of communication. This benefited passengers as much as the town's industry. (B)

The Henley Regatta took place from July 5th until 7th, and from Streatham this was a pleasant day out for Beatrice's brother Ernie and his sweetheart Laura. On this occasion the prizes were presented by Lady Esther Smith. (B)

dear, eh. I hope by this time you have received the Strawberries, altho' they have not yet advised me of sending them off. I told them to put up a good big boxful. I have told you of the Strawberry feeds we have at home about this time in the Year. They are great. We shall be having one next week I expect.

I see the Henley Regatta is in full swing. I suppose Ernie and "Ern Snuff" are having a fine old time "on the river".

Things here don't look much more pleasant yet I am grieved to say, but still darling I keep going on trying to do my duty by everybody and if people are not satisfied I cannot help it. I think of you darling, and your love and that is all sufficient for me. It brightens me up darling and makes me feel I have much to live for, and with such love I know we shall be able to go along and come together through everything.

Well dearest for the present "Au revoir", with my whole love and heaps of kisses.

*Your own devoted
Jack*

Roll on 16th.

"Roselea", July 8th 1898

My own darling Jack

I have so been looking out for a letter. I wanted one so badly, for I must own to you I have felt so awfully depressed and when I find in your letter, that you are so worried, it made me feel worse, in fact dear, I could not help a few tears. Is your Mother vexed because you are coming with us?

It does seem a shame that she will not be alright, it is quite bad enough, you being so far from me and only seeing you so seldom, without having anything else to worry us. Darling, I do wish I could just pop in and have a fond hug. I do so long for the 16th, it seems an eternity waiting for it. I am not looking forward to tomorrow one bit, I only want it to go quickly and pass on to the next saturday. You don't know how I feel today, most wretched, for I do so want you and yet happy to feel how great your love is for me, bearing what you are for my sake. I have been "biking" too much again and knocked myself up again. I have been out every night this week and last night I really could not go. I felt too done up. Now Jack don't think me selfish but I don't want you to ride down to Folkestone for it will make 3 days the less to be with you, so do come by train, in fact Ma has written to the Hotel to reserve you a room for July 30th. Of course I shall take my bike, if they take it in, as I think we can get some nice rides. Mrs. Morris, Mrs. Ware and Nellie Morris are all taking theirs. I hope we have some fine weather, that is all. The strawberries have not yet arrived. I have been looking out for them, but I suppose they will come soon.

Beatrice's brother David was married in 1893 to an American – Katherine, always called 'Kitty' by the family. She was the daughter of W. F. Lawrence of Boston, Massachusetts, and wrote to Beatrice from West Newton, where she lived with their twin sons and daughter Margaret, while David was at sea with the Royal Marines.

I had a letter from Kitty (David's wife) congratulating me, such a nice letter, she wants me to write and tell her what you are like. I have also had two other letters since writing to you last. I wonder when they will have finished coming in. I think I have had 17 already. Ida has never written. I hope your Mother has not told her not to write. Give my love to Jennie when you see her. Where are they going for their holiday? Aimèe and Laura are still here, and have asked me, if I had got the "pip". I told them "Yes, badly".

Pa is so excited about going away, he is just like a kid, running round ordering new shirts, a new suit etc. and he seems so glad that you are going and Mrs. Morris. No dear we shall not need anybody but our two selves, won't it be lovely and there are such pretty walks, I have always said Folkestone is an ideal place for lovers.

Well dearie, au revoir and I do hope you are feeling better. Lots of love and oceans of kisses

Yours, ever
Beatie

A grander summer house at Thrale Place, a favourite retreat of Dr. Samuel Johnson a century earlier. He lived there for some years with the wealthy brewery family, the Thrales. (D)

"Roselea", July 9th 1898

My dear old Jack

Just a note to let you know, that the strawberries have arrived and to thank you exceedingly for your kindness, they will come in splendidly for this afternoon. I went to Dulwich and back last night on my bike and it seemed to do me such a lot of good. I have just been cleaning out the summer house, not before it wanted it, so it will be alright for us next saturday eh dearie? Well darling, I enclose you the letter from the Hotel. I am sorry you will have to be aloft but Ma says the rooms are very nice, only of course on the top floor, she has written and engaged the room for a fortnight.

Heaps of love and oceans of kisses and I only wish I had you here to hug for the strawberries. Write me a nice long letter tomorrow, won't you dear?

Yours ever
Bea.

Linwood Lodge, July 11th 1898

My own darling Beatie

Here we are again. You must almost have begun to think that you were never going to receive another letter from me. I am so sorry darling that the contents of my last letter upset you so, but I was feeling so much harassed, but am much better now. In fact I am not going to allow myself to be troubled any more than I can help.

Buck up darling, we shall be alright soon, only five days now. I was so glad to know you had received the strawberries, and above all that they arrived on Saturday. I hope you received them nice and fresh. It is very kind of your Ma to make arrangements for me. I have arranged to finish up business on the Friday night 29th, so that will be alright.

I am so glad you are thinking of taking your bike, we shall be able to have some nice little excursions. I note you have heard from David's wife. Mind give me a good character won't you dearie, when you write to her. I think she has given you rather a large order. I asked Ida if Mother had been telling her not to write to you, but she says that she has not, and that it is sheer neglect on

A letter of confirmation for Jack's "top floor attic" room at the Victoria Private Hotel, Folkestone. (A)

51. Rhyl, looking West.

her own part that you have not heard from her. I am glad you are feeling better now, the biking is alright if you don't overdo it, but you know darling, you get so tempted to have a little scorch and that won't suit you at all. Are Laura and Ernie coming down to Folkestone with us.

I had a nice quiet ride to Lichfield on Saturday, five of us went over there to tea. Took it nice and quietly, having a halt on the way for a feed of strawberries. Yesterday I went to Church in the morning and felt very much better for it. I should think this must be the favourite season of the year for getting married, there were quite a dozen banns yesterday I should think, in fact I thought Mr. Swindell was never going to stop. Yesterday afternoon I went over to Sutton and had a quiet stroll through the Park with Arthur Harrop. Jack Harrop rode on his bike to Rhyl on Saturday, and wanted me to go with him very badly but I told him that my Rhyl days were over; and so they are, aren't they darling. I am glad you have cleaned out the summer house for Saturday, shan't we be busy, but I am glad we can say that now we shan't be long, and we will make up for the past month with a vengeance. How nice it will be darling though when we are always together, that is what I think about, and what gives me more comfort than anything else, for I feel that we shall always be ever so happy, and that it is a great shame that things should crop up to delay us as they do. But never mind darling there must of course be a little of everything in this life, and things will soon mend I am sure. Whichever way things are settled as regards our business, I cannot help but be better off, as far as I can see, and then things will go smoothly. Mother is still very cool. She has not yet made her arrangements for her holidays yet, but she will be sure to take Ida away somewhere. Ida suggested Folkestone but she said she *should not dream of that*. Well darling "Au revoir" lots of love and heaps of kisses

Your own for ever
Jack

"Roselea", July 13th 1898

My own darling Jack

Yes: I did think you had forgotten all about me. I was so disappointed not getting a letter from you on monday, but I will forgive you this time, if you promise not to do it again. Well dear, I am simply longing for saturday to come and isn't it getting hot? We shall have a time. Aimèe went home last night, Laura and I rode over with her, but somehow I do feel so tired this morning. I have just got home. I had to go to Clapham this morning and there was no train, so I had to walk to Balham, hence my weariness. I do hope all will come right as regards the business. I suppose it will then be in your Mother's hands entirely, and she can make it very unpleasant if she likes, but I do hope she will be kind, for I too, am longing for the time when we shall always be together. I know we shall be perfectly happy and what jolly times we will have, and what nice rides we shall be able to have, you will have to think of all the pretty places to ride to. Our tennis party went off very well, although it was rather a cold day. Your strawberries were delicious and such a lovely flavour, we did have a tuck in, in fact they gave me indigestion, it was exceedingly good of you to send them. I do hope we shall have fine weather for our holidays, did your Mother make any remark about you coming with us? I feel sure you will like Folkestone, at least I hope you will.

Our two servants leave tomorrow and the new ones come in, I do hope they will do. Laura is staying on here, because she wants to see you, so I know you will not mind having the little room will you dear? Of course, you know, I shall be at Streatham Hill to meet you, I only wish it was tonight. How long will you be able to stay? I am so glad you went to Church last Sunday and you will go this won't you darling? and take your wife that is to be.

Tomorrow night Ernie is coming home early and wants Laura and I to ride to Kingston. If I feel alright I shall go, but I shall wait and see. Give my love to Ida and tell her I think she might write and how I wish she and your mother were going to be at Folkestone. Shall you take your bike with you?

Well my dearest I must close now. With heaps of kisses and my whole love

Yours most devotedly
Beatie

Ernest playing tennis. His father had refused to allow him to go into the Navy when he was thirteen and so Ernie ran away from school at sixteen and joined the Merchant Navy with the Shaw Saville Line. After four years he came out and worked a seven years' apprenticeship before joining the 'House of Rothschild' in 1905, as his grandfather and father had before him. (H)

⬩⬩⬩⬩⬩⬩

Linwood Lodge, July 19th 1898

My own darling Beatie

Now for a chat with you my own sweet one. I do miss you so dear, for it was such happiness to be with you, but alas we are far apart again. What a sweet good night we wished each other on Saturday and Sunday, but last night how different. But we must hope on and look out for our happy time together at Folkestone for it will be a truly happy time won't it dearie. Who could possibly be more happy than we who have such perfect love one for another, and such faith in each other. We shall always be happy together I know darling under any circumstances whatever.

On returning from their blissful weekend together Jack sent to Beatrice the remnants of the torn up letter from his mother to Beatrice, which he had saved in a drawer. He had not tried to piece it together and read it. If he had he would have found her still cold and unforthcoming about her feelings towards Beatrice.

An earlier letter from Jennie, as well as an anxious letter from Jack on July 18th revealed the anxiety the family felt at Uncle John's announcement to dissolve his partnership with the business. Jack hoped to persuade him against it and "thinks Uncle will come to terms", otherwise "there will have to be a split up".

Because of Jack's many contacts with the jewellery trade in Birmingham he was able to buy and have jewellery repaired more cheaply than Beatrice could in London. One of these contacts he was later to wish he had never met, however.

The time when Beatrice and Jack were likely "always to be together" was a long way off, but sufficient in itself to keep Beatrice's spirits up during their long separation. (A)

Of course you received this morning the remains of that letter I told you of and I have been wondering all day as to what you will do with it, or whether you will be able to decipher any of it. Mother seems as cool as ever and I have not yet given your love to her for I consider it would be wasted on such a cold creature, at all events, at present. Don't trouble yourself any more than you can help, on that score my darling, for I do hope the sun will soon begin to shine for us, altho things are not too bright at present.

I understand that Uncle John returned yesterday, so we may soon hear something now as to the future conduct of the business. It will be truly a relief to know what has got to take place, and as soon as I know anything I shall let you know for I know that you are most anxious, dear.

I have made enquiries about the ear-ring and will you tell Ma that I can get it matched exactly for her, and that the cost will be £6=0=0 (six pounds). Of course I have not yet given the order for it to be done, as you remember we arranged I was to let you know first what the cost would be. If the price is alright let me know and it shall be done at once.

Well, darling, I received a letter from my Captain yesterday, and had an interview with him this morning. My resignation had been reported to Head-quarters and he tells me that it created as much surprise there as it did at B'ham. They do not mean losing me if they can help it, but they will have to, I believe. The Adjutant seems to be interesting himself in the matter and says if the work I have been doing (Signalling) takes up too much time for me, I can do something else, which would not need so much time putting in. He has some new work which he wants taking up, Range Finding by means of instruments, and he says I could soon train the few men required to a good state of efficiency and is anxious for me to take it up. It is no use for me to think of it though, as of course I should have to do the full week in Camp and that is impossible. He has granted me leave of absence over Camp, and I have to attend Gun Practice in October, two days that will take and then I shall be returned efficient for this year. Then he says I can let him know if I will take up the new work for next year or if I am still in the same mind as to resigning.

Well darling, I do wish I were with you to comfort you, and myself as well, for I am so lost without you, but it is comfort to write to you dear for it is like having a chat together. We must both look out for the 30th and then we shall be happy again. What a sweet time dear when all these partings are over, and I have claimed my dear little wife. We shall be then truly happy. Well dear good night, heaps of love and many kisses.

Your own devoted
Jack

"Roselea", July 20th 1898

My own darling Jack

I was so glad to hear you had arrived safely and not quite melted all away. Wasn't it hot? I do so miss you, this separation is awful and each time we part is harder for me, but I must think of the time, when we shall always be together and won't that be bliss.

Well dear I am about used up, this housemaid nearly drives me mad, she does not do anything properly and I have to do it again after her, then today Flora has gone home until tomorrow and I have had to do the cooking etc. and was down this morning at 7 o'clock and have been hard at it ever since and I don't know which way to turn, I have such a lot of small jobs to do before we go away. Well my darling, I have pieced that letter together and do you know she does not mention you or our engagement, she utterly ignores it, so I don't see how she could say it was putting matters right. Ma surprised me very much, this morning, by telling me she had written to your Mother, asking her and Ida to come to Folkestone. I wonder what she will say? Ma will be very glad if you will get her earring done for £6, and thanks you very much for all the trouble you have taken. Just fancy not wanting you to leave the Corps, I am not surprised and I shall not have a word to say on the matter, you must decide for yourself.

I shall long for the 30th, won't it be lovely to have a fortnight together, we shall enjoy our little selves. I hope all your affairs will go on satisfactorily and try to get friends with your Mother. I don't like to hear of this coolness and I am sure she does not like it.

Excuse short letter darling, but I will make up for it next time I write. Heaps of love and hugs and many kisses

Yours always Beatie

Linwood Lodge, July 22nd 1898

My own darling Beatie.

I was so glad to receive your dear letter, but am afraid you must begin to think dear that I am rather neglecting you, as you did not hear from me this morning. The plain fact is, however, that I have really not been able to find time before. I have just come up to bed now, and am penning these few lines before retiring and intend posting this very early in the morning, in order that you may receive it tomorrow, Saturday. Of course you will be at Folkestone, then darling, and I must address it to you there. I do wish we were just one week older and then I should be with you tomorrow. I am sorry you have been having such a stiff time of it lately, but then darling it all helps to fill up the time, altho I hope you will not be any the worse for it. I am so glad that I had kept that letter after all, and that you had seen it dear; but I felt all the time that it was too much to expect that she would write such a letter which would, to use the expression again "put everything right". She was only trying to annoy me more, if possible. Everything is right already, eh dearie, so far as we ourselves are concerned, and what matters further, I saw the other morning that a letter came from your Ma to my Mother, but she has never mentioned the matter to me; and but for your dear self I should still be ignorant of the contents. All arrangements are now made for the Holidays I believe; and Mother and Ida are going to join Jennie at Barmouth on the Thursday in Bank Holiday Week. Nin and Alec are going to Corwen just for the Holiday time and Alec returns and Nin goes on to Barmouth. Barmouth is a very stuffy place,

DOMESTIC SERVANTS' WAGES.

From a report compiled by Miss Collet, and issued by the Labour Department of the Board of Trade, it appears that one-third of the occupied female population of the United Kingdom are engaged in domestic service. The number of women and girls so employed in the United Kingdom in 1891 is stated in the census returns as 1,748,954, so that domestic service is not only the largest women's industry, but the largest single industry for either men or women. Miss Collet has obtained, by means of over two thousand schedules, information concerning the wages of 5,453 women and 326 men employed as resident domestic servants; and although these numbers, when compared with the vast numbers of persons engaged in domestic service, may seem at first sight to afford a somewhat inadequate basis for any general conclusions, the number and variety of households from which schedules have been obtained, and the striking uniformity disclosed by the returns in the rates of money wages paid for similar service in households employing the same number of servants, furnish a sufficient guarantee that the returns afford a correct indication of the average rates prevailing for servants of a given class and age, or employed in households of a given type. The following table is given to show the average wages of female domestic servants (at selected age periods) according to class of work:—

	Years.	London. £	England and Wales. £	Scotland. £	Ireland. £
Between maid ...	19	12·4	10·7	—	—
Scullerymaid ...	19	13·7	13·0	—	—
Kitchenmaid ...	20	16·5	15·0	15·0	11·3
Nurse-housemaid	21–25	14·9	16·0	14·0	—
General	21–25	14·9	14·6	15·3	10·3
Housemaid	21–25	17·5	16·2	17·1	13·5
Nurse	25–30	21·0	20·1	19·5	15·8
Parlourmaid	25–30	22·2	20·6	20·1	16·0
Laundrymaid	25–30	27·3	23·6	20·0	—
Cook	25–30	21·8	20·2	20·6	17·2
Lady's maid	30–35	28·1	24·7	24·4	24·0
Cook-housekeeper	40 and upwards	41·6	35·6	22·0	—
Housekeeper	40 and upwards	34·3	52·2	45·0	—

The Mercer household would have had at least two servants – a cook, housemaid and a gardener to maintain the large garden at 'Roselea' and the tennis court. Nevertheless Beatrice was a good cook and very capable in the house. (1)

Jennie, Jack's married sister, was always called 'Nin' by the family, although her real name was Jane. She was married to Alexander Hawkes – known as Alec – and at this time had one daughter Doris.

Jack's Hooligan friends were in Paris around the time of the famous three-day cycle race after which many of the riders were "victims of delusions". One "fell fast asleep upon his machine and did not awake even when he dropped on to the track with a heavy thud". Another rider "climbed a tree in the belief that he was a monkey". The winner, an American by the name of Miller, "finished marvellously fresh".

the rocks are close up to the sea and the town is completely shut up as it were in an oven and I am sure it will not do them very much good to spend a Holiday there. I have got the ear-ring done and am sending it on by same post as this. I have the pair in front of me now and they look fine. They have made a very good job of it, I consider, and feel sure your Ma will like it. What a time I have been having lately, working early and late, I want to wake about 4.30 in the morning if possible to get to the Works by 6. I don't know whether I shall manage it.

I am going for a spin on my machine tomorrow afternoon if fine, and back early in the evening as Alf Bradley is coming over tomorrow evening for Sunday. Three of my Hooligan friends are starting in the morning for Victoria, en route for Paris on that cycling tour I told you of, and I have promised to see them off. I don't know whether I shall be able to manage it though. They will be returning via Boulogne and Folkestone, arriving in Folkestone on the Saturday in Bank Holiday week, and want me to secure them a place in Folkestone for the night as they wish to stay there and return to B'ham on the Sunday, as they are all so anxious to see the future Mrs. Jack. How nice it sounds, eh darling, Mrs. Jack Hughes, just fancy, what do you think. Oh darling, I do so wish we were together now, to have a sweet good night kiss, for I do so miss you. It would be such comfort to me. Pray excuse me closing now darling, but it is so late and I want to be up so early that I really must do so. Well my own dearest one, Good night, and a sweet kiss.

Yours devotedly

Jack

Victoria Hotel, Folkestone. July 24th 1898

My own darling Jack

I was indeed most anxious not hearing from you yesterday before I left home, but I was greatly relieved to hear from you last night and know all was right, I think all sorts of things when I do not hear. Well dear, you see we have arrived, we got here about 4 o'clock yesterday afternoon, Mr. and Mrs. and Nellie Morris about 6 o'clock. Susie Lewcock came to the station to meet us but somehow we missed each other. In the evening we walked on the Leas and listened to the band, it was a lovely evening, I did so wish you were here dear, but I shall be looking forward most eagerly to next saturday, we shall have a lovely time, shall we not dear? This morning we went to Church and afterwards a walk along the Leas, there are some swell people in Folkestone, the dress was splendid this morning. It is a most perfect day. I am writing this in my own room and can see and hear the sea, I do love to hear it rolling in, but it would be perfect if you were here with me. Darling I do miss you more and more, and I feel sometimes as if I must give way, this separation seems so hard to bear and it is worse each time, but I know you will come and see me, as often as you can, until – I am Mrs. Jack Hughes, as you say, it does sound so grand to me. I shall be proud to be introduced to your Hooligan friends when they arrive. I wonder which boat they will cross over in, there is one reaches here at 4 o'clock in the afternoon and the one at about 10 o'clock. I expect you

The famous bandstand which provided an attractive landmark and rendezvous for the crowds, including Beatrice, who flocked to listen on The Leas at Folkestone. (E)

will have to change at Folkestone Junction when you come, for the Harbour Station, we did. First of all there is "Folkestone Central" station, then Folkestone Junction, but of course you will make enquiries about that.

The living here is fair and plain, the place seems nice and clean, but such a lot of old tabs, I do hope some livelier people will soon come and wake us up a bit, we will make it noisy won't we? Just fancy, your Mother has not written to Ma yet. I didn't think she would come here somehow. Well dear take care of yourself and not go overdoing it. Lots of kisses and hugs to be taken out when we meet.

Yours always Beatie

Linwood Lodge, July 26th 1898

My own darling Beatie

I was so pleased to receive your dear letter, when I reached home last evening. I rode into town yesterday morning on my bike, and when I had done business started off for a ride, instead of coming straight home. I went as far as Stone Bridge, then on to Coleshill and home about 26 miles altogether. I went the round in three hours. The road from Stone Bridge to Coleshill is most delightful, and especially so in the cool of the evening. I did so enjoy it dear, and thought of your sweet self, and of the times when we shall be going rides together. That is one of the pretty parts I shall take you to, my darling. I am so glad dear, to know you are now at Folkestone, for I feel that every day I am getting nearer to being with you, and shan't I be happy when I am. I called at the Railway Station today and arranged for my luggage to be collected and sent on in advance, so I shall only have my bike to look after when I come on Saturday. I think that is much the better way to do. I am glad you went to Church dear, on Sunday, altho' I did not myself. It was too bad of me, but I went off cycling. But if I do not go regularly myself, I think of those who do. I thought of you darling and felt sure you would be there. I spent the day at Harrops on Sunday, and oh it was hot. We had tea out on the lawn, it was too hot to be indoors. I am glad you like the Idea of the Hooligans' visit darling, and I am sure when they have had the honour of an introduction they will say that I am a very lucky boy.

I do wish Saturday was here and that I were with you, fancy we shall have a fortnight to look forward to and what comfort that will be. There is nobody at home but Alice and I. Everybody is out. Mother and Joe have gone to the Workhouse today that sounds bad doesn't it darling, but you see it is in this way darling. You remember poor little Mr. Evans, well he is Chairman of the Board of Guardians and has today laid the Foundation Stone of some cottage homes which are about to be built. They are intended for poor old couples, that they may live together in future, when they have the great misfortune to become paupers, instead of being separated, as was the case formerly. So of course it has been a big day. Mother and Joe, and Nin and Alec had invitations and were all there. Of course I have not been. Tomorrow, Mother and Joe are going out for the day with the "Forward Lodge". They train to Malvern, then drive to Ledbury and back. They will be in lovely country and will only need favourable weather to ensure a most enjoyable day.

The Leas was an elegant promenade high up overlooking the sea. The famous Leas Lift, built in 1885, carried the holiday-makers up and down the steep cliff to the beach and pier below.

NEW COTTAGE HOMES AT GRAVELLY HILL.

The preliminary work upon the new cottage homes which the Aston Board of Guardians are erecting at Gravelly Hill has now reached a sufficiently advanced stage for the customary official stone-laying to take place, and this interesting ceremony was performed yesterday afternoon by the Chairman (Mr. James Evans). The decision to erect the homes was not arrived at without a good deal of argument, a controversy having raged round the project for some years past. The Aston Guardians obtained plans from Messrs. Franklin, Cross, and Nichols for the erection of a commodious set of buildings, in which the children of the Board will be placed under the care of foster parents. This decision was only arrived at by a majority of one vote, but some portion of the opposition was no doubt directed against the intention to erect the new buildings in proximity to the workhouse, which it is desired, as far as possible, to keep out of the children's minds. The architects' plans were originally drawn for the accommodation of "families" of thirty, but at the instance of the Local Government Board they have been amended, so as to provide for "families" of not more than sixteen, space being found in the altered designs for a total of 250 children. The new buildings face the workhouse on the opposite side of Union Road, and are divided by a broad roadway into two sections, one for girls and one for boys. In the centre of the former is situated the superintendent's house; at the Fentham Road end is a probationary lodge for the detention and examination of new comers, and at the opposite extremity are the church and schools and the infirmary. In each section are seven homes for the accommodation of sixteen children each, and one for twelve children. The boys' department contains workshops, in which they will be taught tailoring, shoemaking, carpentry, and fitting, and a large swimming bath is also provided. The contract, which amounts to £42,000, has been let to Messrs. W. Lee and Son, of Aston. A large company assembled to witness the stone-laying, among those present being ——— E. Ansell, Alderman ——— Ald——— ing the ———

——— ——— Guardians. After discussing the various means by which they might have obtained the needed extension, he pointed out that opinion was in favour of the separation of the children from the adults, so as to avoid the evil consequences of constant association with confirmed paupers. They might have arranged to erect homes in various parts of the district, but it was thought that the plan adopted would allow of a better system of government. The site chosen was pleasant and healthy, and would allow of the children going out into the district to school. Homes for smaller "families" than sixteen would no doubt have been better for the children, but the Board had also to consider the pockets of the ratepayers. They believed that the children trained in these homes would grow up into good men and women, and intelligent and useful citizens. (Applause.)—Mr. Doggett, in proposing a vote of thanks to the chairman for laying the stone, remarked that there was no trace of "Bumbledom" about the ceremony they had just witnessed. What they were doing would tend to lessen pauperism and crime. Mr. A. Taylor, who seconded the motion, remarked that after much heated discussion a majority of the Board had come to approve of the erection of these homes.— Mr. Evans afterwards entertained the visitors to tea on the lawn in front of the workhouse. The band of the Marston Green Homes played selections during the afternoon.

A newspaper report on the Foundation Stone ceremony for the New Cottage Homes at Gravelly Hill. They were built by the Aston Board of Guardians. Some two hundred and fifty children of the board were placed with foster parents. (J)

Everybody seems to be enjoying themselves, but never mind dearie, our turn will be soon here and then we shall be alright. Well my dearest one I must close, and be off to post with this or you will be disappointed in the morning. Cheer up we shall soon be together again. Meantime, with my whole Love, and heaps of kisses, I am

Yours ever
Jack.

Victoria Hotel, Folkestone. July 28th 1898

My own darling Jack

At last a letter from you, but I was glad to get it dear, the time seems as if it never would get to saturday. I am so longing to see you. I went on the harbour the other afternoon and saw the 4.30 train come in and two carriages in front G.W.R. that will be the one you will come by. There were a good many people and we watched them get into the boat. Cannot you manage to leave here on the monday, when you go back, for if you cannot get a train on Sunday, it will make two days difference, do try and stay until the monday you can if you like you know Jack. Ma had a letter from your Mother, and she does not say a word about Ma having asked her here, she only said that Ida was going to Barmouth with Jennie and that she would follow later on, and she did not mention me at all, isn't she strange, but I don't care, when your love is so great for me dear, and I know we shall always be the same. I was glad you went for a ride it will do you good. How lovely, when you take me for a ride, dear and shew me round. Have you heard any more about your Uncle John? but of course you have not or you would have told me. I have only been for a bicycle ride once, I don't like mouching about here, so I am waiting until you come, then I should like to ride to Dover, it is such a pretty ride, although very hilly; yesterday and today, the weather is perfect. I hope it will keep so. Reg goes to Aunt Parker's today, so Ma and Mrs. Morris are going to Smeeth, just to see them and back again tonight. You and I must go one day next week, I have asked Ma to ask Aunt which day I shall come.

Beatrice was very keen to get a sun tan, though it was not nearly such a fashion at that time. It is doubtful that she would have bathed and if so would have been carried into the water in a bathing machine. This and her modest costume would have allowed very little of her skin to be exposed to the sun in her efforts to "get brown". (N)

This house seems filling up, in fact a friend of Nellie Morris' is coming on saturday and she will have to sleep out. I am trying to get brown, but have not succeeded yet, except my hands and they are like a nigger's. I hope you will excuse the pencil, but I am writing this in my room and have not any ink up here. Of course dear, I shall be at the Harbour to meet you on saturday and shall look most eagerly for the time to come. Won't we enjoy our little selves. We are going to sit on the beach this morning to hear the niggers, we feel rather lazy. Well darling excuse more now, and accept heaps of kisses and my whole true love

All yours
Beatie

The Question Of The Wedding Date

AUGUST & SEPTEMBER

Jack returns from summer holidays in Folkestone to discover new plans for the 'future conduct of the business'. His mother remains determined to obstruct his plans to marry while continuing her own embarrassing affair with the dreaded Phelps. Beatrice visits a palmist and although a wedding date is planned the palmist's predictions seem likely to come true . . .

Linwood Lodge, Aug 17th 1898

My own darling Beatie,

Of course you received the wire this morning and are aware of my safe arrival in B'ham, once more. I did feel it so much darling, parting from you after the most happy time we had had together. They were happy days indeed, eh darling, and how soon they sped away. But we must not feel down hearted dearie, at these partings, at least not more than we can help, for we must feel that each of these comings and goings is bringing us nearer to that happy time when we shall be together always. I did feel so upset dearie when the train took me from you, but when I had been on the way a little time,

No letters were necessary for the first two weeks of August as Jack and Beatrice were blissfully together for a whole fortnight, on the family holiday in Folkestone. Jack's return to Birmingham however was quickly to bring him back to the reality of his home situation and yet more difficulties.

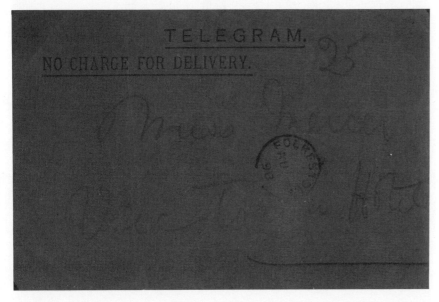

Jack's envelope for his telegram to Beatrice to tell her of his safe arrival back to Birmingham. The charge to send a telegram remained at 'six pence for 12 words' up until 1912. (A)

Pine Walk, one of the many walks in Folkestone. On their favourite walks in the Warren, the famous undercliff, Jack and Beatrice would have been likely to have been accompanied by those there to see the many foreign butterflies for which the Warren was known. (E)

Beatrice had spent many happy hours cycling with Jack at Folkestone, but on his departure Mrs. Morris had become her substitute cycling companion. (K)

strange to say I went off to sleep, and slept the whole way to B'ham only waking each time the train stopped. The train arrived at B'ham at 3.35 and after putting my luggage in the cloak room I walked to the Works arriving there exactly at 4 o'clock. I had a sleep on the couch until 6.30 and then had a cup of tea, and after having breakfast at 8.30 felt as right as rain. In fact I have not felt the least bit tired all day, which rather surprises me. Mother is not at home just now, Ida tells me she has gone over to Blakemore's today. It appears that Nin and Doris, and Mother and Ida are going with them to Aberystwyth in a few days time for their holidays, and Mother has gone over today to make the necessary arrangements. I have not yet heard any further particulars of the arrangement come to with Uncle John, but be assured, darling, that I shall let you know all, as soon as I do hear. I do sincerely hope that we shall all be able to work smoothly together in the business, now after all this upset, and in fact I mean doing my best for I begin to think that Uncle John is not so black as he has been painted, altho goodness knows he is quite bad enough.

It has seemed so strange to me, darling, today, not to have you with me, for we were not very far apart at Folkestone, were we. What lovely times together, especially our afternoons in our little arm chair at the "Warren", and the evenings too in the nice little nooks about the gardens, of course excepting the "Bogie Place". If you walk up Sandgate Rd, darling, in the evening, you must avoid the "Bogie Place" also that walk with the tree in the centre. What fun we had, eh, seeing the couples walk into it. When next we go to Folkestone, dearie, we shall revive happy memories of this visit by paying our respects to all the delightful little nooks that have afforded us so much happiness. I hope you are not yet quite cold, down the side on which I have been accustomed to walk. I shall be looking out on Friday morning, darling, for your dear letter, to know how you are going on; and shall write you Friday night again. Give me kindest regards to Mrs. Morris please. I shall miss your sweet goodnight kiss tonight darling, but we must fancy it until we meet again I suppose. It was so nice of your Pa and Ma to be so kind to me during my stay. Please thank them for me, again, and give them my best love. Well darling I must now conclude, so with my whole true love and a sweet good night kiss

ever

Your own true

Jack

❖❖❖❖❖❖❖

Victoria Hotel, Folkestone. Aug 18th 1898

My own darling Jack

I have only just got in 6 o'clock and it is the first opportunity I have had to write before. I was dreadfully disappointed not receiving your letter this morning. Mrs. Morris sent down directly after breakfast to ask me to go to Lyminge with her on our bikes, so I went it was a lovely ride, I wish we had gone while you were here. I could not get back to the Hotel in time for luncheon, so Mrs. Morris asked me there, so consequently I did not get your letter until 3 o'clock. Reg went for it for me. I was pleased to hear you had such a comfortable journey and do not feel any ill effects from it, just fancy you being able to sleep. I felt parting from you most keenly and I hardly slept all night first crying and then wondering how you were getting along. We went on the pier last night, it was very good indeed. When we got home I went into no. 6 but I cannot bear to stop there now, I feel so dreadfully lonely. You cannot imagine how miserable I feel, I do wish you were here to comfort me and kiss my tears away. Jack you must do something or come oftener to see me, for I cannot go on like this, it makes me feel so bad. Just fancy your Mother going away with the Blakemore's, I think it is a great snub for us, what do you think? I am simply longing for saturday to come, I so want to go home, it seems weeks since you left me, in fact; it all seems a short dream, your stay here, as if I had awoke and found it all a dream and you gone. I shall not want to go to the Warren or Sandgate Rd without my darling unless I found another pebble. I hope things will go on much smoother for you and I should try and keep in with your Uncle and don't forget to tell him about me and that we want to get married as soon as possible and be sure and let me know what he says about it, I do hope he won't mind. I think I had better address this to the Works, or you will not get it until night time and I want a letter when I arrive home. Let me know if you spot any little cabin that will suit us. Mrs. Morris sends her love and so does Ma and Pa. I do hope you are not quite bankrupt after spending such a lot of money on me. I shall look forward most eagerly to the 3rd, how I wish it was this saturday. Well darling, heaps of love and many many kisses. I must fly now and get dressed for dinner.

Yours ever Beatie

The Victoria, or Pleasure Pier, at Folkestone was opened in 1888 and provided an elegant promenade. (E)

Linwood Lodge, Aug 19th 1898

My own darling Beatie

Here I am, just got home and it is 10.45 pm, and I do seem to have had such an eventful time and it seems ages since I left you. I was rather surprised at not receiving your letter first post this morning, but when it came to hand, at the Works, about 11 o'clock, I was so glad, and of course could understand the delay, upon reading it.

You know that an arrangement has been made between us all for the future conduct of the business. Well today we were all to meet to sign the deed, and Uncle John was anticipating that it would all be settled and he would go away with an easy mind; as he is going to Ireland for a Tour, starting tomorrow. It seems it was not to be so. Some big business is about being placed today, and Joe had to leave last night for Glasgow, to be on the scene early this morning. (I hope he will be successful.) I had then to go and see Uncle John and inform him that Joe and I could not sign the deed today, but that Mother would do so and we would do it on Joe's return. He did not mind that of course, as he knew Joe was looking after business. While I was with him last night, we had a good long talk, and it seemed quite like old times. I told him of our engagement and he said if I had got the right girl I had done a very good thing, for he said a good woman can make a good man. I told him there was no fear but I had got the right one. I also told him how Mother was treating us, and he gave the

There was much talk of marriage between Jack and Beatrice on their holiday and a date agreed on between them, although they did not reveal it to anyone for some time.

After an estrangement of two years, this improvement in Jack and Uncle John's relationship was to prove vital for Jack to have any peace of mind.

Whereas the Albion Works had the luxury of a telephone it was still very unusual for private homes to possess one, and although Linwood Lodge did not, it seems as if Uncle John at his house in Chester Road, did. It would have been used only in cases of some importance – as indeed the summons of Jack was on this occasion. (L)

An advertisement for The Private Secretary, *the play to which Frank and Ida went in Birmingham. (J)*

As Jack and Beatrice's story unfolds many of the palmist's predictions seem alarmingly likely to come true.

opinion which I hold myself, that we are old enough to know our own minds and must not think of what other people say about us. He came to the Works this morning and I had another chat with him then. I told him I was most anxious for the business arrangement to be settled, and to have an idea as to how much better off I was likely to be, and he promises to let me know all he can when he returns from Ireland. I was rather surprised to be called up by Telephone this afternoon by Uncle, and he asked me to go over to Chester Rd tonight, as he wished to see me most particularly. On getting there I found there was more difficulty, it appears Mother had declined to sign the deed, saying that some of the conditions contained in it, were not what she had agreed to. Uncle assures me that such is not the case, and that the deed is exactly word for word what she and Joe and himself agreed to while I was away, I told him I did not think Joe would depart from his word, and if he waited until Joe's return for it to be signed no doubt any misunderstanding could be cleared up. I think it will go through alright. I stayed and had supper with him and told him I was anxious to know my position as early as possible, as we want to get married, and he promises to let me know as early as possible, and when he does, I shall let you know all, darling.

I am so anxious for us to be settled down, this suspense is awful and I know you must feel it much more than I, and goodness knows, I feel it badly enough, for I do miss your dear kisses and sweet companionship. I am glad you enjoyed your ride to Lyminge. You will be glad to get home tomorrow no doubt, and I only wish I could be there to meet you, but that is impossible. But still I shall be up on the 3rd. Pray excuse this rambling letter darling, but I must tell you all, and I have told you in the best manner I am capable of. But I am so tired tonight you must pardon the scribble. I hope you can read it. There is no one at home yet. Frank and Ida have gone to see *The Private Secretary*, and of course Mother is out. They will be on the last train. Well darling I must say good-night now, as I must be off to town early in the morning. I hope you will have a good night's rest, and a safe journey home tomorrow. Heaps of love and a sweet good night kiss.

Yours ever
Jack

◇◇◇◇◇◇

"Roselea", Aug 21st 1898

My own darling Jack

You see we have landed home once more, but oh goodness it was a hot journey. Pa got a carriage engaged for us, and we left the harbour at 1.40 and got home about 6 o'clock. I found your dear letter (as promised) waiting for me it quite cheered me up, to think your Uncle was so kind about our engagement. I only hope he will keep to his word and let us be always together. I did so wish you had been here yesterday, when I got back, I miss you dear, more than ever, it makes me feel so dull.

Well duckie I went to the palmist, really she is clever. The first thing she told me, was, to go and get advice, as my heart line was not satisfactory, she asked me if I fainted at all, she says there is no disease, but one of the valves does not act properly and might get serious if neglected. Then she said you have had a great trouble and worry through a worthless man, but that I had sent him about his business and that now my life was smoother than it had been for years, as she thought I had only been engaged about 3 months and to a very good fellow who simply adored me and that we should be married before the year was out (we shall have to buck up don't you think?) she said I had got one of the most clever hands she had ever seen, and that I ought to have made a great name either at a stringed musical instrument or the stage. She says my finger tips are so sensitive. She also says I am very generous and kind hearted and have greater feeling than people imagine even my own Father and Mother have no idea what depth of feeling. I am a splendid manager and love order, most artistic and clever with my fingers. We are to have a very smooth and happy life together (we know that, don't we dear) but that I have a serious illness before me. We are to have 2 or perhaps 3 children (don't laugh). She said that you had loved me some time before you spoke to me and that when I first knew you I had not any thoughts for you. She says that there is a woman, who is trying her utmost to put every obstacle in the way of our marriage, but that we are not to take any notice of it, but go on. I cannot think of any more, but don't you think it is wonderful.

I hope all your affairs will be alright and that the deed will be signed satisfactorily also that Joe will be successful with that business at Glasgow. How long will your Uncle be away. When you see him, give him my kind regards and tell him, how pleased I am, that he approves of our engagement, I believe after all, he cannot be so bad. You remember that old lady at Folkestone Mrs. Wynne, well she was so very kind to me the day we left, she kissed me and wished me goodbye and wished me all the happiness and prosperity in my married life, which she knew I deserved, and she was sure you would be good to me, you were so nice and gentlemanly she turned to Ma and said how she felt for her, at the prospect of losing such a daughter, but she must console herself, by thinking she had gained another son. Well, this is a long letter, I hope it won't bore you, do write back as soon as you can and cheer your poor little Baby up. I did not get up until dinner time today, I felt so tired so consequently did not go to Church. Last friday we went to see *La poupée* at the theatre, it was so good and funny. Well my own dearie Goodnight and heaps of kisses and hugs

Yours ever

Beatie

◇◇◇◇◇◇◇

Linwood Lodge, Aug 22nd 1898

My own darling Beatie

I have just arrived home, 8 pm, and how I wish it was to our own little home; for it does seem so dull here. Night after night when I come home there is no-one here but Ida. Mother of course is so busy. She has been at home all day, but went out about a quarter past seven I am told. Gone to meet her darling, I suppose, isn't it sickening. Fancy coming to an empty house night after night; and even when she is at home she cannot be genial. It does seem strange, but it is true, that I never saw her since I came home from

Fortune telling of many kinds was popular in the Victorian era, although some of it was highly suspect. Beatrice's palmist was certainly right about the "worthless" man who was Beatrice's previous fiancé, of whom her parents did not approve at all.

La Poupée, "The Greatest London Comic Opera Success" – guaranteed to give "286 laughs, 68 smiles and 25 roars" at every performance, was also staged at Folkestone.

The fact that Jack's mother clearly had a lover, which accounted for her rarely being at home in the evenings, offended Jack deeply. He could hardly bring himself to face up to the reality of it and even found it difficult to refer to him by name, but he was at the root of many of the problems Jack was to encounter.

The "extraordinary thunderstorms" followed a period of unusually hot weather and the newspapers reported a person killed by the lightning.

Folkestone until dinner time yesterday, and then she did not speak to me; so after dinner I went to Nin's and stayed there to Tea and Supper, got home at ten o'clock and came in and straight to bed. So I did not trouble her much with my company. What an awful night we had last night, a terrific thunderstorm between two and three o'clock. It was such a storm, as I have never known before and wish I may never hear again. The rolls of thunder seemed to be right upon us. I can tell you I did not feel comfortable, and thought of you darling, and hoped that you were not experiencing the same. I told Nin and Alec yesterday, that it seemed as if you and I were in for similar treatment to what they received, when they became engaged to each other; and that we would be married as soon as I could see my way clear, and they sympathised with us, so if anybody can sympathise with us, it is they, for they did go through the mill, I can tell you. I do hope when Uncle John returns that the deed will be signed satisfactorily, for upon that depends all our arrangements. My income, as I told you, darling, is not sufficient at present to warrant our getting married; but when this deed is signed as it stands at present, it will be.

So you could not keep away from the Palmist, eh? I am much grieved darling about the first news she told you, about your heart; and I have often thought, (in fact said so) that cycling does not suit you. But we must not anticipate anything serious, you must seek advice on the matter, that is if you think there is any notice to be taken of what she tells you. It certainly does seem most strange though, that all she tells you seems so peculiarly applicable to the case. Fancy speaking of our engagement and all the rest of it; but I think somehow she is wrong for I don't see how we can get married this year. She seems to be right in every other particular, excepting perhaps the family we are to have. But who knows? One thing we do know however, without being told, and that is to take no notice of the woman who is putting the obstacles in the way of our marriage. She can never alter our love for each other, eh, dearie. I hardly know whether I am glad you went or otherwise, for the news, rather information, seems to be mixed. However there seems to be something in it, and I almost wish now I had gone myself. You will be sorry to know that Joe has not been successful in the business he went after. Uncle John thinks of being away about 3 weeks. I shall look him up when he returns, and I do pray that the business matter will then be settled satisfactorily and end this suspense, and enable me to claim my bride and bring her to Birmingham. Well dearie I must now conclude, with my whole love and heaps of kisses

ever your own Jack.

I went to Church yesterday morning. It was such a service. I will tell you all about it sometime.

Jack's mother, Mrs. Hughes, easily identifiable as the woman who was "trying her utmost to put every obstacle in the way" of Jack and Beatrice's marriage. (M)

❖❖❖❖❖❖

"Roselea", Aug 23rd 1898

My own darling Jack

I was more than delighted to receive your dear letter this morning as I hardly expected one, I thought you might be too busy. But darling, it does grieve me to know how wretched it must be for you at home, I only wish I could come to you to cheer you up, you know dear I would come to you tomorrow if I could, don't you? Never mind dear, cheer up and hope that the deed will soon be signed and then what joy for us both, when you come to fetch me to be with you always, only think of that dearie, I, of course feel very miserable without you, and especially knowing how uncomfortable things are for you. I am sorry Joe was not successful, but better luck next time. I am simply dead tired, you know Flora could not stay after monday so I have to do the work and with only this fool of a girl it is awful, I should be better without her. We have advertised in the morning's paper so I hope we shall soon be suited. Excuse this dirty piece of paper, I have only just noticed it. I do wish the 3rd was here, I am so longing to see you, it is hard to bear this separation in fact sometimes I feel I must give up. Do write to me as often as possible I do love to hear from you, you don't know how it helps me on. Has your Mother gone yet or when does she go? No darling, nothing can alter my love for you, it is too strong and true, as you will prove. I only wish the time was here, or that you were able to, and we could snap our fingers at *some people*.

Nellie's father has given her a bicycle she brought it round for us to see last night, but I don't like it nearly as well as mine and hers cost £13. Laura sends her love, she is just starting to her brother's at Wallington for a few days, on her bike. I shall try and go for a ride tonight, if I am not too tired. I hope you will excuse these awful blots, I really am too tired to write another, and I have got such an awful pen and Laura is waiting to post this. Accept all my love and oceans of kisses and good hugs. I wish we were where we were last tuesday afternoon, I don't expect you have forgotten, have you duckie

*Yours most devotedly
Beatie*

◇◇◇◇◇◇

Linwood Lodge, Aug 26th 1898

My own darling Beatie

Whatever will you be thinking of me for not having written you ere now, but really dearie I have been so busy the last two days that it was absolutely impossible to find time in which to have a chat with you on paper. It was a most strange thing, but we all were at supper together last night, and I thought may be it was the opening of a new era, it was indeed strange to come home and find Mother here. But alas it was too good to last, for on coming home this evening my first question was, "Is Mother in" and I was greeted with the usual "No". A little word truly, but think of what it conveys to me. Visions of all kinds of things in the future, but of course we are not going to trouble of that. I believe Mother has made arrangements to go away on Thursday next. She has been trying to get to know through Alice, when I am coming up to "Roselea" again, but needless to say it has not come off. I don't know why she should be so anxious, but if she must know why not ask me. You know when I am coming don't you darling, and so do I, but altho' I am so busy the time somehow seems so long, and I feel as if the third were never coming. However, it is only another week now, and then when that is passed we shall be able to embrace each other and be happy together, for a time. I am looking ahead,

Hieratica was the writing paper that Jack and Beatrice used for their letters to each other. It was advertised as a vegetable based paper purported to have been 'Used by the Ancient Greeks'. (B)

Alice was the Hughes' servant and likely to have become a 'go between' for Jack and his mother as they were not speaking to each other directly.

As others did, Jack and Beatrice discovered the many secluded and romantic dells in the wooded parts of the Warren. The irregularities formed by the fragments of rock detached from the cliffs above gave this landslip, with magnificent views out to sea, 'a wild and erratic kind of beauty'.

It was likely that Jack was day-dreaming to cause him to hit his thumb with a hammer, as it seems his heart and his thoughts were still with Beatrice in the Warren.

This was not the first or last time that Uncle John was to play a key role in retaining a sense of balance and fairness in the relationships and business affairs of the Hughes family.

anxiously, to Uncle's return from Ireland, I should think he will be back and everything settled before I come to see you after your Birthday. I do hope so, sincerely, and then I shall be able I hope darling to make you feel more comfortable, as indeed I shall myself. I have not forgotten where we were last Tuesday afternoon. In our little Arm-chair, eh, darling. The *last* farewell visit; and we had several didn't we; and hope to again. What a delightful spot; we were in a little world of our own together, up there, weren't we. It is so sweet to me darling to think of our happy days together, but so miserable am I when I realise that you are so far off. I am truly longing for you.

I suppose you heard nothing of the umbrella, after I left Folkestone. It was very annoying to me to lose it; but of course we have to pay for experience, and I can tell you I shall be a long while before I lose another umbrella, under similar circumstances.

Old Joyce seems to have got quite right again after her time at the Vet's in fact she barked on Wednesday a thing she has not done for a long time, in fact they had quite a shock here, when they heard her, it was so unusual. I did a nice thing at the Works, on Wednesday afternoon, I gave myself a severe blow on the left thumb with a heavy hammer. A silly thing to do, of course, but I suppose it is through having a long holiday, I got out of practice, eh. The thumb yesterday morning was swollen up to about 3 times its usual size, but with attention I have now got it very much better. It has been very painful, but not so now. There is a nasty cut, but I think it will be alright now in a few days.

How is Grandma. I hope she was alright while you were all away. Please give my love to her, also to your Pa and Ma. Thanks for message from Laura, you know darling I am always glad to hear of her, dear girl. Well darling I wish I could give you a sweet kiss, but imagine the kiss, and accept heaps of love from

Yours ever

Jack

"Roselea", Aug 28th 1898

My own darling boy

You cannot imagine how worried I felt, not hearing from you for so long. I thought all sorts of things, don't be so long again dear, do try and write oftener. How is your poor thumb, I am sorry you hurt it, and hope it will go on alright. How is it, that you have to use a heavy hammer? I don't see why you should.

Aimee has been here since friday, she wrote to me, saying how miserable she was, as her engagement was quite off, so I wrote and asked her over for a few days, but she has to go back on tuesday. I feel very sorry for her, as she has been treated very badly by that beast of a fellow. I have been out for a ride on my bike every night last week except saturday, when it was wet. This morning I went to Church and only wished you were with me darling. I do feel this awful separation. I am longing for saturday to come. I suppose you will come by the usual train. I am grieved that your Mother is so funny, and only hope that she will soon come round, have you spoken to her, you ought to you know dear. I shall be most anxiously waiting for your Uncle to be back and have every-

Leo's hair

Aug 19 8

Ted – Beatrice's elder brother, and Nellie, had two boys at this time – Leo aged three and Howard aged two years. Beatrice was particularly fond of Leo and she treasured a curl of his pale blond hair which has been preserved over the years along with her letters, in an envelope labelled 'Leo's hair'. (A)

thing settled, for it will brighten me up, a bit knowing how soon I can come to you to be with you always, for I do get most awfully dumpy being so far from you and seeing so little of you. Ted and Nellie and the children have been here today, Nellie is most anxious to know when the happy day is to be. I told her I didn't know she said she did not believe me.

Now dear, do write and answer to this as soon as you possibly can, I shall be eagerly looking out for a letter to know how your thumb is. We have not got any servants yet, so I wrote and asked Ellen if she could come and stay for a time until we got suited, I am glad to say she is here, for a little time, and so it gives me a bit of a rest, for working about that hot weather nearly did for me. No, dear unfortunately your umbrella never turned up, I wish it had, I was very sorry about it. Do write soon and cheer your little girlie up, who so longs for you. Heaps of love and embraces

Yours. ever

Beatie

✦✦✦✦✦✦✦

Linwood Lodge, Aug 30th 1898

My own darling Beatie

    I was so glad to receive your letter at town yesterday morning, and so learn that you were not quite worked to death; altho' you must have been having a pretty thick time of it. It was really impossible for me to

Perhaps the Mercers should have contacted Mrs. Webb's First Class Agency – she was that week advertising in The South London Press: 'Parlourmaid disengaged; aged 27, wages £20–£24, character four years. Also Housemaid, wages £16–£18, character four years.' Domestic service was regarded as a good training for marriage and a respectable occupation for women, although the work was hard and the wages for women half those for men servants.

Although Beatrice was somewhat shocked to discover that Jack had to do manual work at all at the factory despite being a junior partner, he was in fact constantly 'in the wars', having damaged his ear and later his eye. A metal foundry was a hazardous place and Victorian working conditions often led to serious accidents.

write you last night, darling and I am rather late tonight but I trust you will get this first post in the morning. Glad to say the thumb has gone on remarkably well, owing to the careful attention I have paid to it. My right hand was poisoned once, and I was unable to use it for six months; so that if ever I get any cuts on my hands now I am very careful to get them well as soon as possible; as I should dread to think of having such an experience again. Well darling, tomorrow is the last day of August, so we look like getting somewhere near the 3rd of September.

I went to the Solicitors today and signed the agreement. I found that it was already signed by Uncle John, and Joe; but not by my Mother. However, there is no fear but that she will sign it at once now, as she was waiting for Joe and I to sign another agreement with her, which we did this morning. So that when I see you, darling I shall be able to say, at last, that the business matters have been settled on satisfactory lines. How much better off, by the arrangement I shall be personally, I cannot say definitely just now. But if my expectations are realised, when the profits are declared on this year's trading, there will be nothing to prevent us carrying out our idea which we planned out at Folkestone. You know what that was don't you darling. I am so longing for you, and I know you are the same for me and I can assure you darling that I shall hasten the time of our wedding as much as possible. There is one thing I blame myself very much for, and I feel that I have been exceedingly foolish, and that is that in the past I have never saved any money. Rather I have saved, but have spent it again. But I feel now that I ought to have a bit by me that I have not; and it makes me feel very wild with myself, as it would have been so useful now. However, it is no use crying over spilt milk, the past is gone, and we must look to the future. I shall do all I can darling to make up for my past foolishness. I cannot say that I have had any conversation with Mother yet, we

Linwood Lodge, which still stands, is a large detached house which then had groom's quarters, cellars and a splendid billiard room. A mosaic-floored terrace with sandstone pillars and a balustrade provided a dance floor for the many social evenings and 'musical entertainments' Jack's mother held. Jack's father had been a keen gardener – a mulberry tree, pagoda and five ponds were features, but the show piece was the rockery for which he paid £250 to build and plant. (T)

were at Supper together last night, but the conversation was general, and she and I never addressed our conversation to each other. She requires an abject apology from me, and I don't feel that one is due to her, so you see that is where we differ. It is truly a happy state of things, but really darling I cannot bring myself to feel towards her all I should, since the Phelps affair. It is too much, I can't take it on for it fairly sickens me. I have not heard yet when the wedding is to be, but I hope with all my heart that ours will be first, for if she had married him before our wedding took place, I should not care for her to come to ours, what do you say.

I see Nellie is getting anxious, only natural I suppose for her to want to know. There must have been a guilty look upon you though darling when you said you didn't know. We do know dearie, if things will only run straight a bit; don't we. Well, cheer up, dearie and look forward to Saturday when we shall be able to have some good hugs and kisses. and make up for lost time. Really I must close now, or shall be too late for post. Heaps of love and kisses from

Yours devotedly
Jack

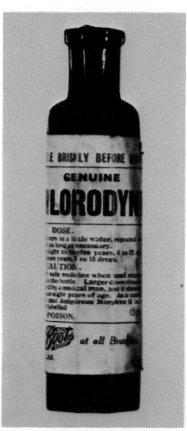

Phelps and Jack's mother shocked the family and distressed Jack more than anyone. He clearly spoke his mind about Phelps to his mother which contributed considerably to her hostility towards him and Beatrice.

"Roselea", Aug 31st 1898

My own darling Jack

I am very pleased that the deed has been signed at last, as now things look a little more hopeful for us. I am delighted that your thumb is so much better, you were wise to take so much care over it. Why don't you have it out with your Mother and have done with it, it would be ever so much more pleasant for both of us and I don't suppose you shewing your disapproval will make any difference to her arrangements. Of course I shall feel I never can receive him as her husband, but I do wish she was her old self to me once more. I have been so seedy the last two or three days, I have had indigestion so badly, I have taken something for it and today it is certainly a little better. I really have been afraid to eat anything. A friend came yesterday, an old lady, and bought me a hand painted bell for the table, such a curiosity so that has gone in my bottom drawer. How I do wish that saturday was here, I am simply dying for a sight of you. Do you know, we have not got any servants yet, I don't know what we shall do, they seem scarcer than ever.

We shall have to have a good old talk about things when you come, and see what we really are going to do. Of course a year seems a long time to look forward to but after all it soon slips by. Good old Folkestone. I wish you and I were at the Warren this afternoon, we would have a time wouldn't we dear? Never mind, we must wait awhile for that and then perhaps, who knows? I suppose your Mother goes tomorrow, is Ida going with her? Did you go to Church last Sunday, I am afraid you did not or else you would have mentioned it. Have you seen the three fellows who came to Folkestone. Jack dear, I do hope you won't have too much to do with them, they are bad enough for companions, for those, who like themselves have no tie, but not good for such as you at all. Aimèe wants to know if you can recommend her to some nice fellow who would take care of her, she wouldn't mind him being a bit old, so

Beatrice's travelling case, in which her letters from Jack were preserved, still contains bottles of powders and potions. One of them, 'chlorodyne' contains cannabis and morphine and bears a 'caution' on the bottle. Many other commonly used mixtures contained opium and these were taken without their danger being fully realized. (A)

Dr. Tibble's Vi-Cocoa, widely advertised as used successfully by men and women in all walks of life, fulfilled the popular belief that 'prevention was better than cure' for the many ailments that Victorian living conditions encouraged. Aimée's ailments were problems of the heart, however, and not even Jack felt disposed to help her find a husband. (X)

After spending a happy weekend with Beatrice, Jack caught the early morning train back to Birmingham in time to be at the Works before lunch. His effort did not seem to be appreciated by brother Joe, however, for whose sake Jack had made the effort, determined not to let him down.

long as she could trust him and live comfortably. I tell her I must keep my eyes open for her. She tells me that in the letter which is in answer to hers breaking off the engagement, he never expresses a regret, the brute I believe he had someone out there all the time. Just fancy she has been engaged to him 8 years. Goodness, we couldn't wait all that time could we darling? I am going out for a walk this afternoon so excuse more, and do write soon.

Lots of love and kisses

Yours ever
Beatie

Linwood Lodge, September 2nd 1898

My own darling Beatie

I was so glad to receive your dear letter yesterday and have been too busy to write you since receiving it until now. I am afraid though darling it must be a short one this time as it is now 8.35 pm but still I shall see you tomorrow so I know you won't mind this time. . . .

. . . I am sorry for Aimèe but I am afraid I cannot recommend anyone suitable, in fact if I knew anyone suitable I don't think I could recommend him, as I feel that such matters are best left alone, and let people find out for themselves. I don't think she should grieve though, but think herself well rid of such a fellow after being engaged eight years. Someone will come along one day and find her out, same as I did you. She must not brood over the past, but hope for better things in future. Just fancy though 8 years. I feel I can't wait so many months.

I am so tired darling and time for post so near so I must conclude now.
Never mind think of tomorrow.
Heaps of love and kisses.

Yours ever
Jack

"Roselea", September 6th 1898

My own darling Jack

Glad to hear you arrived safely. What a pig Joe is getting and I should like to tell him so. I wish you had stayed later now. Pray excuse this writing I can scarcely write with this awful pen. Well Laura and I did feel a bit tired yesterday afternoon, so we both laid down and rested, and felt all the better for it. We went for a ride in the evening when Ern came home.

We had a letter from David on monday a very nice one as far as we are concerned he congratulates me, and says if you are the right sort of chap and can give me a comfortable home and keep me in comfort he doesn't see why we need mind about your Mother treating me as she has, and says we are not to wait for him for the wedding, as it is so very uncertain, and it will be some time when he does get to Portsmouth before he can leave and then he is going to fetch Kitty and the children. I feel almost as if you had never been up at all so recently, it seems such a long time ago, but I shall be looking out for October 1st and counting the days until then. I had a letter from May in Cornwall, she simply raves about the place St. Austell. They leave there on friday by the midnight train and want to come here until Sunday so I have written and told them to come. I only wish your next visit was to fetch me don't you dear? I suppose your Uncle cannot make your position any better on his own account, the more I think of that agreement of your Mother's the meaner I think her but never mind we shall be happy enough as we are.

Ma seems to be coming round a bit but she is still very cool and off handed. Be sure to write again as soon as you can darling. I long to hear from you. What about those two houses? But I suppose you haven't had time to go to look.

Ma has gone this afternoon to see about a servant's character I do hope she will do, she comes in on thursday if satisfactory.

Pa made very kind enquiries about you and how you got home, he is a real good sort, and most kind and thoughtful. Laura thanks you for your message and sends her love and she says she gets excited already when she thinks of our wedding what about us?

Darling I must dry up now or else I shall lose the post. Heaps of love and many many kisses

Yours ever Beatie

Beatrice's eldest brother David, six years older than her, was serving in the Royal Marines aboard H.M.S. Edgar, at that time in Chinese waters. At the age of nineteen he had been presented to the Prince of Wales as a Lieutenant and from that point on was to have a highly eventful and distinguished naval career.

The Mercer family moved only a few years previously to 'Roselea' in Thrale Road, Streatham Park, from a house, coincidentally called 'Beatrice Villas', in Barry Road, Dulwich, although Beatrice was born at a house in Bermondsey. 'Roselea' like Linwood Lodge, was then a substantial family house with a large garden and grounds, including a grass tennis court bordered by rose beds. The tennis court is now overgrown and unused, but the roses still bloom. (H)

A photograph of Jack wearing the uniform of the First Worcestershire and Warwickshire Volunteer Artillery Regiment, Birmingham Division. He was soon to give this up for Beatrice's sake, although not prompted by her to do so. (M)

The working conditions at the metal works furnaces would have been intolerable in a heat wave. When it was too difficult to work in the day the men were prepared to work all night, rather than miss a day's wages. Many of the men would have been the only bread winner for a wife and five or six children.

Woodcock St. September 8th 1898

My own darling Beatie

I was so glad to receive your letter on Wednesday morning, and I am sorry I could not write you last night, but you see it was on account of Lodge meeting. We meet on the first Wednesday in each month, and I have to leave here about 5.45 to be there in time. However I have now finished for today and I am taking the opportunity of writing from here, as before I go home tonight I have to go to the Drill Hall to get information about Gun Practice. When I got home from Lodge last night, my orders were waiting there. I have to parade at New St. Stn. next Thursday morning at 7 o'clock, and proceed by 7.20 train to Aber. I expect it will be late on the Friday night when I get back, but when I do I shall have done all that the Corps. requires of me. I notice your opinion of Joe, and it is about right too. I am glad dear that you have heard again from David, and that he writes so kindly concerning ourselves, for I am sure you must feel much more comfortable. We must not think so badly of my Mother as far as her agreement is concerned, for you see she has Frank and Ida and Jennie to think of and Uncle has nobody. But of course it would not be wise to let him know of the arrangement. It is not likely he will make my position any better for me himself, (at all events during his life time) of course what may happen after, well we must not trouble about that. My position though will now be good enough for us to live comfortably, and I know we shall be as happy as possible together. I have not of course been to find those two houses, you spoke of yet, but I shall do so as early as possible. Every day I look down the lists of houses to let, in the daily papers, and yesterday I cut one out, it was an advertisement for one at Erdington in Orchard Road with a Greenhouse and Garden for £25, and I thought of having a walk that way on Saturday just to have a look at it. Joe picked the paper up later, and noticing a cutting had been taken, asked if I was looking for a house. I told him I did not want one just now, but that I certainly was on the lookout. He said he had been thinking of suggesting to me, that we took a house between us as things generally are so unpleasant at home, but of course if I was thinking of marrying soon that was out of the question.

I told him I was, or rather we were going to be married as early as possible, as I would rather furnish from my present capital and live moderately for a few years to put back the amount, than wait for 2 more years or so, to save the necessary amount, under existing circumstances, for I said we really can't go on long like we are. He seemed to think that was quite right. Fancy an organ has just struck up outside here, "I am going to be married in the morning". Don't I wish that were so. I am simply dying for you, dearie but still we have something to look forward to haven't we darling, for we have made up our minds when it really will be, and I shall be so glad when the time comes for me to claim you as my Bride, and I know you will. Well darling how are you now, I hope much better. The heat here is terrible it has nearly killed me today, and oh it was most trying last night. We had a very full meeting too, to make it worse still. Some of our men here are working at night as the heat is too much for them in the day.

I am glad your Ma is thawing a bit, as it must be very unpleasant for you when she is so funny. Your Pa is alright I know very well, and anyone can get on with him who are only alright themselves. Well darling cheer up and keep hoping for Oct 1st, for the present "Au revoir" with lots of love and heaps of kisses for your dear self

Yours most devotedly

Jack

I do hope you didn't feel knocked up today darling, through getting up so early: it was so nice of you to come and see me off.

Beatrice's father was an amenable and generous man. He adored, and somewhat indulged Beatrice, his only daughter.

❖❖❖❖❖❖

"Roselea", September 9th 1898

My own darling Jack

Isn't this weather simply too awful? I feel nearly dead I don't know what you must feel like shut up. I am melted sitting in the shade in the garden. I do pity the men having to work over the furnaces. Mrs. Morris came over for the day yesterday and she and I went for a ride when it got cooler, she wants me to go and stay with her for a few days. I didn't promise, for somehow, I do not seem as if I could this hot weather, their house is so crowded and stuffy. Be sure to let me know what the house is like, you saw advertised, how cheap, to include a garden and greenhouse surely it cannot be much of a house. Just fancy Joe wanting to share a house with you, poor fellow I feel rather sorry for him, perhaps he knows more about the Phelps business than you do. I am glad you told him we are going to be married as soon as we can and I should also tell your Mother to prepare her and get that over. I went to Kate Hogan's to tea the day before yesterday, she wanted to know when the happy day was to be, I told her the early part of June, she says we have got plenty to do in the time and she is quite right at least, I have. I shall work at my things, house linen etc, and not do any other needle work. I had a letter from David yesterday a very nice and kind congratulatory letter and asking me when it was to be and what I should like. I answered by today's mail and told him a silver teapot and I also told him I expected it would be in June. Ma read the letter, so she knows now but she did not say anything. Mrs. Morris says it is not any too soon to be looking out for a house for some houses will be up to let at Xmas for March quarter and she thinks you are wise in keeping your eyes open and looking at some houses so as to get an idea.

Just fancy I dreamt I was married last night, but the best of it was there was not any man in the business, sort of married to myself. Ma is quite alright now, I am glad to say, it is so unpleasant when she is so contrary. Both the dogs are sitting at my feet they seem fearfully hot. Aimèe started for the Isle of Wight last wednesday. I have not heard from her yet. Poor Laura rode to Orpington on wednesday and got a slight sunstroke, she was very bad for a day but Ernie said she was better last night. She, Mrs. Morris and I are going to ride to Kingston next thursday to see the Lewcocks. Well dear au revoir and do write soon. Heaps of love and kisses.

Yours ever

Beatè

Beatrice would have spent a large proportion of her time at school learning needlework, sewing samplers and practising stitches. It is less likely that she would have made many complete garments, or learned how to use a sewing machine. (B)

Cycling was a very sociable activity as well as a healthy one and large parties of cyclists would often rendezvous at a popular meeting place. (B)

Linwood Lodge, September 11th 1898

My own darling Beatie

I was so glad to receive your dear letter yesterday morning, but sorry to find that this hot weather is so distressing you, and trust it is now a little cooler with you as it is here. I did not write yesterday, knowing you could not receive a letter until Monday. By the way, dearie, I think this is the first time I have written you on a Sunday, isn't it. I have just come in from Church, went on my lonesome, and managed to find the right pew.

I am quite alone here this week end as Joe has gone to Aberystwyth, until Wednesday I think.

It was about four o'clock when I left the Works yesterday, and I rode home on my bike and had tea, and feeling so lonely and miserable afterwards thought I would go and lose myself for an hour or two, so started off on my bike, but when just through Sutton, a Mr. Simmons overtook me, so I rode with him to Lichfield. He met some nieces and nephews, (about eight) there, so there was quite a big party on the return.

I looked out for the two houses you spoke of, darling, but could not see anything answering the description of them, but I did notice the four I spoke to you of and thought they looked particularly nice just now, however, they are all occupied. I have not yet seen the house which was advertised. Alice is here with the dinner so I must adjourn for a while.

Here we are again! What an experience I have been having, fancy me trying to carve a shoulder of Lamb, I am afraid we shall have to live on chops and steaks, when we are married darling, unless I have some practice in carving. I read accounts of two local weddings this morning, don't I wish one had been ours. So you have heard from David, eh, I told him what you would like. Rather clever your way of informing your Ma, as to when our wedding is to be.

I have not heard from Ida yet, Alice handed me a letter she had received from Mother, a day or two ago, for me to read. I thought there must be something in it concerning me, but fancy she never mentioned me at all. Never mind darling, buck up, for the present au revoir. With heaps of kisses and my whole true love

Yours devotedly
Jack

◇◇◇◇◇◇◇

"Roselea", September 12th 1898

My own darling Jack

I was looking out most eagerly for your letter this morning and I was not disappointed. I have had the "blues" most awfully badly for the last few days I have so longed for you and it has seemed so hard, that you should be so far away and such an age before I see you again I cannot make Ma out she has been so awfully funny again the last few days and if anybody mentions my marriage to her, she most promptly turns the subject. May is

As if she had not enough to contend with, Beatrice's own mother was strangely difficult and cool towards her.

staying here today and she mentioned to Ma, that she supposed she would be very busy getting my things ready, she did not answer, and again changed the subject. I think perhaps she does not like it because she has not been told about the date personally so I think you had better tell her when you come up next time.

I cannot make it out about those houses, I feel sure I am not mistaken and I believe I could walk quite straight to them, if I was there. What rent would those 4 houses you speak of be, is there any chance of them being empty, you see people do not usually move the Xmas quarter, if they can help it. I was glad to hear you went to Church yesterday, I, too, went all alone, and I did feel so lonely, and wished you had been with me, next time you come we must go, eh dear? How strange of your Mother not to mention you in the letter. Jack dear, I really think that for my sake, as well as your own you should try and make friends with her. Why don't you write and say you wish to be friends. Now think about it and let me know the result. I have made several little things for our little shanty and they look so pretty and I feel so proud of them and think such a lot when I am making them, of the happy time when we are one and got a jolly little home of our own.

Laura is coming tonight, she is much better and I will give her your message. Just fancy we cannot get a cook anywhere we have advertised 3 more times and have had no answers and Ellen has to go next monday, that means I shall have to turn to again.

Well darling do write very soon and cheer up your poor miserable little girlie. Lots of love and kisses

Yours ever
Beatie

Beatrice knew how to handle both her parents quite well – and usually got her way eventually.

Linwood Lodge, September 14th 1898

My own darling Beatie

Pray excuse the letter card, which I sent you from town this evening; but as it was too late for one to write a proper letter for you to receive first post in the morning, I just sent that (or you would have felt disappointed I know) to let you know that you would hear later in the day.

I was so glad darling to receive your dear letter on Tuesday morning, but what a shame that your Ma is so funny again, for I know it must trouble you so, but I will try and soothe her over (as well as your dear self, for I know you will need it) when I come up next time. I wish you were here dearie, that you could take me to see those two houses, although I fancy you have made some mistake. You may no doubt have seen the houses you mention, but I think you are under a wrong impression as to the locality. I don't know how I shall be able to make it up with my Mother, for really you know I feel so very raw on the matter, and she has treated me in anything but a proper manner, but still I suppose one must put up with a lot in these times, and we seem to have got our share to go on with, don't we dearie.

But for your dear sake I could do anything, and so will try and bring about a reconciliation, if I can.

Draycott
62, NEW STREET
BIRMINGHAM
ALSO
NORTHAMPTON
& WALSALL.

Jack's mother – implacable and inscrutable to Jack at that time. Beatrice's mother was likely to be much easier for Jack to 'soothe'. (M)

Joe had spent a few days with Mrs. Hughes, Ida and Frank on their holiday in Aberystwyth. Meanwhile Jack had been left to carry on business at the Works.

Joe has returned from Aberystwyth tonight, so that I can go to Aber for Gun Practice tomorrow. He is loud in his praises of Aberystwyth, and says he thinks of going down again this Saturday as he has had no proper holidays. I expect to get back home from Aber on Friday night, and should so like to have a letter here when I return.

It has not been very lively here since they have all been away, but then I have not seen such a lot of home; for I have been going out at 25 to eight each morning and getting back about 9 p.m. a tidy day. It has made me very busy, having both Joe and Frank away together. Of course there is no reliance to be placed upon Frank, but still he can be made very useful in his way. I have not had a single line from any of them at Aberystwyth, it does seem strange.

Oh for one of our sweet goodnight kisses, you know dearie; but it is not to be tonight, except in imagination. Never mind, we will imagine it, so here goes. Goodnight darling, heaps of love and kisses from

Yours most devotedly

Jack.

Uncle John is still at Llandudno

⬥⬥⬥⬥⬥

"Roselea", September 15th 1898

My own darling Jack

Here I am again more dead than alive for you know Maud left last monday, so I have had to do the house work, which has nearly done for me this hot weather. I cannot stand it and it strikes me so long as I do it Ma won't bother about getting servants. She is not doing anything to try and find a girl. There is one thing, I shall have to give up if it lasts much longer. I am up every morning at 7 and hard at it all day until bedtime except about an hour in the afternoon when I lie down. Yesterday we rode to Kingston in the afternoon we left here at 3 o'clock, got there at $\frac{1}{4}$ to 5. The river runs through the Lewcock's ground, so after tea Hettie took Laura in the punt and as Laura went to get out she fell in, we did not see anything of it, but Hettie called to one of the servants, and between them they got her out, of course they had to lend her all fresh things and gave her a stiff glass of whiskey and she left here this morning and does not seem any the worse for the ducking. Ernie came and fetched us home, and coming back I was fairly done just like that day coming back from Dorking. I had not the strength left to mount nor could I dismount. At last in the middle of a country road awfully dark, I didn't know where we were I told Ernie I could not go any further, he said I must as there was no help for it. Mrs. Morris suggested getting to the nearest railway station and riding home, so at last after roaming about we found a station and Mrs. Morris and I rode home and thankful I was. We got home about 11 o'clock having left there at 5 o'clock and today as you may imagine I feel very much off colour. I felt two or three times as if I must go to bed but I have been so busy I have not had time, but I have struck this afternoon and am going to lie down. I hope you have had a jolly time at Aber. you have had fine weather. I suppose your Mother will be home on monday, thanks dear for promising to do your best towards being friends I am sure it is the right thing.

Punting on the river, a gentle and popular pastime for ladies, nevertheless required a degree of skill which Hettie Lewcock did not have! (B)

Jack you are a naughty boy to talk of spending more money on me, of course I know it is your nature to be kind and generous, but I did not expect anything after my handsome ring. Well dear, it is as I thought I believe, the reason why Ma is so cool, for she asked Mrs. Morris if she had heard anything about our getting married in June. Mrs. Morris said, yes, Beatie had said that was the time they thought, so Ma said it was a strange thing that Jack had not mentioned it to her, but Mrs. Morris told her, you would not do so until you were certain and then you were not, but I am glad to say Ma is a little better now. I shall look for a letter on monday, I shall not be able to go to Church on Sunday, too much to do. By the way, I don't know what time your letter reached here yesterday, but it was not here at 3 o'clock when I left.

Well darling I know you will excuse more I am so tired, I wish October 1st was here, I do so want comforting and it seems such an awful time to wait. Lots of kisses darling

Yrs most-devotedly Beatie

◇◇◇◇◇◇◇

Linwood Lodge, September 18th 1898

My own darling Beatie

I was so glad to receive your letter yesterday morning, but it grieves me to hear of you feeling so knocked up through having so much work to do this very hot weather.

I hope you will soon be able to get some good girls in, and so be relieved a bit. I know you don't mind a bit of work, darling, but it is really too much for you to have the whole thing to do day after day, and especially in such tropical weather as we have been experiencing just lately. I am wondering how you feel this morning darling, I feel quite lost all alone here on my own. Joe is at Baker's for the week end, the people are just passing on their return from Church, I have not been this morning, for I felt a bit tired, and did not get up until nearly ten o'clock, and have been having a quiet prowl round the garden. What an experience for poor Laura, she was fortunate in having assistance at hand, and I hope she will not feel any ill effects of the immersion. You must be careful what you are doing, dearie, in the way of cycling, for I am afraid it is not doing you very much good. I don't like to hear of you feeling so done up.

Well we went to Aber. for Gun Practice on Thursday morning, there were twenty altogether from B'ham, and there was a saloon put on the 7.20 for us. We arrived at Llanfairfechan (nice name, but a very pretty place) at 11.45, and marched to Aber. 13 miles, on arrival we were served with a hot dinner at the Hotel; and at 2.30 were marched to the Battery for the Practice. There were 81 rounds fired, and some capital shooting made, and we returned to the Hotel just before 7 o'clock. We were surprised then when we were informed that we were not required further. Our return tickets were handed to us, and we were told that we were at liberty and could proceed home if we chose. There was only one train though, that night, the Mail train, 9.13 from Bangor, and arriving B'ham 2.30 a.m. so as I had thought we should be away two days

Jack had remembered that it would be Beatrice's birthday at the end of September, and had written that he had already planned her present for that day.

A photograph of Joe Hughes taken at Rhyl on horseback with the Warwickshire Yeomanry. Joe was later to express his disappointment not to have gone to the Boer War. He could not be spared from the Works, then heavily engaged in making ammunition. (A)

*The unexpected night off in Rhyl and
steamer trip to Llandudno was likely to be
quite a jolly interlude – these being lively
seaside resorts.*

I had arranged accordingly at the Works I did not trouble to come home on
the night train, but took train to Rhyl and spent the evening there.

You remember young Millard, the Pierrot at our dance, well he was with us
at Aber. and went with me. Next morning we took the Steamer to Llandudno,
and returned to B'ham in the afternoon. We saw Uncle John in the train, he
was coming home from Llandudno but we could not ride with him as he was
travelling first class. However, we had a chat with him on the platform, and he
was quite jolly. Fancy we were away two days and were really only at work
about five hours. The weather was very hot indeed, and very trying to be about
in uniform.

We expect them all home from Aberystwyth tomorrow, as Ida, goes to
school again on Tuesday. There is no letter this morning, but I suppose we
shall hear tomorrow. I do so wish I could have been with you today darling,

IX.—SOME SHORT SPINS AROUND BIRMINGHAM.

*The Midlands provided many long cycle
routes through beautiful countryside. In
1898 Jack would have been able to reach
open countryside very quickly even though
Linwood Lodge was not far from
Birmingham town centre. (I)*

for it is so miserable here, or fancy what a jolly time we could have, if you were
here now. The Warren over again. I shall let you know all that happens when
the Mater comes home. When I come up on Oct 1st darling, I shall have to
have a little chat, with your Ma, if we can spare a few minutes, and try and
console her. But of course darling you quite know my reasons for not telling
everybody of the approximate date. I am going to Wylde Green this afternoon,
to Harrops. We all went on our cycles to Lichfield yesterday afternoon (it was
hot) and they asked me to go up this
afternoon. Please give my love to
Ma and Pa, and Grannie. Well
duckie, for the present "Au revoir",
with heaps of love and kisses for your
dear self

*Yours ever
Jack*

◇◇◇◇◇◇◇

"Roselea", September 19th 1898

My own darling Jack

     You don't know how I was looking out for your dear letter, really it
was a comfort to me, for I feel just worried to death. Just fancy we only
had 17 here to tea yesterday not many to see after, was it? and of course it fell

*It was uncharacteristic of Mrs. Mercer
to be unkind deliberately to Beatrice but
it seems as if she too was feeling put out
about the question of the wedding date.*

on me, Ma never offered to help with a thing and at night I could hardly keep from crying, I felt so tired. I was up yesterday at 8 o'clock, no breakfast in bed and of course I could not go to Church. You will think I am always grumbling, but really dear I am sure if you were here you would say I had cause for Ma never helps with a thing, not even to help make the beds and just fancy, she has invited a cousin to stay with us, she came here yesterday until next week, she makes extra work. I do call it inconsiderate of Ma and I get so tired and irritable. Ma goes out enjoying herself. I do wish I was with you, for if I had you to see every night, I should not mind, I only wish the time was here for me to come. Oh by the way, surely you don't think we shall have to wait longer than the beginning of June, that seems an eternal time, so I do hope not. I hope you will speak to Ma when you come up, perhaps that might smooth her a little. I do hope all will be right with you and your Mother, do your best dear. I shall be so anxious to know. Do write as soon as ever you have an opportunity it is the only thing that keeps me up at all. Laura was here for Sunday and left this morning again, she sends her love and does not seem any the worse for her ducking not even a cold. She goes to Herne Bay on friday, so two more people will be miserable, Ern and I will have to console one another.

Reg went back to school last friday, I am very glad, he got such an awful nuisance. I am glad you had such a jolly time at Aber. Well to be you gadding around. What a long holiday your Uncle has had but I suppose he won't go away again this year. Remember me kindly to him when you see him. Has Jennie been away with your Mother all the time? I am thankful to say that the weather is a bit cooler today. Hasn't the weather been trying, on saturday it was simply awful. Well dear au revoir and write soon. Heaps of love

Yours ever
Beatie

Beatrice's youngest brother Reg had been little more than a schoolboy nuisance to her during her engagement. He was later to become a debonaire young man, however, and a great one with the ladies, being rather fond also of Jack's younger sister, Ida. This picture of Ida with her German relations shows Reg on the left. On the right of the picture is Manfred von Richthofn who was to become the famous 'Red Baron', the First World War flying ace. (M)

◇◇◇◇◇◇◇

"Roselea", September 21st 1898

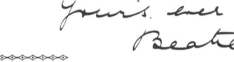

My own darling Jack

You cannot think how I was consoled by your dear letter this morning, it was good of you to write so soon, and will you be good again darling that is if it does not try your poor eye. My dear, I *am* sorry you have been in the wars lately haven't you? I hope it won't hurt the eyesight at all, be sure and let me know how it goes on. I shall now always look for June until it comes, and that ought to do me good when I know, what a dear good fellow I shall have to look after me. Your mother did not lose much time in going out to see her dear Phelps did she? but I do hope you will soon be friends, it would make me much happier for I feel that it is all through me. Give my love to Ida and Jennie and Alec when you see them. I wonder what they will say when they know we intend being married at June. Say dear, I should like to see the list of people you would like asked, you dear old boy, just fancy you thinking about that all to yourself. I am afraid dear if they had to come up the same morning, they would not have much time if they came by the 8.45, for they would not get home much before 12.30 or 1 o'clock, but there I don't know of course what time the ceremony will be yet. You remember Mr. and

This letter from Beatrice did not reach Jack immediately, the reason for which was discovered only days later. Its disappearance caused a flurry of telegrams. Jack's letter also of the 21st, telling of the damage to his eye and return of his mother from Aberystwyth, is missing from the collection.

Derry and Tom's was one of the many
large department stores to be opened and
flourish in the nineteenth century. They
employed many young women and shop
work became a respectable occupation,
though the hours were long and tiring.
Beatrice's friend May was exceptionally
well paid by her Bond Street furrier, £180
a year being well above the average wage
for shop work.

Mrs. Weston, who sat next to me at Folkestone, well, they are going to drive
over tomorrow afternoon to see us. We have not got a Cook yet and we seem
as if we could not get one. I believe a housemaid is coming in tomorrow, at
least I hope so as it will give me a little rest, but not for long as Ellen is obliged
to go on saturday, that means me doing the cooking. I do hope we get a Cook
before you come, or else it will be horrid. I have just bathed the dogs, the
young monkeys, they are now sitting at my feet while I write.

Well dear, Ma has actually bought me my first things towards my trousseau
and I don't suppose I should have got those, only May is leaving Derry and
Toms and that is the only place I can get these necessary articles and she gets
them at a great reduction, so when I knew she was leaving, I asked Ma if I
could order them, there is a bit of a joke on about them but I will tell you when
we meet. Just fancy May has got a berth at a big furriers in Bond St., salary
£180, isn't that splendid? I do think she is a lucky girl. Laura is coming over
tomorrow to wish us goodbye. Poor girl she does not like going, after such a
long holiday. I too, am sorry, for I shall miss her very much. I am going out to
tea today. Ma is going to take my Cousin to the theatre tonight. Well dearie I
shall look for a letter on friday morning, don't disappoint me there's a ducky.
I do hope you will be able to say that your eye is better. Have you spotted any
nice little cabins yet. Au revoir, I am counting the days till 1st Oct. Lots of
kisses

Yours most devotedly
Beatie

◇◇◇◇◇◇

Telegram from Beatrice to Jack,   September 24th 1898

Beatrice's letter of September 24th
expressed her fears that Jack's mother
might have intercepted the letter as "there
was something inside it I did not want her
to see". Another explanation could have
been that she had given it to Reg to post.

WROTE WEDNESDAY ALL WELL

One day without a letter threw Jack and
Beatrice into sufficient panic to telegraph
each other for re-assurance that all was
well. Jack suspected some "mischief at
work" to account for Beatrice's missing
letter. (A)

"Roselea", September 26th 1898

My darling Jack

Just fancy that awful Reg had got your letter in his pocket and had never posted it. I was angry with him, I shall never trust him with another, I suppose you will get it when you get home tonight as you are up at Wylde Green. Well I went over to Dulwich in the afternoon yesterday and went to our old Chapel at Barry Rd. it did seem funny seeing the old place once again. I wouldn't go back for anything, I passed our old house that looked nice. I did not get up until dinner time yesterday for I have got such a frightful cold and I thought it would perhaps do it good but I am afraid it is not any better. I am going over to the Morris's one day this week I think wednesday or thursday.

You do not say how your eye is, but I presume it is better, at least I hope so. Have you spoken to your Mother yet? I am longing to hear that you are friends once again. Hasn't the weather turned cold? at least it has here you will want your overcoat travelling on saturday I expect. Will you come by the same train? of course I shall meet you, and I hope you will be able to stay longer this time. Such a joke Ma sent an envelope of yours to a graphologist, so we have got your character, a very good one too, I am proud of it, but do you know she never told anybody about it and when it came she passed it over to me, she had given "Pickles" as your "nom de plume". I thought it was supposed to be hers, so I said, why there is not a thing true, then she laughed and said it was yours. "Pickles" pretty name don't you think dearie?

However it really is very good. Well darling you have had a letter from me 3 days running, so I hope you will write me a good long letter, yours this morning was very short, I suppose you couldn't spare any more time. Well, ta-ta heaps of love

Yours lovingly
Beatie

◇◇◇◇◇◇◇

"Roselea", September 28th 1898

My darling Jack.

I don't know what to say to you, to thank you sufficiently for your lovely present, it really seems to make me feel how unworthy I am of such a dear fellow, and your kind letter also, I shall prize both immensely being my first and only birthday during our engagement, only think dear, my next, you will give a present to your wife, at least I hope so. Jack dear I wish you could look at that house at Stechford, it is just lovely, if it is alright what do you think? I enclose the cutting, I don't know if you want it again.

NEAR Stechford Station.—Langham House, Cotterell's Lane, double-fronted; three reception, four bed rooms, bath, and dressing room; two acres garden, 200 fruit trees, greenhouse; stabling, coach-house, &c.; immediate possession if required. Rent £30.

There were no sinister reasons for the missing letter after all – only young Reg to blame, for forgetting to post the letter.

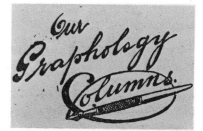

The art of interpreting a person's character from their handwriting was the subject of regular columns in local newspapers. Beatrice's mother had enough faith in it to have ventured to take one of Jack's letters to a graphologist to 'get his character'. (I)

The advertisement for the house at Stechford which was some miles south from Linwood Lodge on the eastern edge of Birmingham. (A)

September 28th 1898 was Beatrice's twenty-eighth birthday and £5 was a handsome present from her father – enough to buy herself four or five dresses from her dressmaker. Jack was fond of giving her jewellery, though the best present for Beatrice would have been for Jack to 'pocket his pride' and put things right with his mother.

I had such a nice letter from Jennie this week, it quite cheers me to know she sides with us, she says "the sooner we marry, the better". I think I have come off very well for presents. Pa gave me his usual £5 note. I must tell you the rest on saturday, how I am longing to see you, and to give you a good hug and kisses and try to thank you personally for your generous gift. The Westons did not come after all, they have postponed their visit, as she was taken ill, no, I didn't care for her at all, but I think she took rather a fancy to me. I wish dear, you would pocket your pride and if your Mother wishes for an apology why, give it to her and have done with it, if that is the only thing to be done. I am sure it is your duty to do it. You cannot go on like this, think how miserable for me when I am your wife. I am going over to Morris's tomorrow and will then give them your message.

I am so thankful that your eye is better, I felt so anxious about it I don't think you take sufficient care of yourself, mind you are mine now, so please treat yourself gently and with care.

Ernie is expecting his machine home this week, he is getting quite excited over it. Poor Laura has been nearly mad since she has been back, she has had an abscess in her mouth. She wrote me a very nice letter this morning, and I have just answered it and sent her your love. She says it is getting better and hopes now it will go on alright. My cousin goes home today, and I am very glad of it, she is such a wet blanket.

One of the more rare occasions when both Jack and Joe visited 'Roselea' together. They are seen outside the front door at 'Roselea' which was at the side of the house and protected by a small verandah. Joe is on the right of the picture. (A)

Well darling, we have not much longer to wait and be sure you stop longer this time, or I shall have to severely Chastise you and Joe too, so look up. Lots of love and hundreds of kisses to be administered when we meet, and many many thanks for your lovely bracelet

ever yours devotedly
Beatie

Jack Tries To Put Things Right

OCTOBER & NOVEMBER

> **'Bust ups' and late night family rows threaten Jack's position in the business. Jack's refusal to try to put things right with his mother now comes between the lovers. For Beatrice's sake Jack tries to talk things round with Mrs. Hughes – he fails and so the rift seems final. Life becomes intolerable for Jack at Linwood Lodge.**

Linwood Lodge, Oct 4th 1898

My own darling Beatie

You will be glad to know that I arrived safely here last night. The train to Victoria went up very well, and there was plenty of time at Euston, which I utilised by getting some tea. The train I came down by, was the 5 o'clock ordinary, a slow train, of course I was obliged to come by that, having an excursion ticket. It is due in New St. at 8.30, and it was 8.40 when it got in last night. When I reached here, it was 9.30. I came up from town by the 9.15. Mother was out, and I have not seen her until just now when I came in.

She is at home tonight, something wonderful for Tuesday. She has two lady friends here with her, the Misses Rogers. They are very old friends of hers indeed, perhaps you will remember them, as the people who helped with the refreshments at our Fancy Dress Ball. Well now Beatie I don't think much of them now, for do you know, you remember you said to me that you wondered where she met Phelps, now I believe these are the people who are helping her in her affair, for she seems to have been making so much fuss of them lately. You know I told you some time ago, what she promised Jennie, if she would help her to bring her desired end about, and how Jennie declined; now if she were to make any such overture to these people, I know they would quickly embrace the opportunity, and I feel sure she has done so. Of course I may be mistaken, but still that is my opinion, and I don't think it is very far wrong. But it is no use to trouble you with all this darling; only I must tell you all that is going on.

Well my little dearie, how are you now, better I hope than when I left you. Has that pain gone, from which you were suffering. You know what I told you about under-clothing, well you really must do it, if you wish to keep strong. Don't laugh, and think I am too fussy about these things. Really it is quite right what I say, and it is only because I am so anxious for you that I tell you. You must really look after your dear little self now you know for me. I did so think of you darling last night, when I was going to bed, and would have given

The Fancy Dress Ball, given by Jack's mother, was one of the rare occasions when Beatrice visited Jack's family, early in their relationship and before Jack's mother was aware of their feelings towards each other. It was held in February of 1898 at the Vestry Hall, Gravelly Hill and was in aid of a children's fund. Joe went as a pirate. (.T)

Jack's return from a weekend with Beatrice, as always, had left him missing her more than ever. Once back to Birmingham he had to face Phelps and the seemingly devious plots of his mother.

anything for a sweet good-night kiss; such as we had on the two previous nights, but alas it could not be. But you know we must take comfort in the fact that each one brings us nearer to June next, when these flying visits will be a thing of the past, and we shall have our future together. Give Aimèe my very kind regards, and tell her to be a good girl and stick to her work. I shall have to leave off here and run to post, or you will be a disappointed darling. *Ever your own true* Longer one next time. I will write to *Jack* your Ma when I come back from post, and send it on early in the morning. Heaps of love and kisses

◆◇◆◇◆◇◆

"Roselea", October 5th 1898

My dearest Jack

       I was looking forward to have your letter this morning and I was not disappointed. What a long time you were getting home, I hope next time you won't go by that train.

      I am not surprised to learn what you think about the Miss Rogers and I should think the same, for did you notice how thick your Mater and the Rogers' and Phelps were at your dance? Does your mother speak to you? I shall be most anxious to see the effect of your letter upon Ma, perhaps she will take more interest then. Aimèe is still here and she is a great help to me for we have not got a girl yet. She sends her kind regards to "Pickles" and she is at present doing my tablecloth and very nice it looks. Ernie's new machine came home this morning and it is a beauty, he is delighted with it.

      My pain is much better dear, although not gone. I think I shall take your

The Misses Rogers may well have been acquaintances of Phelps and been responsible for 'helping her in her affair' but Jack's mother was reputed to have first met Phelps when he called on her to show her jewellery samples. He was clearly not quite in the same social class as the Hughes family which contributed to the distasteful nature of the relationship in the eyes of family and friends.

A view of Thrale Road from the Mitcham Lane end, looking north. On the left is the group of shops which would have been the Mercer's local suppliers. 'Roselea' can just be seen looking down Thrale Road, on the right. (D)

advice and wear woollen things. Reggie asked me last night if it was true that I was going to be married June 1st as he should be thinking what suit he would have, so I told him to ask me another day as Ma was there, as I do not want to say anything until you tell her. I did miss you darling, time does fly when I am with you. Nellie is coming to dinner today and we three are going to Clapham this afternoon to order my coat and skirt. Ma is going to see Mrs. Weston who has been very ill. She lives at Paddington so she will have quite a way to go. Ellen left on monday, she did cry and said she wished she could stay on and I shouldn't be surprised if she did come back, for she said if she wrote to come back would we have her, it is only that wretched old mother of hers that is the trouble.

Well darling you must excuse a long letter this time, as I am cooking the dinner. So write soon. Heaps of love

Yours most truly
Beatie

Beatrice was not taking to woollen underwear simply for warmth. Dr. Jaeger's pure wool underwear, including drawers, chemises, petticoats, corsets and even suspenders, and the importance of 'wool next to the skin' was part of the health cult which swept Europe at this time. Dr. Jaeger's theory was that animal fibres prevented retention of 'noxious exhalations' of the body and therefore the cure of numerous body ailments. Beatrice suffered from rheumatism. (N)

Linwood Lodge, October 7th 1898

My own darling Beatie

It was so good of you to write on Wednesday, and I was so glad to receive your dear letter when I got to the Works on Thursday morning.

Well dearie, I wrote your Ma, and posted the letter early on Wednesday morning, and I should think she would receive it some time that afternoon or evening. I have no doubt you would be looking out for its arrival, and I can quite understand your anxiety as to the effect it has upon your Ma. I should think perhaps I may hear from her tomorrow. I told her the reason I had not spoken of the date of our wedding, to her, was on account of the business arrangements here being so unsettled, but that now all was satisfactorily arranged, there was nothing I could see to prevent the wedding taking place as we wished as long as we had their approval; and you know this is the fact; don't you darling. Last night, when I got home (last train), Mother was still up, (she arrived home by the 10.15 Bus I find), and she conversed with me all night while I was having some supper, but she gradually assumed an offensive tone, and eventually became most abusive and stormy, and in fact there was no alternative but to walk off to bed and leave her at it, for it was impossible to talk with her, she seemed so mad.

The fact is, she was so thoroughly full up I suppose with something the lovely Phelps had been telling her, and seemed as if she could not annoy me enough. I am anxious to hear from your Ma, to know what she and your Pa think of my letter. I do hope she will not think that my reason for writing, instead of telling her, was because of any lack of courage on my part; but you know darling that while I was with you, we were so busy that there was no suitable opportunity presented itself, for a conversation with your Ma. I think she will be very nice over it though.

I am so glad dearie, to know that that pain is better, and also that you are going to take my advice as to woollen clothing. You could not do better, I am

Jack could not do anything right as far as his own mother was concerned and it looked as if he had now upset Beatrice's mother too.

Jack attended his masonic meeting in his Volunteer Artillery uniform. The Installation Meeting would have been to instate new members at Jack's masonic Lodge. (A)

Even though Jack wrote about Jaffray Road frequently, Beatrice persisted in spelling it incorrectly. Not only was her spelling sometimes curious but her lack of punctuation was also.

Beatrice had been so busy that she forgot to tell Jack she had received the grapes. Domestic help – or the lack of it – was a constant preoccupation for middle-class households as good servants were notoriously difficult to get and to keep.

sure. I met Uncle John in the train on Tuesday night, he was very pleasant. I had a letter from him the following morning, about an investment of mine, about which I had consulted him.

Mother was in at the Office this morning, and she talked with me quite properly. How strange. It was a veritable calm after the storm. I hope your Ma found Mrs. Weston much better. We had our Installation Meeting on Wednesday, and everything went most smoothly. In fact it was an ideal meeting. I attended Lodge in "Mess Uniform" and it was the last occasion on which I shall wear the "Queen's Cloth", as my time will be up on Oct 31st. The time does seem long darling, when I am not with you, but thank Goodness there will soon be one week gone of the three, through which we have to wait before seeing each other. I have not yet had any time to go round and enquire after those houses in the Jaffray Road, but shall do so this week end. I do hope we shall find something there to suit us, as it would be most convenient there. I am glad Ernie has got his machine, it will of course, take his attention and thoughts somewhat; I hope he has quite got rid of that pain at the chest, and also that your Pa and Reggie have now recovered from their colds.

You promised, darling, to let me know how the Grapes tasted but have not done so. Never mind. I hope you found them very nice. I am glad Aimèe is still with you, as you have not yet secured a servant she must be a help to you. Tell her not to leave that table-cloth for anything though. For the present "Au revoir". With lots of love and heaps of kisses.

Yours most devotedly
Jack

"Roselea", October 9th 1898

My own dear Jack

Don't laugh at the red ink but Reg is using the black and I cannot sit too near him, it might be dangerous so I am using this. I rather like it, it is a change. I was delighted of course to receive your dear letter, and shall be most anxious to receive your next, to hear about those houses in Jaffary Road. I do hope they might suit us for I feel it would be so very convenient for you and another thing, I know that part, and it would not be quite so strange for me. Really your Mother is a curse, what made her so angry with you the other night? I hope she is alright now. Does she ever mention me? but I suppose not. Your letter of course reached Ma, has she answered yet? She has not made any reference to me at all about it but Nellie was here the day it came and Ma told her about it and said she did not know how to answer it, but she said she did not see any objection to our marriage if you could give me a comfortable home, I suppose she will answer it tomorrow if she has not already done so, let me know what she says, won't you dear. Now you really must forgive me for not mentioning the grapes, when I last wrote, but the fact was I wrote in such an awful hurry but I thank you for them now, they were simply delicious.

Well darling we have got a Cook in at last, she came in yesterday she has not got a very good reference as regards cooking but Ma thought she would be

better than nobody and then if she does not suit we can look out for someone
else, anyway she cooked the dinner very well indeed today, so she may do after
all. At least I shall get a rest for I was well used up and shall be thankful for a
rest. Mr. and Mrs. Pattenden want you to go with me, Pa or Ma to supper on
the saturday you come up. She said when does Mr. Hughes come up again.
I told her and she said she wanted to arrange for us to go there one evening, so
it is arranged for the saturday you come up. I accepted, I hope you won't
mind, but I thought it was so kind of her, and they are very hospitable people
and now they are a bit down in the world it would look as if we refused on that
account, if we did not go, and when they were well off they used to entertain us
most splendidly. I went to Church this morning, they had still got the decorations on the pulpit. I was all alone and only wished you were with me. I had
my breakfast in bed this morning. Did you go to Church this morning? I hope
you did. Do write soon I shall be looking out for a letter, I hope you have got
particulars of the houses. Ernie asked me if I would ride to Dorking next
Easter Monday, rather a long way ahead isn't it? but I think it would be nice,
it won't be so fagging to me this time I hope. Well I have written quite an
epistle this time. Aimèe went home yesterday, I am going over to spend the
day with her on tuesday. Au revoir my dearest and heaps of love and kisses

Yours ever
Beatie

Linwood Lodge, October 10th 1898

My own darling Beatie

  I was so glad to receive your dear letter this morning, really I have
been feeling anxious this last day or two, not having heard from your
Ma, don't mention it to her though, please. She has not written to me yet. I am
looking forward to receiving her letter, and as soon as I do, I shall let you know
the contents. But I cannot feel surprised that she should say, she did not know
how to answer it, for of course she must begin to realise now that it will not be
very long before she will lose her only daughter, and as you have been and are
such a good one, of course it must be very trying to her and she must feel
anxiously for you. But darling when she sees us settled down, and how happy
we shall be, I know she will be pleased, and will not regret trusting you to my
care: I have made enquiries after the houses in Jaffray Road, and all I have
found out at present, is, that they are being built by Mr. Dawson, the Pastor of
the Baptist Church here. The next thing will be to see him, and find out
whether he has any tenants in view, and if not, what accommodation the
houses will contain and the (last but not least of all) rent. I do hope that we can
find one there to suit us, as it would be so convenient. No, dearie, my Mother
never mentions you at all, and you don't know how I feel this separation from
you on that account; for I am not only so far from you, but have no one here
who seems to take any interest in us and to whom I can speak of my dear little
girl, and our future, excepting of course Nin and Alec, and them I see so
seldom. I did see Alec today, and he told me that when the time came for you
to come down to B'ham in connection with our arranging for our home and

*The Pattenden's were close friends of the
Mercers, who had clearly experienced some
fall in status, about which Beatrice was
very sensitive, not wanting to hurt their
feelings by refusing their dinner invitation.*

*A cycle ride from Streatham to Dorking
would have been a distance of twenty-five
miles. Beatrice would almost certainly have
needed extra energy from something to stop
her flagging. (B)*

*Jennie, Jack's sister, and Alec, having
experienced similar hostility from Mrs.
Hughes at the time of their own engagement provided Jack with some comfort.
The Phelps affair was a new issue,
however, and had much more worrying
implications for Jack's future financially
and chances of marriage.*

Packhorse Bridge at Hampton-in-Arden in the 1890s. Phelps and Jack's mother – who was quite a large lady – presented an undignified but amusing spectacle on the weighing machine at Hampton-in-Arden Station. (F)

the furnishing, that if my Mother would not invite you down, that they would do so with pleasure and that I was not to be afraid of letting them know. What he really called in to see me for, in the first place was to let me know of something they chanced to see on Saturday afternoon. My mother called at their house on Saturday morning, and left at a few minutes to one in the Carriage. Alec came home to dinner as usual, and as it turned out such a very fine day he asked Nin if she would like to have a little trip into the country for an hour or two. They made up their minds all at once, and caught the 2.55 to Hampton-in-Arden, and judge of their surprise, as they passed through the Booking Hall, on leaving the Station, to see a lady and gentleman whom they knew; the lady on a weighing machine, and the gentleman putting on the weights. The lady was my Mother and the other thing was the lovely Phelps.

They too had gone into the country for an hour or two. They had their backs turned so Nin and Alec passed through unseen by them. Alec told me Nin was coming over here today to have it over with Mother, because some time ago my Mother told her that the affair was off, and now it seems thicker than ever. Of course, I suppose she has a right to please herself, but why does she carry on in this manner. She might be a foolish young girl instead of a woman old enough to have some sense. I don't know whether Nin has been today, or not.

There is nobody at home but Frank and I, as Mother, and Ida and Joe have gone to Harrison's Concert. It is the first of the season, and Patti is singing. I went to see the Football Match on Saturday, there were about 25,000 people there, the Villa were victorious. After the match I went to Wylde Green, and stayed until this morning, four of the family from there are at Llandudno so the old gent needed a little company.

It was a wet day yesterday, but I managed in the morning to get just far enough to have a view (from the outside) of a house at Wylde Green which is to let. It is occupied at present. It looks as if the people in it were very untidy, and took no pride in either the house or garden, but it is a place which could

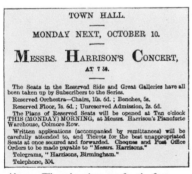

Above: The advertisement for the first night of the Harrison's Concerts, at which the Hughes were present, at the Town Hall, Birmingham. (O)

Right: An illustration of the Old Inland Revenue and Telegraph Office in Pinfold Street, Birmingham, advertising Harrison's Concerts, which Jack attended in 1898. (F)

be made very nice and comfortable to judge from the outside. I should have gone in had it not been Sunday, but I think I may have a look at it next Saturday. It is nice of Mr. and Mrs. Pattenden to ask us to their house, but really darling our time is so precious isn't it, during these flying visits, that we can ill . . . . .

The end of Jack's letter is missing, but he clearly went on to say that he would rather spend the short and precious time he had with Beatrice with her alone, and not have to waste it making social visits to neighbours such as the Pattendens.

<><><><><><>

"Roselea", Streatham Park, S.W. Oct 10th 1898

Dear Jack

I never realised until I read your letter what it will mean when the sunshine has gone out of our home. I had looked upon the matter of marriage quite in the dim future, just as we do about our long sleep. We know it must come sooner, or later: but we like to make ourselves believe it is so much in the far future that we need not trouble ourselves about it for a long, long time.

I am devoutely thankful that my future Son is one we can look up to with love, and respect. And as far as we short sighted mortals can see there is a very happy future before you both.

I pictured to myself a seven years engagement. I realize all the difficulties there are, in the way of being so far apart, and the coldness of your Mother. We Mothers are strange beings when they realize handing their children over to some one else, and another sharing the love which has been all theirs; but it will all come right: her Motherly love will be stronger than her prejudice and she will be ready when the times come to say "Bless you my Children".

Now to go back to your suggestion about the wedding bells ringing in June. I expect you two have made up your minds about it and all my persuasive powers will not induce you to a seven year engagement, as I had fondly hoped for. If that is so, it will be more graceful on my part to give the approval you ask for, and bow to the inevitable.

Long engagements of several years were quite common in Victorian times, in order to allow a couple the time to save up enough money to set up a home. Beatrice's mother was party to the plan for Jack and Beatrice's wedding date but yet a further formal approach to Mr. Mercer would also be necessary.

The very slightest remark about it gives Pa a fit of the blues, what he will be when he has to face it I cannot imagine. Accept my best love, Believe me,

Lovingly Yours M. Mercer

<><><><><><>

"Roselea", October 11th 1898

My own darling Jack

I was more than delighted to get your dear letter this morning as I thought perhaps you wouldn't have time on monday night. What time did you get my letter at the Works, I should like to know, for I went with Ernie to the post on Sunday night and it went out 11.30. Well, Ma has written to you at last, be sure and let me know the contents. I wonder what the accomodation and rent will be of those houses in Jaffary Rd. I do hope they won't be beyond us for I feel I should like that part. Be sure and thank Jennie and Alec for their great kindness in offering for me to go there, I do think it nice of them to take so much interest in us. Just fancy your Mother and old Phelps going out

A postal collection at 11.30 on a Sunday evening seems a luxury indeed – especially as a letter posted then was fairly well guaranteed to reach its destination the next morning.

Wylde Green was a few miles north of Linwood Lodge, and the home also of Jack's friends, the Harrops.

Ernie would have clocked up about forty miles on his new bicycle to Leatherhead and back. (B)

Jack was by now so despondent that even Mrs. Mercer's agreement to the wedding date had done little to cheer him. It was fortunate that he was able to pour his heart out to Beatrice and that she was so understanding.

together, doesn't it seem ridiculous, they would be surprised to know that Jennie and Alec saw them. What sort of looking house is the one at Wylde Green? I had a post card from Aimèe, asking me to go wednesday instead of today as her sister is going out today, so I am going over tomorrow. We are very agreeably surprised at our new Cook. We had really an awful character, as regards cooking, the only good point was that she was honest, well, up to now she has cooked everything very nicely indeed. She may not be as methodical as we could wish but you cannot expect everything, I only hope she goes on alright then we shall be nicely suited and give me more time for my needle-work, for Jack dear, you know I shall have a lot to do now. Aimèe did not finish my tablecloth, but I shall stick to it, but there is a lot of work in it.

It has turned awfully cold here today, so we have started fires and very cheerful it looks. Couldn't you write to Mr. Dawson for particulars, you would know sooner and I am simply dying to know. Mrs. Morris wants me to go and stay with her, but I shall not go if I can possibly help it, although they are very kind, the place seems so full up and I never am well. I had such a funny attack yesterday afternoon I half lost my senses and every nerve in my body was on the twitch, I felt so bad, I got some brandy and I soon felt quite well again. Ernie is very pleased with his bicycle and he wanted me to go for a ride with him last saturday, but I felt too tired, after I had finished doing the work, but I hope to go soon. He and Reg went to Leatherhead and back they said it was very cold. Well darling I think I must say au revoir I have several things to see to. Accept heaps of love and hundreds of kisses, you know the sort I mean.

yours most devotedly

Beatie

Linwood Lodge, October 12th 1898

My own darling Beatie

When I reached home last night there was a letter from your Ma, and I was so glad, for you don't know anxiously I had been looking out for it.

I enclose the letter with this so that you may know exactly what she has to say on the matter. I need not of course tell you how delighted I was to find that your Ma so gracefully accedes to my wish, or rather our wishes. You can give me the letter back when I come up on the 22nd. Only ten more days to wait thank goodness for that. I do wish you were with me now darling, for I have had a most awful day today, and have fairly got the hump, and if you were here to comfort me I should be able to feel different. I cannot explain, but everything seems to have gone wrong today, from the very start, (sometimes it happens that way) and now I have come home to an empty house, no-one here but Ida, no-one to say a cheering word.

It makes me long more than ever for the time to fly, so that June may come and I can have my own little home and dear little wife to come home to, after my business; for I know you will cheer me up darling. However, don't trouble about this, for we must take things as they come I suppose, but really I feel so miserable tonight, and there is no disguising the fact, for I cannot smother my feelings. I was so glad to receive your dear letter this morning, I had hardly expected it as I thought you would be spending the day with Aimèe yesterday. Your letter of Sunday arrived at the Works about eleven o'clock, or shortly after, on Monday. When you say about going to post with Ernie on Sunday night, I picture both of you there, each sending words of comfort to one miles away, dear Laura in one direction and I in another. How strange.

I am so grieved dearie to hear of you having had such a bad turn. Are you feeling quite better now, and also have you started to wear the woollen underclothing. If not you really should do so at once. Time is very short, and really I am unable to write more tonight. Do pray excuse this short letter, and with heaps of love and kisses, from,

yours most devotedly
Jack

Ernie and Laura had been sweethearts since childhood, having met at Sunday School. Laura was at this time teaching at Herne Bay so Ernie too relied on the postal system to keep them in touch.

"Roselea", October 13th 1898

My own darling Jack

Cheer up dearie I cannot bear to think you are feeling grumpy and I so far away, and not able to pop in to try and comfort you, I feel so sorry for you, but nobody's life runs perfectly smooth does it dear? It wouldn't do for us. Thank you for sending me Ma's letter, I will keep it for you until you come. I went to Dulwich yesterday morning, I left here at 10.30 and Aimèe met me at Peckham Rye station and I went shopping, it is so interesting buying things for my trousseau for it feels more as if it was really reality and the time will soon slip by dear, and then think and picture how happy we shall be.

I suppose you have not heard any more about those houses? I called in at Morris's on my way home, they send their love. I told them our wedding was settled and they, like everybody here think we have got a lot to do in the short time, and so we have haven't we, but we shall manage it alright I know. I have been thinking, I believe I shall have to come to Birmingham twice, the first before the March quarter to choose the house and then it would be too soon to buy furniture, so I should have to come again to buy the furniture, don't you think so? I hope Jennie wouldn't mind that, if I had to do so. Nellie rode round this morning to ask me to go to tea, so I am going to ride on my bike. She does not seem at all well, she is so worried just now. When I got home last night Mr. and Mrs. Ware were here they wished to be very kindly remembered to you. Mrs. Morris wants me to go up to town with her on saturday and go to a matinée, but I shall not go, I don't care about saturday's matinée without a gentleman but the following saturday I shall have my dearest with me, that is what I am longing for. I hope you will write again soon dear and I hope you will be able to say, you are quite your own cheerful self once more.

The new Cook is most satisfactory I am pleased to say, if she only continues, it is a comfort to me, as you may imagine. Well dear, I cannot stop any longer, I must be off to Nellie's or I shall lose the post, heaps of love and kisses

yours ever
Beatie

Saturday matinées were a fashionable rendezvous for men and women in London's West End. The local theatres and music halls provided relatively cheap entertainment and were one of the most popular ways of spending a night out for both the middle and working classes. This painting was by Hal Hurst RBA. (B)

Woodcock St. B'ham. October 15th 1898

My own darling Beatie

You cannot tell how comforted I was by your dear letter, which I received yesterday morning, for I had been so much down in the dumps, but thank goodness I feel more like myself again now. I am so sorry that it was impossible for me to write you last night, but I was here until nearly 8 o'clock, and then had to meet a gentleman on business at the Health Exhibition now on at Bingley Hall here, and did not get home until 10 o'clock. The Band of the Life Guards is playing there this week, and I heard them play the Music from the *Circus Girl*. It made me think of Folkestone and your dear self, at once, and our visit to the *Circus Girl* there. I have been trying all morning to get away just for a little time to write you a few lines as it would be too long for you to wait until Monday morning, and I hope that even now this may be in time for you to receive it this evening. There was to have been a cycle party to Bracebridge Pool, Sutton today but it is a very wet day and so that will be off. I have not found anything more out about the houses in Jaffray Road but am going up to Wylde Green this afternoon and shall have a look over the one there, about which I told you. I am sure dearie that Jennie would not mind having you there, *anytime* it is necessary for you to come down, no matter how often. What an experience we shall have, buying the furniture. I often catch myself now looking in the furniture shop windows, "A thing I have never done before". I am sorry Nellie is not very well, please remember me to her very kindly when you see her, and I hope she will soon be better.

How strange you should find Mr. and Mrs. Vane at home, when you reached there for do you know the same night when I reached home Joe and Mother were talking about them, Mother had evidently received a letter from them recently. I am so glad to know that Mr. and Mrs. Vane feel so kindly towards me now, for you know all about what happened years ago, however there is no need to go back to that now, eh darling.

How shall we do for time next Saturday. When you write dear, will you please enclose one of the local time cards for the trains, then I can see how I can get down to Streatham by leaving here by the two o'clock train. I am being continually called away so you must please excuse the scribble. You don't say how you are in your last letter, but I sincerely hope you are better, and have got quite rid of all those funny feelings. Well darling really there is not time for more. Heaps of love and kisses

Yours most devotedly

Jack

Jack's misreading of Beatrice's letter was to get him into yet more trouble.

⬥⬥⬥⬥⬥⬥⬥

"Roselea", October 16th 1898

My dearest Jack

I did feel so neglected when I did not find a letter from you yesterday morning for I thought I should not get one then until monday. However I was surprised to receive one by the last post last night. You must have read my letter very carelessly or my writing is very indistinct for I never mentioned Mr. and Mrs. Vane's name. I went to Church this morning I suppose you did not. Hope you had an enjoyable time at Wylde Green, they must be very fascinating company I should imagine for you seem to spend most of your time with them. I would rather not live up there I think, for I should not care for you to be always going with him, as you know I did not take to them at all, and do not wish to have anything to do with them and I know what it would be if you lived near them, they would be always coming and fetching you out, and I shouldn't like that. I enclose you a time card, I am glad you are coming by the 2 o'clock train, I suppose you will come to Kensington and then change for Streatham Hill. I reckon you will catch the 4.53 from Kensington, let me know and I will meet you. Pattenden's want us to go as early as we possibly can, of course I don't really care about going, only as they arranged it specially for your benefit, I felt rather flattered and accepted so you must grin and bear it for once.

Don't think I mind you going to Wylde Green now for I know you are not any too comfortable at home, but I don't want you to have anything to do with them when we are married, if we ever are. I really think, even if your Mother asks me up, I would not care to go, if she treated me coldly so don't you suggest it, if she offers of her own free will I don't mind, but not unless. Ask Ida if she would care to be one of my bridesmaids? Perhaps your Mother would not allow her. Do you go to see your Uncle at all, I think you might do so; I am sure he would be pleased. Ma was naming a few people who she would ask to the wedding, quite a few and they numbered nearly a hundred so with your friends we shall be a large party shall we not? I shall be glad when next saturday comes, it seems as if it never would come, I somehow feel such an uncertainty tonight and want you to re-assure me. Well I think I must conclude, I am not feeling at all well thank you dear! Hope you are alright and don't keep

A photograph of Ida taken as a bridesmaid at her older sister Jennie's wedding in 1895. Ida would have been eleven years old at that time. To be asked to be a bridesmaid to Jack and Beatrice, would have put Ida in a difficult position. She was too young to make her own decision about such an event and her mother was certain to be against it. (P)

It is very evident from Beatrice's emotional letter that she was feeling insecure. She had never been too enamoured by the Harrop family and had already told Jack that she thought they were a bad influence, but this letter suggests that she might also have been a little threatened by the Harrop girls. At least Beatrice was honest about her feelings towards the Harrops.

me without a letter as long, you don't know how anxious I get, for, of course I think of everything bad. Aimèe asked me to remember her to you when I wrote, it is her birthday today. Lots of love

Yours wholly
Beatie

Linwood Lodge, Gravelly Hill. October 17th 1898

My own darling Beatie

I was so glad to receive your letter this morning, for I knew then that you had received mine of Saturday, and you cannot tell how anxious I felt over that lest you should not hear from me until this morning, but I reckoned you would get it on Saturday night, and was so glad to know that you did.

Now dearest I did not read your last letter carelessly; nor do I ever do so, but when I read in your letter today that you had not made mention of Mr. and Mrs. Vane in your last letter I could not understand it, and got out your last letter and read it again, and found that you had written about Mr. and Mrs. Ware.

Now the reason I had misread your letter was that the letter "W" looked very much like a "V", and the letter "r" had a blot on it, and hence my reading it for a letter "n". I am sure darling that I am most sorry for the mistake, but pray don't attribute it to any carelessness on my part. You don't know dearest how it pained me when I read in your dear letter this morning, where you say, "when we are married, if ever we are". I have been thinking over that all day. Of course we shall be married, and who will be happier than we. Your confidence in me is not shaken, in the least I sincerely hope, for I have done nothing to cause it to be, goodness knows. I am the same Jack to you darling, and shall ever be. Do tell me in your next darling that you trust me as ever.

I asked Ida today if she would like to be one of your Bridesmaids, and she said she would most certainly. It appears they were in town today, Mother and Ida, and the subject of our Wedding was mentioned to them by a friend. Ida said she would certainly be there, and Mother said she was not offended with Beatie at all, but that she required a most abject apology from Jack, as he had offended her and until he had given it she should not think of attending the Wedding. "Everybody else could go, but she should not".

Now dearie I have told you all the circumstances of how Mother came to be offended with me, over and over again; but when I come up on Saturday, we will talk it all over again, and whatever you think best for me to do, I will do it. I have not been to Uncle John's house since I told you, but have met him several times at town. However I have to go to see him, and should have gone tonight but for writing to my dear little girl, so I shall go tomorrow. He is alright now, and always very pleasant to me. It is very bright and cheerful here tonight, no-one in the house but Alice, and it does so make me long for the time to come when I shall have my own little home, and you my dear little wife to come to. Cheer up darling, don't look on the dark side of things. I am afraid we have been doing too much of that lately.

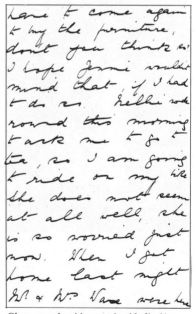

Clear enough evidence to justify Jack's difficulties in reading Beatrice's letter and subsequent confusion over the Vanes. (A)

The time is up and I must be off to post, and when I come back I am going to write a letter to Mr. Dawson, for particulars of the houses in Jaffray Road, so hope to be able to tell you about them on Saturday. Au revoir for the present dearest with heaps of love and lots of kisses

most devotedly

Jack.

The contrast of the lively household of the Mercers, and memories of his own youth when his father was alive and his mother was not "always out" in the evenings, must have made Jack feel desolate and lonely but for Beatrice's love.

"Roselea", October 18th 1898

My own dearest Jack

I received your kind letter this morning and very glad I was to get it. I have had such horrible feelings lately, so you must forgive me if my letters were rather funny you know I didn't mean it, for you know what my love is for you, don't you dear? Now, I am going to talk very seriously to you about your Mother. You know, as I have told you before, your Mother will never be the one to give in, you cannot expect it, one thing being your Mother, and then you have hurt her feelings, which she says she needs an apology for. Now I have thought it very unkind of you, not to have done so, after me asking you, when you know it is the only thing to be done. I feel it very much that you cannot do that little thing for my sake, when it means so much to me. Of course, if she won't come to the wedding I cannot help it, and really I am getting quite sick about it, if she still feels the same, *she must.*

I am glad Ida likes the idea of being a bridesmaid. We are having awful weather, I cleaned up my bike and got it already but I have trotted it upstairs again, for now I shall not be able to use it yet awhile. Just fancy, for about the last week, I have been able to fill our flower vases with roses from the garden, isn't it wonderful? The Cook is still going on alright as I hope we are now settled for some time to come. I went out with Nellie shopping yesterday, got caught in the rain beautifully. If it holds up a bit I want to go out this afternoon to post this. You ought to feel very flattered I assure you, for last Sunday it was raining in torrents when I went to post your letter, but I make it a rule always to post them myself now. I am feeling a little better today, but last night I came over very bad, I think this weather is so trying. Poor Chief's legs have been very bad, this last day or two, he cannot get upstairs. I am going to ask you a favour, haven't you a friend in the paste diamond business, I have been wondering if you could get me 1doz paste diamond buttons, about the size of a sixpence if you can, would you mind enquiring the price for me, but don't put yourself out at all, for it really does not matter much, only, Ma, Nellie and I want 4 each, and here they are so expensive. I hope you wont mind me asking you. You can but say *no.*

Well, darling I shall be so anxious to know the result of your letter to Mr. Dawson be sure and let me know as soon as you can. Do you think you could stay monday night? For they have got such a good bill on at the Palace theatre, and we thought it would be nice to go, I am longing for you my dearest, but for the present au revoir.

all yours
Beatie

Beatrice no longer trusted anyone else to post her letters even in the worst weather and she frequently went to the post in pouring rain for that purpose alone. This picture is from an advertisement for the Liebig Company's Extract, to be taken for winter ailments. (B)

Linwood Lodge, October 19th 1898

Jack's earnestness and honesty was now in conflict with a more pressing need to be practical and – above all – to keep Beatrice happy.

My own darling Beatie

Your dear letter reached me this morning and I am sure you cannot tell how anxiously I awaited it. I am sorry indeed to know that you have been feeling so poorly lately, but suppose that the weather is responsible for that in a great measure, but I am glad to hear that you are now better. The weather here, for a week, has been simply vile; raining and dull, and quite enough to give anyone a fit of the blues. Now, to talk about the much vexing question, as to apologising to my Mother, of course I will do anything for you my darling, and as soon as possible, but I feel I shall be making a liar of myself, if I say I am sorry I said what I did. What I said I quite felt and meant, and how can I say I am sorry for it, but still I am of course sorry that it should have put her about. However I can waive all these feelings for you my dearest, for I can see that it is the only thing to be done to bring my Mother to receive you as she ought. She is out tonight, (in fact she is always out) and has left word that she has gone to Mrs. Rollason's, but I don't believe it for a moment.

I wrote to Mr. Dawson for particulars of the houses, as I said I should, but at present have no reply. Perhaps I may receive one in the morning, I hope so for I am most anxious, and so do hope that the houses will be suitable for us. Last night I went up to Uncle John's and spent an hour or two, I got there just after 8 o'clock and after supper we had a hand at cards. He was very jolly, and seemed quite pleased to see me, he came in to the office this morning and I met him again tonight coming up in the train.

Now he is alright I think I must keep him so, and not stay away as I have done, for so long a time. When I got home last night Joe was very much upset in fact he had had quite a turn for there was a man killed at Gravelly Hill Station last night, and from what they said at the Station he thought it was Frank, and it made him awfully bad, but thank goodness it was not Frank. It was an awfully sad affair, so sudden, and the poor fellow smashed beyond recognition. Some poor family have a great trial. What a chapter of accidents are happening lately, it really makes you feel it is hardly safe to go about. I have enquired about the paste diamond buttons, and they quite know what is required, having made many of them. The price is somewhere about $1^s/6^d$ each, and I am going to have a sample one made, and will bring it up with me on Saturday, and if it is suitable you can have the dozen in about two days after I return. I am so longing for Saturday to come darling, that I may be with you, but it is only three more days now, but somehow the nearer we get to it the longer the days seem to be. I should like to stay over Monday night, dearie, quite as much as you would like to have me, but am afraid that it cannot be. Ida is quite pleased with the idea of our Wedding. Doris is coming over here tomorrow, for about a week I believe, as Jennie's servant is going away for a time, not being well. I must try and get home as early as I can and play with her and amuse her. It will be a bit of good practice for me, don't you think.

They are coming in now getting the supper about and it is nearing time for post, so I must conclude. For the present dearie, Au revoir. Heaps of love and kisses

Yours most devotedly
Jack

An account of the accident at Gravelly Hill station in the local paper. Jack's brother Frank was always a worry to the family due to his 'affliction'. (J)

Beatrice did not respond at all well to Jack playing with his little niece Doris. Perhaps she was anxious that Doris would be so delightful to Jack that he would set his heart on having children, which she was afraid she may not be able to provide for him, being already twenty-eight. There certainly would have been even less hope of it should they have waited seven years before marrying, as her mother wished.

"Roselea", October 20th 1898

My own darling Jack

It is so nice to hear from you every other morning, but young Ernie does chaff me about it, but I can put up with that, and am only too proud to think that you do take the trouble. I have only just got back, I have been out the whole morning with Ma and am feeling so tired. Many thanks dear for troubling about the paste buttons, but we can get them for that here and I think it is too much to pay for buttons, so unless they keep a cheaper sort don't worry about it, I must go without. I am so glad that your Uncle is so nice once again and I should certainly try and keep him so. I am longing to see you my darling to have a good hug etc., be sure and let me know what time you arrive at Streatham Hill, or perhaps you would rather come alone eh? I believe Pattendens will give us a very good spread on saturday. She did not tell us if any one else was going. You know they only have one servant and she told Ma she had hired a waitress for the evening. I have got my vests to wear at last, so I hope now not to have any rheumatic pains. Whatever makes Joe think that Frank would commit suicide. I remember he telling me that it occurred very similar to this affair once before and I am sure Frank would never do such a thing, poor fellow.

I shall be anxiously waiting to hear what Mr. Dawson says. I do hope they will suit us for I feel I should like to live just about there.

It does not look as if it was going to be fine tomorrow so our ride will be off. We have this morning received card and cakes from an old flame of mine who once declared he should never give up hope until I was really married but he, like the rest, has found Miss Wright and was married on tuesday, time he did settle down I think he is quite 38 or 40, another good man gone wrong they say. Wait until our turn comes eh dearie? We will show them something. Please do not practise playing with Doris. You won't require it you know.

Well dear I really think I must stop now and keep all the rest until saturday. Au revoir darling and be good

Yours wholly

Beatie

Frank was two years older than Jack. Despite his affliction, of which Jack never wrote in detail, he was able to go to the Works and do simple tasks. It would not have surprised the family too much if he had fallen under a train as he was a sad figure. He was not to live many more years and died in 1903 at the age of thirty-five. (P)

"Roselea", October 26th 1898

My own dearest Jack

I was looking out most anxiously for the postman this morning and Pa teased me and said he supposed that was why I was up so early. I was down before breakfast. Well dear your letter has quite excited me, for I shall be most eager to know how things will turn out. Just fancy Phelps coming to the house, but no doubt your Mother told him to, I am very glad that Jennie took her stand, now how about Phelps getting the push, I cannot think what will happen. Of course, your Mother will be very indignant about it I think, (although I should be glad if he went) that perhaps it is hardly the course to pursue, for she will be more likely to marry him, that is my idea, out of spite,

The Phelps affair had finally come to a head, Uncle John having played a key role in "Phelps getting the push". Phelps presence at Linwood Lodge and at the Works, and the furious row that ensued made it clear that he was not going to be tolerated by the family. This turn of events is detailed in a letter that, sadly, Beatrice did not keep.

and as her husband she could put him to manage the business couldn't she? How unkind of her to be so cruel when you kissed her, but of course I can see what it is, she wants the actual apology from you. I feel sure she will say it is your fault about your Uncle acting as he will, but I do hope things will come alright for all our sakes. Keep in with your Uncle whatever you do.

Well my darling, I did feel so lonely and miserable after you left me, but I am consoling myself that each parting brings me nearer to when we shall be *one*. I really am feeling better today dear only I have got rheumatism in the muscles of my back which is very painful. I have found the photos darling and will send them next time, as I have not a large enough envelope.

Ma and I have been talking about getting my house linen. I want her to get it before Xmas, for I shall have as much as I can do after getting my own things. Also she has been speaking about having Laura here when I am gone, and I believe if it can be arranged, that she will ask her, I hope so, for I should like to see her here wouldn't you dear? How long is Joe going to stay in London. I suppose he will not call here. How is Jennie and is Doris still at Gravelly Hill? I was asking Ma about the amount of housekeeping money I should want, she says some weeks come less than others, but that she should say 35/-. I said £2 to include laundry etc, she said I should have enough to save out of that so I feel sure that we shall be very comfortable. I wrote to Ida yesterday. I wanted her to get me some fringe nets. I cannot get them so large anywhere here and I also asked her about being bridesmaid, I thought I may as well, so I suppose she will write now. Do write the same day that you receive my letters, that brings it that I hear every other day and I can't wait any longer than that. Well dear I shall lose the post if I do not buck up. So I will conclude with heaps of love and kisses.

Yours most lovingly
Beatie

❖❖❖❖❖❖

Woodcock St. B'ham. October 28th 1898

My own darling Beatie

Well dearie I was so glad to receive you dear letter yesterday morning but how horrid for you to be having that Rheumatism again, I quite thought you were going to be free from that now. Still I hope it will not be very painful and that it will soon be quite gone altogether. This Phelps business is fairly sickening me, as you may easily imagine, but I feel that Uncle John has quite made up his mind that he (Phelps) must go from here. The only thing really though that troubles me about his going, is that I feel sure that both Phelps and my Mother will think that I have been instrumental in bringing it about. Now really such is not the case, for I never told Uncle a word about their goings on together, or had any conversation with him on the matter until he told me all about it himself on Tuesday morning. You need not be afraid about my Mother placing him here, to manage the business, in the event of their becoming married. But still of course there is this to be looked at, that after he had left this business he would be nothing to Joe and I, and so of course if my Mother cared to have him at Linwood Lodge, it would be no use

Jack had already sealed his letter with red sealing wax when he realized he had no stamp. (A)

for us to grumble. We should have to grin and bear it, or get out, and of course which I should do is a foregone conclusion. We know I shall clear out in June (in any case) don't we darling, but how if I have to do so before. Do you know since this affair has assumed such an aspect, I positively hate the very sight of the man, for I feel that we have been so had, all along. Joe got home from London on Wednesday night. I had quite a little surprise, when I arrived here yesterday morning and saw the letters, for I could not mistake the handwriting on the first letter I saw. It was the envelope from you darling, containing the photos. It was really so good of you dearie, to send them on so soon, I expected I should not get them that day. It is very nice to have them to look, but really Ernie has not done you justice at all has he darling.

How lovely it is to read your dear letter and see how busy you are getting all ready for our little home. Don't we both wish we were in it now. What a jolly thing it will be for Ernie and Laura, if your Ma has Laura to come to "Rose-lea". They will miss you so darling I know, when your Jack takes you from them, but then they will think of our future and when they can see you happily settled in your own little home, they certainly will not mind, but will feel that their loss is our gain, and feel rather pleased than otherwise. Doris is still at Linwood Lodge. She is very amusing (for a little while). On Wednesday night I was amusing myself with her, and she told me that Auntie Beatie sent her a nice dress, a white one.

Ida told me she had received a letter from you and that she would send the nets on Thursday. She is quite pleased with the idea of our wedding. I am so sorry dearie that they tease you because you look out for my letters every other morning, whatever will they say now, two mornings in succession. You know

Beatrice's envelope with her familiar and very feminine handwriting, which contained the photographs that Ernie took. Perhaps Jack should have taken one of her letters to a graphologist, as Mrs. Mercer had done his. (A)

With great pride the Mercer family was associated with Waterloo. In 1815 Beatrice's grandfather, Thomas Mercer, the Master Mariner, had brought the news of Napoleon's defeat at Waterloo to the 'House of Rothschild', where he, the first of four generations of Mercers subsequently worked, before even the British Government knew of it. Her grandfather died in 1862 having left the sea some years earlier to finish his working life with the famous banking firm.

dearie, I told you I went to a lecture, on Waterloo last Friday night, well I am just going now to hear the second part, and completion of it. It was very well given and most interesting and instructive and I have been looking forward to tonight to hear the continuation.

Well dearie nearly one week gone, of the three. Heaps of love and kisses.

Your own devoted
Jack

Granny desires her fondest love   "Roselea", October 29th 1898

My own dearest Jack

Many thanks for your two letters which you know I was very glad to receive. I should have been rather anxious if I had not had a letter yesterday morning and I feel so disappointed, in your yesterday's letter you wrote, "All's well". I quite thought it was alright with your Mother and I feel so concerned this morning when I find it is not so. Jack dear why don't you apologise, I shall begin to think, that you are not a man of your word. I do hope you won't have to leave home before we are married, I shall feel so miserable if you do. You might have a look at *our* house and see how it looks and let me know. I do feel this separation so darling I only wish we were married and together. I had a letter from Ida, she sent me the nets, please thank her for me, and tell her that I will write to her in a day or two. Ma and I went shopping yesterday I bought some of my sheets and pillow cases, it *is* lovely getting my things together for I picture us in our little home. I have started my undervests and certainly I am better of the rheumatism, I shall have to be more careful for I know how I got it and it was quite my own fault.

Just fancy little Doris remembering I sent her a dress. Tell her that Auntie Beatie sends her some kisses, which please administer for me. I wonder Joe did not call here and you can tell him we think it very funny of him. When do you think Phelps will go? Does Joe agree to it? I feel sure there will be ruptions over it but we must hope for the best. My only advice which I begin to think you ignore is to apologise to your Mother. Let me have a letter on monday morning, won't you dear? I shall be looking out for the postman, so don't forget. Ida never mentioned her Mother in her letter, I am wondering whether your Mother knew she wrote, she tells me that she is taking part in that dramatic performance your Mother is getting up. Will you go to see it, is she taking part in it? I have nearly finished that tablecloth I was working and I don't mean to leave it until it is, I expect it will be done today or early next week. Have you seen Jennie since? What does she think of Phelps going? No I certainly don't think Ernie has flattered either of us as least I hope it is not supposed to be or else I am uglier than I thought I was. Well dear I must be off. I am just going to have my annual, so ta-ta and be sure to write tomorrow. Lots of love and reams of kisses

Yours ever
Beate

A photograph of Jack's small niece, Doris, in 1896, the year she was born. Beatrice was often sending Doris clothes that she had made for her. (M)

Linwood Lodge, Gravelly Hill. October 30th 1898

My own darling Beatie

Pray excuse the pencil but I started to write in ink and have had to give it up as the pen was really so bad. I was so glad darling to receive your last letter this morning, but just fancy I was in bed when I got it.

Ida and I have just come in from Church, and we walked home by way of Jaffray Road, so as to have a look at out house. I was surprised to see how far they have got on with them. They have got right up to the top, and got the rafters on to carry the roof. As I imagined there are not any cellars. The call has just gone for dinner so I must adjourn.

Here we are again. Well about our house. The rooms do seem small but then there are no floors in yet so I suppose one cannot very well judge. From what I can see of the Dining Room, there will be a square window standing out. The window frames are not in yet but you can judge what they will be like from the construction of the brick-work. I think darling we shall find they will suit us. Now about that burning question again, my Mother. Well dearie, yesterday afternoon there was to be a rehearsal for the Dramatic entertainment and I did not come home until the 9.15 p.m. train. Joe came up by it too. When we got home they were at Supper, there was Mr. and Mrs. Austin and their baby here, and also Mr. Phelps. Joe went into the Dining Room, and took supper with them and I had mine in the kitchen, for I felt I could not treat Phelps as a gentleman, so I had better not see him. I don't know whether or not this is to continue until the Dramatic entertainment is over. Mother did not go to Church this morning and I did not see her until Dinner time today, and we have had no conversation together. Little Doris was in here just now, and pointed up at your photo, and said "nice Auntie Beatie up there", and I told her you had sent her some kisses, and gave them to her. She then lifted up her pinafore and showed me the dress you had sent her. She has been put to bed for a while now. It is a dull and cheerless day here, and missling of rain. How different I feel to what I did last Sunday when I was with my little dearie. I do so wish I were with you now my darling, for I am so lost and miserable without you. I feel so glad I went to Church this morning for I am sure it makes me feel better. It is Hospital Sunday here today. I am so glad darling to know that you are better of that rheumatism, and do now pray continue to wear those under-vests now you have at last started them, for you will surely be better if you do so.

You would of course think it strange that Joe did not call at "Roselea" when he was up in London, but I am sure it was only because he had not time. He was only up two days, and was obliged to come back when he did, and his time was fully occupied. I don't know when Phelps will go from the Works, but think it will not be very long. Joe's views on the matter are not very defined. In fact, I think Uncle John almost seems to think that he approves of the affair, but I am sure such is not the case. There will certainly be a bust up when it comes to it, and what it will end in I don't know, but I do know that my Ma then cannot upset our position, if we look after ourselves and work Uncle John the right way. It will be to our interest to always keep him alright for if my Mother were in sole control it would be a bad lookout. I have not seen Jennie since Monday night. She definitely thinks that Phelps ought to go, in fact she was the first I think to suggest it.

Jack had no excuse to have such a bad pen. There were so many different kinds of pens advertised at this time that it is surprising he did not have several fountain pens. (B)

Dramatic and musical evenings were popular social events in Victorian households and Mrs. Hughes organized these on a grand scale. Perhaps it was here that Ida gained her first experience and desire to go on the stage.

'Bust ups' seemed to be fairly regular events in the Hughes family at this time. Beatrice was quite right to keep reminding Jack that he must "keep in with" Uncle John.

'Grannie' was Anne Trigg, Mrs. Mercer's mother. She was a strong old lady and outlived her daughter, ending her days at 'Roselea' where she died in 1906.

It is so nice to read of you going buying all these things for our home. I wish darling it was time for us to buy the furniture and then we should know that the happy day was not far off. I read this morning of a couple spending their honeymoon on Mont Blanc, think that would be cool enough for us dearie? Dear Old Granny, thank her and give her my love in return. Bless her, we shall all be old someday I suppose. Please give my love to your Ma and Pa and accept heaps of love and oceans of kisses for your dear little self.

your own devoted

Jack

You will notice, the Mayor of Stratford on Avon, is mentioned in the enclosed cutting.

◇◇◇◇◇◇

"Roselea", October 31st 1898

My own darling Jack

I was looking out for your letter this morning, as I was quite hoping that you would have made it alright with your Mother. Jack you very much disappoint me, if you wanted to, I know you would find an opportunity, but enough I shall not mention the matter again, you know my wishes. I think, as Mr. Phelps was there only for Rehearsal, you ought to have gone into supper, it would have been quite a different matter had he have been there alone.

Just fancy, the house being so forward, I do hope the rooms won't be too small, I should hate it, if they were, but, as you say, one can hardly judge yet awhile, what sort of bricks are they using, I hope some red. But if I do not like it, we are not obliged to have it are we? Do you know, when I wrote to Ida I asked her if she would be one of my bridesmaids, but she never mentioned a word about it. I think this treatment I am receiving is abominable, I cannot stand much more of it I can assure you. I know very well Joe could have come down here at evening time, if he had wanted, but I suppose he like the rest, wanted to give me another slight. Yesterday was a shocking day here after dinner, it simply poured with rain. Nellie Morris and I went to Church yesterday morning, but as it was so wet the children could not get round. I am glad you went to Church it certainly does you more good than cycling. Ma and I are going up West on wednesday, we are going to the dress-makers at Kensington. I want to order a new evening gown. We always have to give her plenty of notice, she is so busy. Granny says she is very much obliged for your kind message and hopes that when we are as old as she is, we shall be as well looked after. I think it beastly of Joe, that he should have gone into supper as you did not, it appears to me that he says one thing and does another, I begin to quite despise him, he has not got any pluck.

I hope you delivered my message to the Harrops, for I really think it was very good of them to invite me. It looks as if I should come to Linwood Lodge doesn't it and you are going the right way to bring it off aren't you? It is a most glorious day here, although much colder, we have taken to fires again. My Rheumatism is quite well again now, and I hope it will keep so. I am going to write and ask Jim and May over for next saturday. Well, excuse more now, I am just going out and I am so busy. Write soon I shall look out for a letter

AN EVENING GOWN OF WHITE CHIFFON DRAPED WITH BLACK LACE.

The fashion writer in the 'Mothers and Daughters' column of the Streatham News, *predicted that: "fruit is to be used more for trimming evening gowns during the winter months than flowers, while the use of chiffon continues to be universal". (B)*

wednesday morning. How about the buttons, I am waiting for them, as the dressmaker is here today, let me know if you are not able to get them and I must get others.

Heaps of love

Yours devotedly
Beatie

A West-End trained dressmaker in Streatham would have charged Beatrice one and a half guineas for a fashionable tailor-made 'costume', consisting of a jacket and skirt with a blouse or waistcoat.

Birmingham, November 1st 1898

My own darling Beatie

I was glad indeed to receive your dear letter this morning, but oh it has upset me. I have been thinking of it the whole day. It has been too bad of me, I quite feel, not to have apologised to my Mother, before this, when the present state of things is putting you about so much. But, darling I really will do so now, it cannot be tonight, as she is never at home on Tuesday night, however if by chance she should be I will do so tonight, and if she will come to, you shall hear so in my next letter. It does so worry me darling when you are so put about, but God knows, after the treatment I have received at the hands of my Mother, there can be no wonder that I should be loath to offer her an apology.

My love for you Beatie is too strong to allow of your happiness being upset in the manner, and if apologising to my Mother will make you feel happier of course I will do it, as I have told you. But don't think so badly of Joe, darling, for not coming to "Roselea", I am sure he had not time. I got the Buttons today and have sent them off, and no doubt you will receive them by the same post as this. They have been on hand a long time, but darling, don't think it has been any fault of mine. I hope you will receive them safely and that they will please. Really dearie I am so upset I cannot write you a long letter tonight. Excuse me just now. I will apologise to Mother and write you again. Meantime with heaps of love, I am,

ever yours devotedly
Jack

A relaxed picture of Jack. Straw boaters were fashionable for both men and women in the late 1800s, particularly on sporting occasions in the summer. (A)

"Roselea", November 2nd 1898

My own darling Jack

The buttons came safely to hand this morning, we like them very much and very many thanks for all the trouble you have taken over them, when you write again, let us know how much they are, and shall I send the money on, or wait until you come saturday week. I don't see any reason why you should have been upset over my letter, I only spoke the truth and gave vent to my feelings and I don't think I spoke before I had cause. I have long felt this exceedingly, and you cannot deny that I am being treated very badly by your people, and you could have ended this long ago and it made me very

As the only and much loved daughter in a large family of boys, Beatrice was used to getting her own way. The difficult relationship with Jack's family was particularly frustrating to her therefore, as she was used to having people do what she wanted.

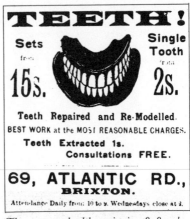

There was no health service in 1898 and a visit to the dentist would have been a costly and painful experience, as dentists did not use anaesthetics at that time either. (K)

angry and I could not help telling you, I never meant it to upset you though, you are too sensitive like me, but I hope you have forgotten all about it by now and are feeling better. I am getting so nervous, I am going to the dentist today, to have several of my teeth stopped, I know I shall be bad and have to go to bed when I get back, as I did before but I feel I ought to have them done, I have such a dread of fake ones. Mrs. May is going with me, Ma is too much of a coward. We are having frightful weather, the wind is blowing high and pouring with rain. Mrs. Tory said she was coming for the day, but we hardly expect her, as it is so wet. Mr. and Mrs. Morris are coming over tomorrow to spend the evening, it is Ma's "at home" day so Mrs. Morris is coming in the afternoon.

If we have that house in the Jaffary Rd. I suppose the landlord would let us choose the papers and decorations to our own taste up to a certain amount. He ought to. Mrs. May is just taking a house not quite completed and her landlord says she can choose her decorations up to a certain sum. Well dear, I wish you were with me now, I do so want you, and the 12th seems such a long way off, but I suppose I must be patient, it won't come any the quicker for worrying. I hope you will answer this so as I shall get a letter on friday morning. On Nov. 13th at Church the Bishop of something or other is going to preach something special, so we must go dear. Well dearie, I cannot stop longer, we are turning out the drawing room (good old room) and we want to get it finished for when Mrs. Tory comes. Accept heaps of love and many kisses to make it well.

always yours own
Beatie

Woodcock St. Birmingham. November 2nd 1898

My own darling Beatie

I have at last taken your advice, and when I got home last night I apologised to my Mother, as I told you I would. She altogether stood off from me, and quite resented me. She told me it had taken me a long while to find out that I was sorry, and that it would take her as long to believe that I really was sorry. In fact she said "Don't be sorry for me, for you have no need, be sorry for yourself, for you will have cause to be". She further said she wished me well, and if I looked after those belonging me, and did my duty as well as she had, I should have nothing to reproach myself for. But she impressed upon me that she did not believe a word I said, as far as apologising to her was concerned. Well dearie I have done as you wished, and now you know my experience. I don't think that she is altogether so annoyed with me, over the Phelps matter entirely, for don't you remember darling, the day when I bought you your engagement ring (the Phelps affair had not been mentioned then) I went to her bedroom to show her your ring, before bringing it to you, and to wish her Goodbye. She would not see the ring, she refused to absolutely, and would not wish me Goodbye, and said rather cutting things, which I told you all about at the time. Now darling you know what the Palmist told you about a woman who would put every obstacle in the way of your marriage, well I can't say that I attach much importance to what she said, but really all of it looks true, doesn't it.

Jack's supreme effort to apologize to his mother didn't seem to help matters much. The palmist's predictions were already beginning to come true.

We do know though, that the course of true love never runs smoothly, this we know to some tune, for really matters seem to have been very strained ever since our engagement. But darling we must stick together and we can live it all down. My love for you is greater, if possible, than ever before, for I know how hard it is for you to keep up and continue to have such confidence in, and love for me when you are so far from me, and never receive a cheering word from those who ought to welcome you amongst them and be proud of you as my future wife. We are the victims of circumstances, and darling so long as you can continue to love me and I love you, as we have done until now, what need we to trouble for any thing further. It would certainly be so much more agreeable, and calculated to inspire greater confidence in yourself towards me if matters were more amicable, but then we are the people immediately concerned, and must think and act of ourselves. I quite appreciate your dear good love darling for me, when you have put up with all this coolness from this end for so long. It is bad enough for me and has troubled me a lot, but I know darling it must have been worse for you. Never mind dearie, let us continue in our love for each other, and the time will soon pass by, and when the anniversary of our engagement comes round, we shall be happy in the possession of each other. You know darling I have shown to you, that I shall be in a position to provide a comfortable home for us, and you know and so do I that when we are in it we shall be quite happy together, so do not let us worry ourselves any more than we can help over all this unpleasantness which occurs in the meantime.

I have made up my mind, and nothing will ever alter my love for you, now darling if we are both in the same mind, what matters anything else. Nothing will estrange any affections from you dearie. Whatever will your Ma think of it I wonder; but still Beatie I think they have sufficient trust in me, both your Pa and Ma, to let you come to me, even under such circumstances as the present. At least I hope so, but then of course my Mother may be alright towards us before the time of our wedding comes round, for I am not going to let the matter pass, on this one effort, but try consistently to bring her round. I am writing from here darling during lunch-time as I have to attend Lodge this evening leaving here at 5 o'clock. Cheer up dearie, and with heaps of love believe me *ever your own devoted Jack*

This final rift between Jack and his mother made him even more desperate that he would not lose Beatrice's love also, and with it his only chance of happiness.

"Roselea", November 3rd 1898

My own darling Jack

I do feel so sorry and upset. I have just read your dear letter, and I hardly know what to make of your Mother. You have done your duty dear, and you cannot do more, I have told Ma, and she says, you have nothing more to do, and she thinks your Mother most unmotherly to behave in such a manner. I wish I was near you that I could pop in and have a talk with you, but be the same and try to be just your old self to your Mother, she may come round in time, at least I hope and pray so. I feel now, more than ever, that I am the cause of all this unpleasantness, but so long as your love for me does not

Beatrice's hat was typical of the period – decorated profusely with birds' wings and ribbons. This, together with her serious expression, so typical of the formal Victorian photograph, did not flatter her. (A)

Beatrice had at least got Jack to do what she wanted and though it was a wise attempt to make peace with Mrs. Hughes, the basis of her antagonism was clearly a much more complex issue than something a simple apology would repair.

alter I don't care, it did worry me that you did not apologise before, when she let you know that was what you wanted but know that you have done that, I feel happier on that score, but miserable to think that you are having all this to put up with and all for me. Darling, you won't regret it, for when we are one, we shall have forgotten all these ructions and live for one another and have the happy future to think of. What does she mean by saying "you have more cause to be sorry for yourself", does she refer to me, or what? I hope you never will be sorry it won't be my fault that I know, for it will always be my great aim to make you happy and be my lover always. If she is always going to be as she is now, it will never do to live so near her, so keep your eyes open and look about for other houses to look at.

I did not go to the Dentist yesterday, I have an appointment for tomorrow morning, I do dread it, but it will be a good thing over. Now darling, don't let all this bother worry you, you must feel now that you have done all you could and now I don't care so much, we must look to June 1st and then What ho! Ma sends her love and dearie cheer up for my sake, we must not worry or we shall get too thin and we shall not be able to find one another. Excuse more now dear, I want Pa to take this and I am hoping you will receive this tonight. Lots of love and I do hope all be well *always your own Beatie*

◇◇◇◇◇◇◇

Woodcock St. B'ham. November 4th 1898

My own darling Beatie

Pray excuse the hurried note I wrote you last evening, but I was busy here until nearly a quarter past 8, and then I wanted to get home, as Mother had Mr. and Mrs. and the Misses Blakemore to Supper, and if I had stayed here and written you a long letter darling I should have missed the train, and she would have told me that I had stayed away purposely. Now as I told you in my last, dearie, I am going to try consistently to bring her round, of course I don't mean by that, that I am going to be always on my knees, imploring her, as it were, but that I shall not do anything that she can take exception to.

Of course the news as to my Mother was sure to upset you but my darling don't worry, we shall come through it all right. If she is pleasant and proper to us when we get married all well and good, but if not we can't help it. She was most cutting in her remarks, I consider and most ungracious to you but never mind my dearie, we know each other thoroughly, and I know I shall never be sorry for it, as she says, nor will I give you cause to be.

Now it is a strange thing, but I had been thinking the same thing myself as to whether it might not be better for us to live a little further away from Gravelly Hill. What I had thought was this, that I might buy a couple of Villas (with my money, which I have at present on Mortgage) and live in one and let the other. I think if we did that way, we should do better with our money, and have a better house to live in, only of course there is the fact that the money could not be so quickly realised, if necessary. There are two freehold villas for sale, in

Jack's hurried note of November 3rd was written from the Works, where he had been working late. It was unusual for him to take part in a social event with his mother, and this was an attempt to make his amends with her.

Beatrice's own brooch, in the design of a stamped envelope with her name engraved on it, is a charming souvenir of Jack and Beatrice's courtship by way of letters. (A)

Chester Rd. Near the Station between the Station and Uncle John's and I think if we did that kind of thing, that it is a property which would suit us well. What do you think of the idea darling?

I hope you did not feel very ill after your visit to the Dentist today, it is an awful experience I know, having been through it myself. You need not trouble to send the money for the Buttons, that will do when I come up. I am glad you like them.

You cannot tell darling how much better I felt after reading your dear letter today, I am not going to worry myself over all this about my Mother anymore. It is you I want dearie, and I know that nothing is going to part us, so what else comes, well we can put up with it. Mother is out with Ida tonight at a Conversazione so as there is no-one at home, I had arranged to go to the Promenade Concert at Curzon Hall tonight at 8 o'clock, but it is a quarter past now, so I shall be late.

Yours most devotedly
Jack.

Give my love (or rather some of it) to your Pa and Ma. and Granny, and accept heaps for yourself from

◇◇◇◇◇◇◇

"Roselea", November 5th 1898

My darling Jack

I was eagerly looking out for your letter this morning but I am afraid it was not very cheering. I know dear, it is not your fault, I like you to tell me all, so please tell me in your next what were the cutting remarks made by your Mother and how she was ungracious. I am more than ever disgusted with her, especially when I think how she has pretended to be so fond of me, but I can see now that was when she thought you boys did not take any notice of me, it shows how shallow natured she is, I shall never like her again and when we are married, the less I see of her the better, if she thinks so badly of me. I certainly should not upset her more than you can help. I can quite see through it, she is trying her best to set you against me, but I don't think she will be able to will she dear? at least I hope not, that is what Ma says, she thinks she has such influence over you that she will talk you out of it. Do write and reassure me darling. Goodness knows I feel miserable enough, without having to think that. How horrid of Joe to forget to give you my letter, I should think he did it purposely.

Now dear about buying the houses, certainly it would be very nice if we could always insure the one being let, but as Pa says it is an uncertainty and of course there are all repairs to be done aren't there, but of course you would not buy houses that were not well built and that would not be in demand. I should like to know what they are like, give me full description when you write, what sort of windows have they, are they pretty and what accomodation have they? don't laugh at all these questions, but you know dear I love to know. I am feeling awfully seedy this morning. I went to the dentist's yesterday. I wanted him to put my teeth right and thoroughly examine them, well, I am glad to say I did not want any stopped, but he says they are too close together and he is going to file between every tooth. I had half of them scaled and the rest are to

Jaffray Road was only a short walk away from Linwood Lodge – much too close for comfort if there was to be continual bitterness between Jack and his mother. Chester Road station was two miles further north.

The Curzon Hall was a popular meeting place for middle class ladies and gentlemen – concerts being a much more popular way of spending an evening out than they are today. (O)

Beatrice's dread of going to the dentist was justified. Even without having to have any fillings she had fully expected to faint – a tendency of Victorian ladies, perhaps due partly to the tightness of their corsets.

The Beeches, the house in Chester Road, Erdington, where Joe Hughes, Jack's brother, lived until his death aged eighty-seven. (V)

be done on monday, I was so bad he had to leave off. I did feel dreadfully bad. Of course I fainted and consequently I feel very washed out today, I went to bed all yesterday afternoon, got up to tea, then I went to bed at 9 again. I promised to go to Morris's today for a week, but I had to get Ma to write and tell them I felt too bad. I wish you were coming today you could cheer me up. It makes me feel so mad that I am such a coward, but the dentist says it is my heart, not that I am nervous and of course I cannot help it. Do you know how much those houses are in the Chester Rd. I don't know where they are, are they anywhere near your Mother's houses? Granny sends her love and thanks you for being so thoughtful of an old woman. Well I have given you quite an epistle, I hope I have not bored you. Do write so as to get the letter here on monday morning, I shall be looking forward to have it.

Well dearie I must conclude and I do hope you will be able to write and say that your Mother can never influence you to break off the engagement. Lots of love

Yours ever
Beatie

❖❖❖❖❖

Linwood Lodge, Gravelly Hill. November 6th 1898

My own darling Beatie's

I was glad indeed, dearie, to receive your letter this morning, but pray do not worry yourself over all this business about my Mother. The cutting remarks she passed about you, were what I have already told you, and I do consider that she was most ungracious to you, to say such things as to say I should have cause to be sorry for myself. I don't fear that at all darling, and you need not be afraid that anything she can say or do will ever alter my

It must have been a great shock for Beatrice to know that Jack's mother had been so cutting about her. She was used to being adored by all her family. Beatrice was fortunate to have such a loving and understanding Jack.

affection for you. I love you too dearly Beatie, to be turned from you by anything or anybody. I am the same Jack to you as I have been all along, and shall always be. I wish I were only with you now, to reassure you, if such were needed, but never mind darling, it is not very long to the 12th, and then we shall be able to soothe each other, and be comfortable and happy together, if only for a little while. I have not been to Church this morning that is too bad of me, isn't it dearie, but I was so anxious to see those two houses in Chester Rd. that I went for a walk instead. I have not been to Chester Road in the day time for a long while so had not seen them. Well darling they are nearly finished, and are two very nice looking houses. They have square Bay windows, and the front room is intended for the Drawing room I can see. I did not go inside. There is the old fault about them though, the usual long narrow strip of garden, and there is no width of land at all close at the back of the house. The rooms look very nice and pleasant, but then it would be so much nicer if there were a nice bit of garden, for of course you will not want to be stuck in the house, all the time. I called at Uncle John's but he was out for a walk, and I did not wait for him as I wanted to get back here for dinner, I came back by way of Jaffray Rd. and had another look in at those houses there. The Dining Room there would be about as large as our Drawing Room here, I should think, and then there would be the square window besides, the Drawing room is about as long, but about 3 feet narrower, rather a small room. There is not much depth of garden. They will be very good looking houses when they are finished I think. There is only one place with anything of a Garden that I have seen, that would be likely to suit us, and that is the one I told you of at Wylde Green. I don't know if it is to let now though.

I am sorry darling that your experience at the Dentist's upset you so much, and hope you have quite recovered. It is hoped you will not be so bad tomorrow. I don't know the price of those houses in Chester Rd, but Uncle was to enquire for me, and I called at his house this morning thinking he might know by this. It is very kind of him to enquire, but still if they were likely to suit us I should not think of buying them without taking further advice. In fact, before I did anything definitely I should want my little wife to come and see the place I thought of bringing her to. It was a wretched day here yesterday, but is quite nice and bright today, and my walk this morning seemed to quite brace me up. I walked about 6 miles and had such an appetite when I came in. Mother is expecting Clarence Brotherton here today, I understand but I don't think I shall see him, as I think of going out. I am anxious to know the price of the houses for I think after all they would suit us, and if the price is right, I should get Harry Hawkes to go over with me and see them, and if we thought they were alright then perhaps you would come down dearie, and have a look at them.

Now dearie, do please try and make yourself as comfortable as possible, and be assured that whatever comes or goes I am yours for ever. I shall love you more and more if it were possible, but don't imagine for a moment that anything will ever part us for I am sure it will not. We have given ourselves to each other, and Beatie, I know we shall never regret it.

For the present, dearie, Au revoir, heaps of my dearest love, and lots of kisses

Your own devoted

Jack

Berwood House in Chester Road in the 1890s. A large detached house typical of this part of Birmingham. The two villas Jack had in mind were much smaller and more modest than this, though his mother was later to look at houses like this one. (F)

Clarence Brotherton was married to a cousin of Jack's. He lived in Belfast and was an agent for a company selling oil. He was an irritable and unsociable man, dissatisfied with Ireland and keen to save every penny in order to go to live in America, which he did.

Beatrice's prescription for tooth powder and a mouth wash, from Day's the Dispensing Chemist, of which there were many branches, especially in London and the south of England. (A)

"Roselea", November 7th 1898

My darling Jack

Your dear letter has quite cheered me up in fact I feel quite my own self and I am quite excited at the prospects of you buying the houses. I really think I like the idea more, now that I have thought the matter over and about the garden, never mind about that if the house is nice. I am so glad that they are new, I somehow thought they were old places. Well dear, I hope they won't do the decorations before we buy, I want so much to choose the papers and another thing, couldn't the front room be used as a dining room, it would be so much more cheerful. Don't give all your money for the houses and forget you have the furniture to buy etc. I am glad you are going to ask Harry Hawkes to look at them, he can tell you the real value, can't he? do let me know if anything fresh crops up. I shall love to hear about it, naturally dear I shall like to see them before you decide, I suppose I could go to Jennie's from friday till monday some day, if it was necessary. Well I have been to the dentist's this morning and thank goodness he has finished. I feel sure they will be alright for some time now at least I hope so, it cost me 15^s/6^d so it ought to. I do begrudge it, but it had to be done. I went to Church yesterday morning, young Leo met me and he spent the day with us, he was such a good little chap and he does get so funny. Of course I will excuse you for not going to Church this time under the circumstances. There is one thing, if you buy these two houses I don't suppose you would let the one until March. Don't you know how many rooms there are? I wish your Uncle would give us the houses for a wedding present, he would be a brick wouldn't he? However, we must not be greedy.

Ma and Pa went over to Dulwich to hear the funeral service of our friend who died last week. I did not go as I felt too seedy but I am feeling much better today, in fact I am going for a ride this afternoon. Do you know that saturday was a lovely day here and it is exactly like spring today. Does your Mother speak to you now. Did you go to your Uncle's to tea yesterday? I have finished the tablecloth and it really looks very nice I think although I say it as shouldn't, I am now working something else for our dear little home.

Well my own darling, I feel perfectly safe now as regards your love for me, I have no fear now, I am sure nothing can alter or change your love, I have my whole confidence in you and can trust you through anything. Lots of love

your own
Beatie

✦✧✦✧✦

Woodcock St. B'ham. November 8th 1898

My own darling Beatie

It was a real treat to receive your dear letter this morning, and to find that you are now feeling your dear self. I am sure darling you need not have worried so much, but then of course I know, you could not help doing it, when you felt it possible that influence might be brought to bear on me to

Uncle John was still an important ally for Jack and Beatrice, though Beatrice was over-estimating both his generosity and wealth if she expected him to give them a house as a present.

cause me to alter in my love for you, but no darling, as I have told you before that will never be. I am, like yourself dearie, quite excited about the house question. Uncle was here yesterday, and he said he thought he would have particulars of them today, and would bring them in, he has not been here though today, so of course I am unable to say anything further about them at present, of course, if they are likely to suit us I should arrange for you to come down, to see them, and stay with Jennie. I am glad to know that you have finished with the Dentist, for awhile, you got on better this time, eh? It is too much to hope for darling, to think that there is anyone, who would be so generous as to make us a present of a pair of houses on the occasion of our wedding. If there only were wouldn't it be fine, but that is too good to think of.

I am glad you are able to get out for a ride now, for I am sure it will do you good. There has been no weather here for riding lately, we have had so much rain that the roads have been continually in a muddy state, still if the roads had been ever so good, I have not had time to do any riding myself. We are busy at the Works just now, and darling I am glad of it, it has been a very poor year, but the last two months have been much better, and particularly we are busy now, I hope it will continue don't you dearie.

My Mother does not speak to me at all. She went with Joe last night to a Ladies Banquet at his Lodge and when she reached home I was in the Break-fast Room so she sat in the kitchen and as she required a drink, had it taken to her there. Truly a happy state of things, but dearie, let us never mention about her for I think we have said enough, and I know it only makes us both miser-able, to think about it.

I did not go to Uncle's to tea on Sunday. I am so glad the tablecloth is finished you have been patient and persevering. I will repay you for it all when I come on Saturday. I don't know yet what train I will come on, on Saturday, but will surely let you know, some time before. I am longing for the 12th to come dearie. Only four more days and then we shall be able to have a sweet embrace (or rather a good many). For the present darling, Au revoir. With heaps of love

Ever your own devoted

Jack

As bicycling became more popular, special costumes were designed for the cycling enthusiasts. The Birmingham Weekly Post regularly featured advertisements for coats and skirts adapted for cycling in the muddy and wet weather. By 1898 knicker-bockers and gaiters were beginning to be worn by keen women cyclists. (I)

"Roselea", November 9th 1898

My darling Jack

Here we are again, how goes it? I hope you are alright dear. I was glad to receive your dear letter this morning, I must say I was a wee bit disappointed, I thought I should have heard more about the houses, but you see I am too impatient. I must be patient and wait, when you are so excited you know it seems such a long time waiting. I shall be so glad to see you on saturday dear. I feel we want a good old talk about things don't you think so?

I think it is very good of your Uncle to make enquiries about the houses, it shows he takes a little interest in us, doesn't it? Was it his suggestion that you should buy on your own? I went out for a ride yesterday morning it was a

Beatrice was certainly impatient to have the house question settled. She must have felt frustrated at being so far from Birmingham as there was little she herself could do to help.

lovely morning, but I felt a bit tired. Reg had his half term holiday, so he took me. In the evening he, Ma and Ernie went to Drury Lane to see *The Great Ruby*. I didn't care much about going, it would have been different if you had been going so I stayed and kept Granny company we were quite alone all the evening, Pa being home late. Of course dear I am glad to hear that you are busy, for it will be all the better for us, but I don't like the idea of you having to stick to it so much. Poor old Chief, his legs have been so bad lately, they seem so stiff, he can scarcely walk. I don't suppose your Mother will like giving you your money, does she know anything about these houses? The other day Kitty cabled to Pa to know when we last heard from David. I suppose she has not received his letters and consequently got very anxious, poor girl, it must be awful, this separation. Just fancy if you and I were not to see one another for 3 years, I should go mad I think, but one hardly knows until we are put to it what we can bear. Granny sends her love, says no doubt you are looking forward to saturday, are you dear? I am. I can tell you, I am afraid if shall nearly crush you to death when I do get hold of you. I have been thinking you will only come once more after saturday, before you come for Xmas, it hardly seems possible does it? and then we shan't be long. Well dear I am afraid that I have exhausted all my news so I must conclude with many kisses and all my dearest love

ever your own Beatie

How is the sovereign purse, full?

The silver sovereign purse with Jack's initials engraved on it which Beatrice gave as a present to Jack. It would have held three sovereigns when full. (A)

Woodcock St. B'ham. November 15th 1898

My own darling Beatie

Here we are again, I reached home safely last night but it was rather an anxious time as far as Willesden. The train was delayed so many times that when we got there, it was already time that we had left but still there was the other train waiting, so it was alright. We got into B'ham in good time and I was at home just turned 10. After I had had some supper I went to bed at about 10.45 for I felt rather tired. Mother was not at home so I did not see her, until this afternoon, when she called in at the Works as she was requiring some money. Of course she was as indifferent as ever. She will do all she can to annoy me, I know; and even that devil of a Phelps, altho of course he dare not say anything to me, seems by his very bearing to try and annoy me. But never mind dearie, I can stand it all, and we shall come out quite as good as they, at the finish. Now how are you, by this time, better I hope, it was so painful to me darling, to come and find you so unwell, and I do sincerely hope, that now you have got the turn you will steadily improve and keep better. I sent up for the Bill of Excursion for Saturday, but it is as I expected, to return on Monday by the cheap train, I should have to lose all day Monday from here, and travel during Monday night. Now darling you know it is not the inconvenience to myself I think of, but you see I shall have them all grumbling here if I am away two Mondays in succession. But if you like darling I will come by the half day trip on Saturday, and return by early train on Monday morning, or on Sunday night.

Of course if I come up this week end, it will not interfere with our arrangements for Dec 3rd. It does seem awful when I think of my Mother's conduct towards you, she is quite inhuman; and especially to think she should be turned against us through such a thing as Phelps, for if he had never come on the scene, we should not have had all our anxiety, although perhaps things then might not have gone any too smoothly.

I suppose Ernie got safely home from Herne Bay, remember me to him, and tell him I hope they had a very nice time. I am going down to The Empire tonight. The special attraction is *Herr Seeth* with a troupe of Lions, Dogs etc. You will think dearie, that I am always going off somewhere. Well perhaps I am lately, but what inducement have I to do anything else. If I go home there is no-one there, and I have to sit alone, so I might as well go where I can be entertained a bit.

Tuesday night is always Phelps night. It will be different, darling when I have got your dear little self to come home to. I shall want to come to you as soon as I have done my business, and I know we shall always love as we do now. I cannot express how I wish for the 1st of June to come, but as this is not the age of miracles, I know there is nothing for it, but to wait patiently. You will while away the time, I know darling, by making all kinds of pretty and useful things for our little home, and shan't I be proud when the time comes and we have got the things all in and we are settled down. Perhaps at Christmas, or soon after you may come down with me for a time, and that will all help to make the time go by. Cheer up dearie, and try and keep as bright as you can. Let me know what you think of Saturday. I have enclosed a bill for you to see the times. Please give my love (some of it rather) to your Pa and Ma and Grandma, heaps for yourself, and lots of kisses

Yoursmost devotedly
Jack

❖❖❖❖❖❖❖

"Roselea", November 16th 1898

My darling Jack

I was longing to have your letter this morning to know whether you would be able to come up on saturday. Now dear, I hardly know whether you mean to come or not. Of course you know how delighted I should be if you could manage it, and if you come by the trip on saturday and go back early *monday* morning, surely they couldn't say anything to you for that, why don't you come 3rd class it wouldn't cost you so much then dearie, do come, I shall love to see you and have a good hug. I shan't know where I am, to have you 2 Sundays running, and we won't go to Church eh dear? so as to have more time to ourselves. I was very anxious on monday night and kept wondering how you had got on, but I am very glad you caught your train alright, it would have been awful if you had not.

Don't let that brute of a Phelps worry you darling, I know it is hard, but think we have not got so much longer to be apart. You ask me how I am? Well dear, yesterday I had a very bad day again, but I am pleased to say that today I am feeling better again. It cheers me up to think I shall see you again so soon

Jack's distraction from the dreariness of home was the Herr Seeth circus at the Empire Palace. (O)

A photograph of Beatrice, in later life, at home at The Chestnuts, the house in Chester Road where Jack and she eventually moved to and made their final home. (A)

A third class train ticket would have cost Jack 9s. 5d. single or 18s. 10d. return, from Birmingham to London, compared with a first class ticket at 17s. 4d. single and £1 = 13 = 0 return.

Laura had moved from Dulwich to the school in Herne Bay in Kent in order to follow Mrs. Knight to whom she was a pupil teacher, and whom she much admired. Ernie visited her at her half-term.

and I promise you I will be quite well this time, if I can. Don't go back Sunday night, for it would not be worth while you coming for that short time. Ernie and Laura had a very fine time together and the weather was grand Ern says. Laura sent her love to you. Hope you enjoyed your little self at The Empire, I am only too glad you do go somewhere, it does you good instead of moping at home alone. I shall look forward to coming down with you after Xmas to look for a house, we will make up for a lot then, what do you say? I hope Jennie won't turn against me and not want to have me. Ma and Pa appear to have been talking matters over, Pa says he is disgusted with your Mother to treat me so, and he wanted to come down and see your Mother about it, but I have begged him not to and Ma told him, it would be better to leave things as they are. If you come on saturday, don't forget to let me know what time to meet you, and you bet I will be there. I have at last made up my mind to take to woollen underclothing entirely, so I am going this afternoon to order them for I still feel a bit of rheumatics knocking about, anyway, I can but try it. The grapes dearie, are simply delicious, I only wish you were here to help me eat them, such a lovely flavour and so satisfying. Well I shall look out for a letter on friday morning, so don't forget. Accept my dearest love and oceans of hugs and kisses and cheer up darling, never mind anybody. Chin chin till saturday

Yours devotedly Beatie

November was a time for rheumatics and Beatrice suffered from it. Many doctors at that time had testified to the effectiveness of Dr. Jaeger's Sanitary Woollen System for the relief of rheumatism.

Woodcock St. B'ham. November 17th 1898

My own darling Beatie.

Now I have finished my days work, I can have a little chat with you, these little chats on paper, are not like the nice little tête à têtes, we can have together though when I come up to see my little dearie; so I have really made up my mind to come up on Saturday.

I am so glad darling to know that you are better, and sincerely hope you will be able to keep getting better still, and when you are quite well, to remain so. Really I should not know whatever to make of it, if I arrived at Streatham Hill, and my little dearie not there to meet me. It would seem so strange, for you know you have met me each time yet, darling, and you will this time I know, if you are well enough, and I sincerely hope you will be. Now don't think this too awful dearie, but I shall have to leave Streatham Hill at 7.28 or 38 on Sunday night, so that I can get home and be here usual time on Monday morning. I shall appreciate being with you darling, I am sure, even if only for a short time, for you cannot tell how anxiously I have been thinking of you since I left you on Monday.

I am glad Ernie had a good time with his dear Laura, please give my love to Laura, when you are writing her won't you dearie. There was a fine show at The Empire, the other night, but I don't seem like enjoying anything of the sort just now, it all seemed to pall on me somehow, the only thing I could watch with any interest was the show with the Lions, and really it was marvellous. The thing he did with them seem almost incredible. You need not fear darling, that Jennie will turn against you, I know she will never do that, she is

Even the amazing Herr Seeth with his circus had not amused Jack enough to shake him out of his depression.

too good and straightforward. Fancy it is her birthday tomorrow, the 18th, I never thought of it until now. I will just write her a note of congratulation, I know she will be so glad to find that I have not forgotten her. We cannot feel surprised at all at your Pa getting disgusted at my Mother's treatment of your dear self, but I do hope he will not come down to see her, on the subject, for I know there would be ructions, and goodness knows it is quite bad enough at present. Perhaps though your Pa may think there is some further reason for all this state of things, than what I have told you. But I can assure you darling I have told you all. I have kept nothing from you whatever, for I made up my mind from the start, that there should be no secrets between us, and there are none. I know you trust me implicitly, don't you dearie, but of course your Pa and Ma are naturally anxious for you, and we must give their feelings some consideration. Do please continue to wear the woollen underclothing for you will never be free from these bouts of Rheumatism, until you do. If you write me tomorrow dearie, please address here, as I shall leave home early on Saturday morning. I am just going now to a meeting about the "Hooligan Dance" which it is proposed to hold during Christmas week. For the present my dearest one, au revoir, heaps of love and kisses

Your own devoted

Jack

Jenny would have been twenty-six on her birthday on November 18th 1898. She had married Alec three years previously and her daughter Doris had been born the following year. They lived south of Birmingham centre at Edgbaston. (T)

◇◇◇◇◇◇◇

"Roselea", November 18th 1898

My dear darling Jack

How lovely to think I shall see you tomorrow, I am so excited about it, but my darling, don't go back on Sunday night it will be awful, and what a frightful hour you would reach home. Surely you can be out of business for 3 hrs, for of course you would be in business by 12 o'clock on monday. I cannot really let you go on Sunday night so for pity's sake stop and go early monday morning. I am sure your Uncle would not mind and let Joe go to the very dickens if he likes. My dear, Pa, I am sure never thought that you were keeping anything back, but he thought he should like to come down to your Mother and have it out with her but he has given up the idea, as I asked him not to. I wrote Jennie a little note this morning just to send her my good wishes. Ethel my cousin, came yesterday and bought me a wedding present from her Mother and Father. You remember I have told you about them, how unfortunate they have been, and even now, Uncle is not earning anything and they actually sent us a guinea to buy something for our home, wasn't it good of her, I know very well, they will go without something for it, and I hardly know what to do about it, but Ma said they would be insulted if I sent it back so I must make it up to them in some other way. We must keep it and wait and see what we shall want. Just fancy I am going to be quite frivolous tonight, I am going with Ted and Nellie to see *The Sorcerer* at the Savoy. Nellie has just been in to ask me, I am going there to tea and then go from there. How was it that you did not enjoy The Empire, my dear, you must "buck up", and pull up your socks. I went over to see Aimèe the other afternoon she is very well and she has got on with the embroidery for me.

The popular Gilbert and Sullivan opera, The Sorcerer *was at the Savoy Theatre in the Strand, London. The theatres in Streatham and Brixton were so good that it was a special evening for Beatrice to go 'up West' for the theatre.*

This was a very rare occasion when Jack and Beatrice saw each other on two weekends in succession. It was not to be without its penalties, however, and it was Jack's ill luck that Uncle John should happen to call in at the Works and find him absent.

I will be at Streatham Hill tomorrow at 4.51 to meet you, what joy, isn't it dearie to feel we shall meet again so soon but do stay until Monday morning, there's a dear, kind Jack, I won't let you go, so there. Accept my whole love and very many hugs and kisses to be administered personally tomorrow

Yours ever devotedly
Beatie

Woodcock St. B'ham. November 21st 1898

My own darling Beatie

Here we are again, unfortunately, I mean here I am again, at B'ham, but never mind darling it won't be long till I come up again, will it. It was so foggy going up to town this morning, however, with a rush I just caught the train at Victoria, although I had to get in whilst it was on the move, it was a foolish thing to do, and I won't do it again darling. I met a Birmingham gentleman, at Willesden, Mr. Gothard, and we travelled up together. We came second class, and were very comfortable, only four in the compartment. When I was at Willesden I sent a wire, to say I should be at the Works at 12 o'clock, and very glad I am that I did so. I did it so that Joe might arrange accordingly. Well Joe was ever so late getting here this morning, and Uncle John came about eleven and had been and opened the letters and gone away before Joe arrived. Frank was here and Uncle told him, he thought it was a nice thing, for him to come and find neither Joe or I there but I am so glad I had sent that wire, because he could see what time I should be here, and that altho I was away I had not lost sight of the business. Wouldn't you think Joe would have tried to have been a little earlier than usual, knowing that I was away, but if I had been half an hour earlier, I should have been in here before him this morning. I can't reckon him up sometimes I think he does not mean very well towards me I don't know whether I am right there or not. Well dearie I hope you had a good rest this afternoon, for you must have felt very tired after turning out so early this morning. I won't get you up, like that again darling, if I can avoid it. But I know you would rather do that, than see me off on Sunday night, wouldn't you dearie. I suppose you will get a fine old bit of chaff, off young Ernie, over my coming up two weeks in succession, but we don't mind that do we darling. I shall take an early opportunity of seeing Nin, and find out what their arrangements are for Christmas.

Please remember me ever so kindly to all the Morris's when you see them tomorrow. I hope you will not overdo yourself when you go flying all about up West etc, it is all very nice but don't do too much of it, for I want you to keep well now. I hope the little change will do you good. Well dearie, please excuse more, at present, the stock of paper has run out I find.

Au revoir, lots of love and heaps of kisses

Roll on Dec 3rd
These envelopes are so thin I must use two of them

Your own devoted
Jack

A photograph of Ernest, taken by Mr. Langton, the 'electric light photographer' whose studio was 'nearly opposite' Buckingham Palace. Ernie would have been jealous of Beatrice being able to see Jack again. It was a pity for him that soon after he had given up the sea to come home, Laura then went away to teach, again preventing them from being together. (H)

126 E. Dulwich Rd, E. Dulwich. November 22nd 1898

My own dear Jack

It seems weeks since you left me, in fact I cannot believe that it was only yesterday. Well, dear you see I have got back, we have had such a long day, and I am so tired, so I hope you will be able to make this out. The shops are simply lovely, the dresses most gorgeous they did make my mouth water, I tell you. It was too bad of Joe not to get to the Works until so late, wasn't he well, or what? I hope your Uncle will not turn cross with you about it. I have seen the sword today, which the Sirdar had presented to him, it is lovely. I said I knew you would have liked to have seen it, you would wouldn't you dear? Of course I shall only be too delighted to come back with you at Xmas, if Jennie can have me, it would be lovely being with you, and looking for our dear little house, but I shall not mind at all, if it is not quite convenient, and shall understand and look forward to come later on. I did not lie down yesterday, I started doing something and wanted to finish it, so I had an extra good night instead. You must have felt tired dearie I thought a lot of you, we had it quite as dark as night after you had gone, but I was so glad that you caught your train to Willesden. It was so good of you to come last saturday, I do so appreciate it, especially as the journey is so long. Mrs. Morris sends her love and hopes that next time you come you will come here to tea on the Sunday, I promised to give you her message. I have been to my swell dress-makers today to order a gown and I was asking her about my wedding dress it doesn't seem so far off when I speak of that, I shall long to see you once again and hope the 3rd will soon fly here. Give my love to Jennie when you go up and be sure and not ask me, unless it is quite convenient and agreeable to her.

Well dear au revoir, write here so that I get a letter thursday morning. Lots of love and very good hug, you know the sort I mean

Yours ever
Beatie

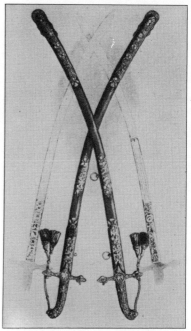

On Beatrice's outing with Mrs. Morris 'flying about' London's West End, in addition to window shopping for dresses, they also managed to get to see the sword Lord Kitchener had just received following his activities in the Sudan and the victories of Atbara and Omdurman. (B)

Woodcock St. B'ham. November 23rd 1898

My own darling Beatie

I was most anxiously looking out for your dear letter this morning and was so glad to receive it. It arrived about eleven, as I expected, you had a big day of it yesterday. I know dearie, you like trotting round and seeing all the nice things but Mrs. Morris must mind and not knock you up, or how shall I go on. Oh those selfish men, you will say, think only of themselves. I went up to Jennie's last night, to have a talk over their arrangements for Xmas, but that was impossible, as I had not been there many minutes, before Joe arrived, and very shortly after Harry Hawkes. I just had a few minutes conversation with Nin, before Joe arrived, and it was about Joe and my Mother. Nin tells me that when the agreement job was on, she had a hard job with my Mother, to get her to agree to my sharing in the profits of the business to the same extent as Joe. She has not much of an opinion of Joe and cannot understand his behaviour, over the Phelps affair.

Although Joe was the eldest son it seemed mean and calculating of their mother to favour Joe who was less principled and likely to take sides as it suited him.

Part of the family's embarrassment about their mother's affair with Phelps was due to the fact that he was considerably younger than her, in fact barely older than Joe, and referred to as 'the old buck'.

It was Harrisons' Concert on Monday. Mother and Nin and Joe went. Jennie did not really feel up to going, but it was a matter of keeping Phelps away. It seems, it was arranged for Nin to go, if she pleased, and if not, the other beauty was to go, so of course Nin went. She says she could not think of them being seen together, there, when it was in her power to prevent it.

I like you to speak of your wedding dress, dearie, for it does me quite as much good to think of that good time coming, as it does your dear self. I shall go up to see Nin again, during the week, and shall no doubt be then able to let you know something about Xmas. I have an advertisement in the Post today for a house, so that I can get to know what is going on, so perhaps I may get some houses in view for us to look at when you come down. There is a gentleman about to leave his house at March at Wylde Green, it is his own, and he is moving into a larger one which he had bought. He wants to let or sell the one he is at present in. I should not care to approach him, but I think the advertisement will bring the required information, although I fear the price will be too high. But still we must not let an opportunity go by must we dearie. When we have got the house, it will seem as if we are not going to be very long. I am always picturing ourselves in our home, aren't you darling. I think from what I can hear from Alice, and the little things my Mother says occasionally, that she is going to leave Gravelly Hill. I should think so too for it will be a bit thick when she marries her Phelps. Altho' she has said all along that she doesn't care a bit what people think. There can be no doubt I feel, but that she has quite made up her mind to have him. The earring has been tried and it is gold the man says, so I cannot understand the trouble to the ear, unless it is, that the wire is too small, and so pinches the flesh.

When I send it back, I shall send so that it will arrive during the day, so that your Pa will not see it. For I know he would be anxious to know what it was had arrived. Well dearie you must thank Mrs. Morris, for her very kind invitation please, but as for accepting or otherwise, well I am in your hands, darling. Whatever you please. There was a heavy fall of snow here during last night, and during this afternoon it has been raining incessantly, so you can tell the outlook is very cheering.

Well dearie, au revoir heaps of love and kisses

Your own devoted Jack

Jack's advertisement in the Birmingham Post stated that he was looking for a house on the Sutton Line, to rent or buy from March onwards. The advertisement would have cost him nine pence for up to sixteen words. (J)

◇◇◇◇◇◇◇

126 E. Dulwich Rd, E. Dulwich. November 24th 1898

My own darling Jack

I was delighted to receive your dear letter this morning, but I cannot help thinking about your Mother and Joe, but there I won't say all I feel, only I am sure they are both my enemies and both working to bring about the same end, but they will never do it will they dear? What a strange thing that Joe should have gone to Jennie's, did he know that you were going? I am sorry that Jennie has been so poorly I hope she is better now. We are having most awful weather so cold and wet. Yesterday we went to see "Tree" in *The Musketeers* but I must say I was very disappointed in it, the plot

Beatrice was staying with the Morris family in Dulwich at that time. They were a large and jolly family and Nellie Morris, one of the daughters, was a close friend to Beatrice.

The Musketeers, *which proved so disappointing to Beatrice, was a play by Sydney Grundy, performed at Her Majesty's Theatre in London. 'Tree', Sir Herbert Beerbohm Tree, famous for his spectacular Shakespearean productions there, was one of the great actor-managers of the period. (B)*

is so disconnected and it does not give scope enough to the actors and actresses.

I hope you hear of a house dear, it will be so much nicer, if I come up to have some in view. Where does your Mother think of going if she leaves Gravelly Hill, do you know, for if she is likely to move, perhaps we could get a house there to suit us. I really would rather not come here on the Sunday that you come up, but Mrs. Morris is so kind and seems to take such an interest in us both, that I feel I cannot refuse, but I tell her, we cannot come until after tea. We couldn't do without our afternoon hug, could we darling? Tonight Mrs. Morris has got a few people to supper for my benefit, so we have been all the morning shopping. Can you find out if Doris would like a cream walking costume trimmed with leaves and bonnet to match, for if I go to Jennie's I want to make her one, and it seems a pity to make it and then not to be wanted, try and pump Jennie, will you dear? and if there is anything else that she would rather have? I expect Ma's earring is too small, unless it is her ear that is wrong, something is not quite right, I should think. Mrs. Morris is lying down, got a fire in her bedroom, she is bothering me to go and do the same, but I have some needle work with me, so I think I shall take that up and do it there. She desires her love and is looking forward to seeing you.

Accept my whole love and I do hope all will end well, I shall not be happy until I am always with you, and then we shall not care for anybody shall we dear? Lots of hugs and kisses

Yours most devotedly

Beatie

I expect I shall go home tomorrow so send your next letter to "Roselea"

A letter card from Beatrice's mother, thanking Jack for repairing her earring. Always kind and welcoming to Jack, she ended her note with "I know someone else who is looking forward to the 3rd!". Although Phelps had been trained in the jewellery trade it is unlikely Jack would have consulted him on the matter. (A)

'Let 'em all come' – a popular song title of the time was a phrase Jack used often in the face of threatening problems. (B)

venience ; immediate possession. Rent 27s.—Henry Smith and Son, James Watt Street.   c6211

EDGBASTON (close Five Ways).—Large Family House ; coach-house, stable, good garden. Rent £125.—Address, 149, Daily Post.   c6749

ERDINGTON.—Four bed rooms, bath, two sitting, kitchen, pantry. Rent £28. ; free till Christmas.—Hooper, 16, Bennett's Hill.   c6678

ERDINGTON (Eton Lodge, Jaffray Road).—Compact house ; very pleasant situation ; four bed rooms, w.c., bath room, large dining room ; early possession.—Address, O. 22, Daily Post. c7125

FARM.—To Let, at Lady-day, 1899, a good Farm in Worcester-shire, about three miles from a market town and railway station, containing about 446 acres, of which 95 are arable and the remainder good pasture and meadow land, with orcharding. The House is pleasantly situated, and the buildings sufficient for the farm.—For rent and further particulars apply to Willmot, Fowler, and Willmot, Land Agents and Surveyors, 6, Waterloo Street, Birmingham.   1080

FURNISHED House to Let, Edgbaston ; two minutes from Botton Park Station. Terms moderate.—Address, 20X, Daily

Unlike the new development of houses in Jaffray Road that Jack and Beatrice had been interested in earlier, this house had already been built and occupied for some time. It was pleasantly situated opposite open land. (J)

Woodcock St. B'ham. November 26th 1898

My own darling Peatie

I hope you were not very much disappointed, when you received my note this morning. There was no time to write, but I felt I must just let you have a line anyway, so that you would not be anxious; but I will try and make up for it now. You are quite right I think dearie, about Joe and Mother being your enemies, but you know that they will never be able to accomplish their desired end, don't you darling. I am sure I feel as if I had not a single friend here. The way Joe treats me is abominable, for there is not anything which I do that I can ever do right. It is one continual grumble with him. Certainly he has not been well lately, but then if a person is unwell I don't think that should be any excuse for making people miserable. I don't like the cool manner, with which he takes to the Phelps affair, at all, for it seems to me, as if he has primed me up to say to my Mother that which he would not care to say himself, and then when she has set herself against me, he goes hand and glove with her, and the consequence is I have them all against me. Never mind, "Let em all come". I know I do my duty, and that is satisfaction to me; and more than that it is such comfort to me to think of my little darling, who is waiting to come to me and make me happy. I received a card, (in reply to my advert for a house), with particulars of a "Pretty Detached Country Cottage", named "Hill Top" at Four Oaks, just past Sutton. I don't think it would suit you though, dearie, for it is quite out in the country, and a mile and a quarter from a station. The owner wants to let it furnished for £65 = 0 = 0 a year, or sell it with the furniture for £800 = 0 = 0. The house is close to Golf Links, and as the owner is at present at Cardiff, I think he must be someone who has been coming up there for Golfing, some swell or other, and now has the house to dispose of. Altho' I don't fancy it would suit us, I shall go over there this afternoon, if it is fine, just to have a look at it.

I am sorry you were disappointed in your visit to *The Musketeers*, it is so annoying to make a journey to town and then see something which you cannot enjoy. There was an advert in the Post yesterday of a house to let in Jaffray Road, "Eton Lodge", I wrote for particulars but there is nothing in this morning's post about it. I think I know the house, though not by name. When my Mother moves from Gravelly Hill, and I should think she will when she marries again I think she will go somewhere right the otherside of the town. I think she and Phelps were house hunting the day they went to Hampton in Arden. She is treating for some property now, but I don't know where it is situated. I am glad you have arranged for us to go to Mrs. Morris' after tea, instead of before, for you are quite right dearie, we must have our afternoon to ourselves. I will find out about the costume you mention for Doris, when I see Nin; I must go and see her early next week, if not tomorrow. I am dying to be with you darling, and don't know however I shall wait until next Saturday. By the way, must I bring my Dress Suit, next week. Heaps of love and kisses

Your own devoted

Jack

I hope you are quite as well after your visit to Dulwich

"Roselea", November 27th 1898

The National Cycle Show at Crystal Palace displayed not only the 'latest inventions and improvements in Tyres, Fittings and Accessories' but for those weary of cycles, also provided entertainment from 'Eminent Humorists, Vocal Comedians and Dancers'. The entrance fee was one shilling. (B)

My own darling Jack,

I do feel so lonely without you dear, I have been wishing you were here, it seems such ages since you were here. I can hardly realise that it was but last Sunday, you were here. I did not reach home until 9 o'clock last night when I found your two dear letters. I flew up to my room and eagerly devoured them. I am so miserable without you dear. I don't know how I shall exist until June 1st for every separation seems longer. Well I have been most gay last week, but I am glad to get back home to have a little rest. On friday Mrs. Morris and I went to the Cycle Show at the Palace. I saw Hornblower there and should have spoken to him only he was talking to two fellows, he looked me straight in the face, but of course he would not remember me, then I suppose. I saw your friend Raby, at least I saw his stall and a short fair fellow in charge, would that be him. I was a good mind to ask him but had not got the cheek. I got awfully tired of looking at bicycles, so we went into the Variety entertainment, which was very good, they had some awfully clever trick riding on machines, 5 people on one all at once then I saw some wonderfully clever elephants, they did all sorts of funny things, which I thought exceedingly good. We got back about 10 o'clock and I was tired. Yesterday afternoon, I went to a theatre to see *Two little maids from school*, a very pretty little play, I liked it very much. Annie Hughes is in it, don't you remember we saw her as "Saucers". How would you like to see *The Belle of New York* on the tuesday after Xmas, they say it is awfully good. We thought if we make up our minds, it would be better to book early as to get good seats, let me know if you would like to go. I am glad you are getting several houses in view for me to see it will be so much nicer to have a choice. What sort of house is Eton Lodge in Jaffary Rd. I am afraid the "Hill Top" would be a bit off being so far from the station. I shouldn't mind the country, but you see, you would have to leave earlier and get home later, which you know I cannot allow, for it will be bad enough not getting home until 8 o'clock. Have you found out if that house at Wylde Green is still to let, for that seems to take my fancy, although of course I might not like it when I saw it. Don't mind Joe dear, treat his conduct with indifference. I am not going to care in the least for either of them I am only glad that I have found out their real characters and shall know in future how to act. I only hope Jennie will remain our friend, or else it will be a bit off for me, won't it dear? Is your Uncle alright? I hope so. Have you been to see him lately?

No dear, there is no occasion to bring your dress suit, it is quite an informal affair next saturday and darling, I hope you will come by the 2.10 train and am sure you can get here by way of Kensington, and would you mind, if I do not meet you, as I know I shall be very busy and the Lewcocks will be here between 4 and 5 o'clock. But if I find I can manage it I will, you know that don't you? so don't wait at the station if I am not there, but let me know what train you come by won't you dear? I am simply longing for saturday, I can scarcely bear it I feel so dull, I hope all is well, and that you are alright. Write soon dear and cheer me up. Lots of love and hugs

Late-Victorian dress for men began to show the styling of modern dress. Jack's less formal dress suit would have been a dress sack coat. This more informal jacket than the frock coat was an innovation of the late 1890s. It had a black waistcoat and grey-striped trousers. He would have worn grey spats and black patent leather boots and possibly a striped neck-tie. (S)

Since Beatrice did not wholly approve
of Jack's Hooligan friends who had
presented themselves to her in Folkestone
following their cycling trip to Paris, it
was unlikely that she would have
welcomed a re-acquaintance on their stand
at the Cycle Show.

*Neuralgia must have been about the last
thing Jack also needed to have to cope
with at this time. He was very run down
and tired and it was not surprising that he
became ill.*

Woodcock St. B'ham. November 28th 1898

My own darling Beatie

      I was so glad to receive your dear letter this morning, and find that after all you were not disappointed on Saturday morning, as I was afraid you would have been. You cannot feel more lonely than I darling. I think it would be impossible. I am so glad you had a jolly time last week, Mrs. Morris seems a rare one for getting about. I only hope you did not get doing too much. That would be my friend Raby, no doubt, whom you saw at their stall at the Show. I am sure he would have been most pleased, to make your acquaintance, but then of course I can quite understand that you would not care to introduce yourself, under the circumstances. Well, darling, I have been through the mill since I wrote on Saturday morning. I had an awful attack of Neuralgia on Saturday afternoon, and was nearly driven mad with it, you have often told me I must get fatter, and when I woke yesterday morning I found that I had succeeded in doing so, but it was only so far as my face, was concerned. I had a lovely swollen face, but not so much pain. I had to stay in bed all day and keep out of the drafts, so that I could be able to be out today. I have not been able to eat any ordinary meals, yesterday and today and have been on the bread and milk diet, but I think I shall manage some supper tonight. I did so think of you all day yesterday, and was wondering what was going on at "Roselea" all the time. I suppose Ted and Nellie came round with the kids. I remember "Saucers" very well, don't you? It would be very nice to see *The Belle of New York*, at Xmas, I should like to go very much. I have not received any reply to my enquiry, re "Eton Lodge", and of course had no opportunity of walking round to see the place yesterday, nor have I found out anything about the house at Wylde Green, but I will do so. Uncle is alright with me, but I have not had much opportunity to go and see him. He comes into the Office most days and he is alright, but he is very much annoyed about the Phelps affair. What do you think, my Mother drove up home with Phelps from the Works, on Saturday, and after they had had tea, the carriage was ordered for a quarter to seven and they were driven to Aston, for a rehearsal. She returned home at twelve o'clock, of course there is no train at that time,

*The view in 1900 from Erdington Parish
Church tower, looking north along the
main street, with Sutton Road leading to
the Chester Road in the distance. Jaffray
Road was a new development south of the
church, uncomfortably close to Linwood
Lodge. (F)*

so I suppose Phelps must have taken her up in a Car. Nice carryings on don't you think. There are about a dozen people coming up to Dinner tomorrow evening, if that beauty is there I shall not be. I can't bear the sight of him, I shall come by the 2.10 on Saturday, but don't know yet what time I shall arrive, I must look out the trains tomorrow.

Excuse this short letter darling but I am anything but well, and want to catch the 7.40 home, and get to bed. Joe is no better, he too was in bed all day yesterday and has had to go home early again today. I am going to look after myself and get in form for Saturday. I had a card from your Ma yesterday about the ear-ring. Au revoir. Heaps of love and kisses

Ever your own true

Jack.

Jack's mother was particularly fond of social evenings, dances and 'dramatic entertainments'. A dinner for twelve had been a regular event when Jack's father was alive. Jack would then have taken part very happily, but his hatred for Phelps had now become very bitter.

"Roselea", November 29th 1898

My own darling Jack

How are you dear? I do hope you are better, it does so worry me that you are not well and I so far from you, I only wish you were nearer that I could run in and see you, why don't you see a doctor, I feel sure you are run down, and need a tonic. I hope you will be alright by saturday, or else it won't improve it travelling. I had such a nice letter from Jennie yesterday she says when I want to go and see a house, they will be pleased to see me, she is disgusted with your Mother, for behaving as she is and to use Jennie's words "to cloud, what; should be one of the happiest times of our lives". She is right so far, but I hope to have still happier when we are always together what say you dearie? I am awfully busy, I have such a lot to see to this week, Ma has taken Ethel (my Cousin) to see the shops today up West so I thought I had better write to you first and then I shall have to "buck up". Ernie is going to book seats at *The Belle of New York* for tuesday Dec 27th. I think we shall enjoy it, the Morris' have seen it and they say it is awfully funny. We had letter and photos from David yesterday he was still at Wei hai Wei and was taken on a pony outside his house, it is fairly good considering it was done by an amateur. He is so surprised that we are not going to be married until June, he quite thought it would be this winter. I have got a nasty cold, but otherwise I feel ever so much better than I did. What is the matter with Joe? how funny that you should be both in bed the same day. Who came to your Mother's dinner party, of course I suppose Phelps did, but I hope you went in, you know dear, it won't alter matters, now. Jennie tells me she thinks your Mother will be leaving Gravelly Hill, as she would never have the cheek to introduce Phelps to Erdington folks, it strikes me, she won't be long now before she is married. I shouldn't be at all surprised if it is before ours, but that won't matter will it dear?

Granny sends her love, hopes you will soon be better, she has got a slight touch of bronchitis. Accept oceans of kisses and all my love

Yours most devotedly Beatie

The British secured the lease for Wei hai Wei from China in 1898 and the name became the subject of many jokes and slogans. David, Beatrice's brother, with the Royal Marines at Wei hai Wei at that time, was soon to leave with H.M.S. Edgar to return to Plymouth. (B)

ASTHMA CHRONIC BRONCHITIS

BRONCHITIC ASTHMA, HAY FEVER, and INFLUENZA.

The "Lancet."—"A convenient and valuable remedy."
Dr. Thorowgood.— "Pure spasmodic Asthma and Asthma due to Emphysema of the lungs with co-existent bronchitis alike appear to me to be materially relieved by the Ozone Paper."
Harrison Weir, Esq.—"Your Ozone Paper has got rid of my Asthmatic affection; it is the only remedy which gave me permanent relief."

2s. 9d. and 4s. 6d. per Box, of all Chemists; or from the Proprietor for the amount in stamps or P.O.O. to any country within the Postal Union.

R. HUGGINS & Co., Chemists, 199, Strand, LONDON.

Influenza and bronchitis were worrying illnesses and very common complaints as many Victorian houses and work places were damp and unheated. In addition to the many home cures the chemist shops were stocked with numerous alternative ways of coping with the winter ills. (B)

Jack was beginning to get over-sensitive about his mother's behaviour to the point that he began to imagine all manner of 'mischief' that she might be causing.

Woodcock St. B'ham. November 30th 1898

My own darling Beatie

Now for a little chat with you. I have been looking forward to this all day, but fancy my little joy being delayed so long, for I have only just finished work, and it is now 9.30. Never mind dearie, I am feeling much better now, and nearly alright, and hope to be quite alright when I see you on Saturday. You cannot tell, dearie, how glad I was to read from your dear letter this morning, that you had received a nice letter from Jennie. I am so glad that she has written you, before I have mentioned the matter to her myself at all. I saw Alex yesterday, and asked him if he knew their arrangements for Xmas yet. He said he believed they were to go to Gravelly Hill for Xmas and stay for the few days. He mentioned by the way, that their girl was leaving them, and just a few days before Xmas but he said he would ask Nin all about it and let me know. I hope we shall have some likely houses in view, by then, and that it will be convenient for you to come to Nin's. Won't it be jolly. I am so glad we are having seats booked for Dec 27th, shan't we have a gay time. I hope darling, that your cold is well now, for I cannot bear to think of you being unwell. Joe's cold is much better and I think he will be alright now in a day or so, but he has been very seedy indeed. Of course Phelps was at the little affair last night. I was delayed in town last night handing over my accounts, to the President of the Sergts' Mess. I used to be Secretary you know. When I got home, 10.50, the people had all left, it was strange that I had that job on last night; but still if I had not I should not have sat to table with that beast. Mother will certainly be leaving Gravelly Hill, and I don't know whether Alice is "smelling a rat", so to speak, or whether Mother has put her on to try and pump me, but she was saying last night she thought she would like to come and be our servant, when we were married. I said, "don't be silly you know you would want too much money for us", and she said, she would come for £14 the first year, and a rise of £1 a year, each succeeding year. I told her that was alright at the start, but how if she remained with us about 20 years, (joking of course).

I am so sorry poor Granny is poorly give her my love, and tell her I hope she is better. I am dying for Saturday to come, it has been a long while going, this part of a fortnight.

Please excuse the scribble into which I have drifted, for I feel so tired. I have received no word about that house "Eton Lodge" yet, and it seems to me very strange. I shall find if there is such a house there, for I believe I have been had, and by my Mother or somebody she has put on to do it, so that she can find out if I am looking for a house at Gravelly Hill. You will of course wonder whyever, I think that, but still I do think so. Well dearie Good-night, I am much better and hope you are also. Heaps of love and kisses

Your own devoted

Jack

An Anxious Time For Beatrice
DECEMBER & JANUARY

Jack finds Eton Lodge and Beatrice visits Birmingham to see their 'sweet home'. Christmas is soon upon them and proves an eventful time of the kind least expected. Subsequent letters are desperate with instructions to Jack to 'destroy my last letter and do the same to this'. Beatrice hints to her mother that she might have to marry next month. . . . Her fears allayed she begins to plan her bottom drawer.

"Roselea", December 1st 1898

My own dearest Jack

Do excuse this hurried note but I know you will excuse me and be sorry to hear that Granny is very dangerously ill, with bronchitis and heart trouble, we have been up all night as the Doctor says she must not be left. We have just got a trained nurse in, so that will relieve us at night. Ma, of course is knocked up, we cannot get her to take any food. I feel all mops and brooms, but I must keep up somehow. It all depends on how Granny is, whether we have the dinner party on saturday but it will make no difference to you coming, am so looking forward to see you. Dearie I think we should be very lucky if we could get Alice for £14, but I am afraid she does not mean it, I only wish she did. I'm glad you are better dearie, how I am longing for saturday, you don't know how much. Let me know what time you arrive at Streatham Hill, won't you dear.

Excuse more I must away. Lots of love

yours devotedly Beatie

Woodcock St. B'ham. December 6th 1898

My own darling Beatie

I know you will be looking out anxiously for a letter tomorrow morning, and you shall not be disappointed. Well dearie, I got back to B'ham safely last night, and went on to Gravelly Hill by the 9.45, so I reached home about 5 past ten. We had distinguished company, on the train, the Rt. Hon. Joseph Chamberlain, travelling from Euston to B'ham, by it. He had been up from B'ham to London, the same morning, in order to attend a meeting of the Cabinet. When I got home Mother and Ida were out, they had

The Mercers were fortunate to be able to afford a trained nurse to come in to look after Granny. Hospitals were at this time still often unhygienic places and doctors were a luxury that only the middle and upper classes could afford without great hardship.

Joseph Chamberlain, one of Queen Victoria's greatest statesmen, first came to Birmingham as a businessman. He was Lord Mayor from 1873 until 1876 and pledged that, "The town shall not, with God's help, know itself". He later became Colonial Secretary and Member of Parliament for West Birmingham. (B)

Joe was not as conscientious as Jack, but then he had less to lose at this time than Jack. The company's profits, and the size of Jack's share of them, were vital to Jack if he was to be able to marry the following year.

A photograph of Jack years later at a time he had so often dreamed about. (A)

Perhaps Beatrice's father, who was fifty-seven by this time, was feeling he needed extra protection of a policeman's whistle when out alone in the dark winter streets at night. Thousands of the poor in London at this time lived by thieving, despite the high penalties for petty crime. (R)

gone to the Institute Entertainment, and returned just before I had finished supper. Joe also was out, at his Lodge, and came up on the last train. It was a nice thing, just fancy yesterday morning Joe never got out of bed until long after ten, I don't know whatever time he reached here. If I were he, and could not get up in the morning, at a decent time, I think I should put a stop to the going out at nights, and see if that would make any difference. Joe seems always very brisk at night. But anyway one would think he would make an effort, when he knows I am away. I had a talk to Alice last night, but think we must not attach any importance to what she said, about coming to be our servant; when we are married. If she does come so much the better, but we had better not reckon on it. If we don't have her, we can no doubt find someone.

Won't it be fine dearie, when we are married and always together. These partings are simply awful, for it seems so dreadfully long from one visit to another; and then when the time does arrive for me to come I seem to be no sooner with you than it is time to leave you again. Fancy having to wait all through this and two other weeks, never mind dearie buck up, one day is gone and that has brought us one nearer. We had a fine old time this last visit though didn't we darling. I suppose you have been a little cooler today than yesterday though. How is poor Granny, better I hope. Tell me all about her when you write, for I am most anxious to know. She and I were quite pals, but I somehow felt when I wished the dear old creature Good-bye that it was for the last time. Still we cannot tell, but I hope that whatever time she may remain with us, she may not be tortured with pain, but that she may be comfortable, for she deserves to be I am sure. I hope your Ma is keeping up, and that she is better than when I left, I am afraid though that this illness of Granny's will knock her about a lot. Have you heard from Aunt Parker and Aunt Renard? You must try and keep your spirits up dearie, as much as you can, and cheer up both your Ma and your poor Granny as much as you can. When I was up, your Pa was speaking of a Whistle which he would like to have. I have got one today, and sent it on to him. I expect it will reach "Roselea" same time as this. I hope it will be suitable, and tell him I also hope that he will never have any real occasion to use it, however, if he should, I have no doubt it would prove quite effective. I am going up to Jennie's now, and will mention to her about the Coat and Bonnet: the answer is a foregone conclusion though, I know, she will be very pleased and proud to think that you will take so much trouble. I am going to see the house tomorrow darling.

What a strange thing, there will be two more houses to let in the same road very shortly, in addition to those now being built. Well dearie, Au revoir Heaps of love and kisses

your own devoted

Jack

❖❖❖❖❖

"Roselea", December 7th 1898

My darling Jack

I had such a fright this morning, when the letters were brought in there was no letter for me, I couldn't imagine what had happened but presently Lydia brought your letter in and said she had left it in the letter box,

I was so glad. Well dear, Granny has certainly taken a turn for the better and yesterday she was able to take a little boiled sole and some oysters, which she thoroughly enjoyed, so we hope now with care, she will go on alright, she tells me to give her love to you and thanks for your kindness. The whistle has not arrived yet, but no doubt it will, what is it for, policeman's whistle or what? it is the first I have heard about it.

What did Alice say to make you think she did not intend to come to us, I thought she was only joking, but never mind. I hope we shall be able to find a nice girl when we want one. Well dear, this is the day of the bazaar, Ma and I are going over, it is a pouring wet day so I should not think there will be many people there. Ma is dreadfully nervous about it, but I hope she will get on alright. She is far from well, her nerves are so bad, but she is able to eat a little more now. We heard from Aunt Parker and Aunt Renard but they did not say anything about coming up. Of course Aunt Renard will be here for Xmas, when you will have the pleasure of meeting her, don't cher know. Well dear, I shall be anxiously looking out for your next letter to hear all about the house, what other houses will be "to let", will they be likely to suit us. I hope the road is alright, drains etc, for the houses seem to be "to let" pretty often. How mean of Joe not to get to the Works earlier, I am sure he does it on purpose, and I feel he is only jealous of our happiness. Granny asked Ma to write to Cousin Ted and order a pair of pictures for my wedding present from her, she says I have been so kind and attentive to her, and I am sure I have not done much, but I shall be glad of the pictures for I know they will be good. I hope he will send pretty subjects. Well darling, I must go now accept all my love and oceans of kisses and a real good imaginary hug

Yours ever most devotedly
Beatie

Nursing had become a respectable occupation for young ladies by this time. An experienced nurse could earn £50 a year and those who worked in private homes had a much less harsh time than their colleagues working in hospital wards. (K)

Woodcock St. December 8th 1898

My own darling Beatie

I was so glad to receive your dear letter this morning, and to know that poor old Granny is so much better. I do hope she will keep improving and that she may have a few more happy years of life before her. Please give my love to her, dearie. It was a policeman's whistle, which I sent to your Pa, and I am rather surprised to learn that it had not come to hand yesterday. Alice said she supposed she would have to stay with my Mother so long as she remained at Gravelly Hill. I have no doubt though we shall be able to find someone when we are ready.

I hope your Ma is keeping better, and that she got through the ordeal of yesterday quite successfully. Now darling for the house question. I went to see "Eton Lodge" yesterday, and was not carried away with it through the furniture being in, as you were afraid I might be. There was no furniture in but still I was carried away with it for it is a delightful little place, and I am sure you will like it very much. The tenant went out yesterday, and has removed to Handsworth. I enclose herewith a ground plan of the house, on which you will see marked the dimensions of the Rooms and Kitchen. *The Dining Room* is

At last Jack had found the house he knew was right for them and this time he was confident enough that Beatrice would like it too that he was prepared to go ahead without her seeing it.

A house similar and adjacent to Eton Lodge in Jaffray Road, which is no longer standing. Many of the houses in Jaffray Road made way for modern flats. (W)

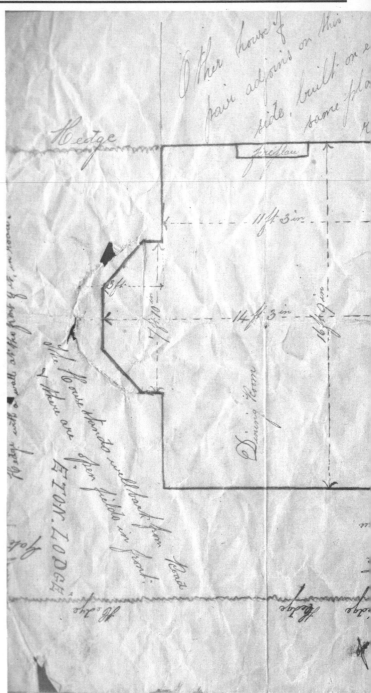

The detailed ground plan that Jack drew of Eton Lodge for Beatrice. He outlined important features in red ink and must have spent several hours measuring up beforehand. (A)

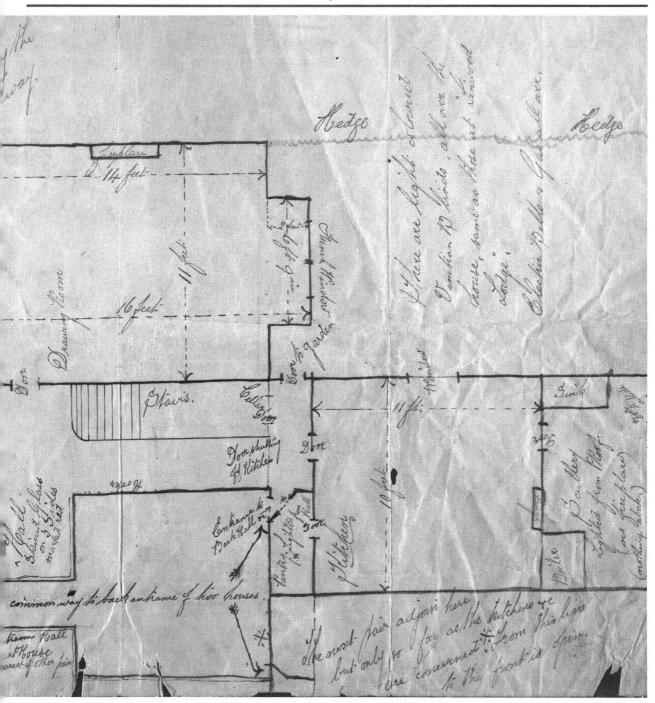

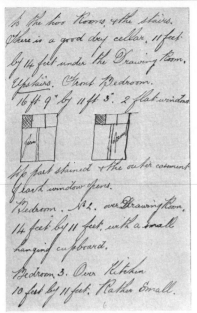

Jack's drawings of the casement windows with stained glass in the top sections. (A)

For many years Jaffray Road was unsurfaced and made hazardous by large puddles which were particularly bad outside Eton Lodge.

16ft 9″ × 11ft 3″ exclusive of the Bay which is 7ft 10″ wide and stands out 3 feet at the furthest point. The windows are casements, and stained glass at the top part. Nice Brown Marble Mantel and tiled hearth, and 2 Gas Brackets on chimney-piece. There is also an Incandescent Gas pendant with a red shade in the centre.

Drawing Room. 11 feet by 14 feet exclusive of Window which stands out square 2 feet, and is 6ft 9″ wide and opens down to the floor, making the room 16ft long measuring from the window. White Marble Mantelpiece and 2 Gas Brackets, also 2 other Gas Brackets, 1 in the centre of each other wall.

Kitchen 10ft by 11ft with half stained window to prevent being overlooked. Good Range and Cupboard, Pantry leading off which is lighted from Back Wall and ventilated from front.

Scullery, with Boiler. Sink with Hot, Cold and Rain Water supply. The Scullery is lighted from the roof.

You will notice that the entrance stands out from the Body of the House. It is all of stained Glass and has nothing above it, but is tiled on the top. There is also you will notice another entrance by which can be approached the Kitchen or Garden without coming into the front of the house.

There is a door in the Hall shutting off the Kitchen etc, so that when you enter the house, you need see nothing but the Hall and approach to the two Rooms, and the stairs. There is a good dry cellar, 11 feet by 14 feet under the Drawing Room.

Upstairs. Front Bedroom. 16ft 9″ by 11ft 3″. 2 flat windows top part stained and the outer casement of each window opens.

Bedroom No 2, over Drawing Room. 14ft by 11 feet, with a small hanging cupboard.

Bedroom 3. Over kitchen. 10 feet by 11 feet. Rather Small.

On the landing and over the Pantry there is a combined W.C. and Bath Room, lighted to the front, by stained windows. In fact there is stained glass in all the windows which could be overlooked, and in the tops of windows in Reception and Bed Rooms making the place very pretty, and when your clever little hands have been at work arranging things I know we can make a charming little home of it. There is a fine attic, I did not measure it but it is about 16 by 11. It is in the roof, but has a nice lead glazed window, glazed diamond pattern, looking out to the front and is very pleasant.

Gas and Electric Bells all over house. W.C. and Coal House outside. The Garden is narrow near the house, but *where it is clear of* the *outbuildings*, it opens out to about 7 yards wide and is about *24 yards long*. There is a nice piece of grass also in the front; the back land is grass by the way. The rent is £30=0=0. Rates £8=0=0. I have seen the Agent this morning and he tells me that the man who has just got out, has given notice to leave in March, and has to find a suitable tenant to follow him. He says he will keep the house in abeyance for me, to see the present tenant, and arrange with him to come with me to his office so that we may come to some arrangement about the first quarter of next year, his unexpired time.

I did not of course wish to take a house before March, but I am afraid it looks like paying a half quarter's rent before that, but I must not mind that if we get the place that suits us. I know you will like it, and if I can come to a satisfactory arrangement with the present tenant, (the Agent is alright for March) about his unexpired time, shall take it at once. I know your tastes darling and am sure you will like it, but even if you did not, (which is impossible) we could do a year or so in it, and then be looking out for another. But I am confident you will be pleased with it, I am going to see the tenant now and when I come back will finish the letter off, and tell you result of the interview. Oh, do please thank Granny ever so much, for me, for her gift to us. There is hot and Cold water laid on to the Bath, and the Hall is prettily tiled. There is a gate out at the bottom of garden into a kind of small drying ground, and a passage round coming out into the road, round which would be wheeled the Coals etc, to prevent same coming near the front of the house. I must now be off and see the tenant his office is in Newhall St.

Jack was so excited about Eton Lodge that he almost forgot to mention Granny or anyone else in this letter. The luxury of hot and cold water for their bath and other details about the house were pre-occupying his mind much more.

Well I have got back from seeing the tenant, and think I can come to an understanding with him by paying $\frac{1}{2}$ quarters rent previous to March qrt. but the difficulty seems now to be with the Agent, as to how much money they will spend on the house for us to go in. However, he has told me to get a man to go over and give me an estimate for doing it up, which I am to let him have, and he will see the trustees of the property and let me know how much they can allow me towards it. I shall get two different men to give me an estimate I think. I have told you all about the house darling and given you fullest particulars. Leave it to me I am sure you will like it. The place is very healthy, and the reason the present tenant is going is because they have been persuaded by their friends at Handsworth to go back there again. They are an old Handsworth family, and only came to Gravelly Hill about $2\frac{1}{2}$ years ago. Mr. Lilly is leaving Jaffray Road, because his family has got too large for the house, and another thing he is getting on now, and I suppose his position is better than formerly perhaps, and he feels that he can afford to live in a larger house, further out. If you will, darling, as the Spotter said. "Leave this to me". I am sure you will be pleased with the house, for there is everything we shall require, plenty of room, and not too much. Two minutes walk to the bus, ten to the train, and about six minutes walk to a post office. (There is a new one now opposite the Baptist Chapel). You show the plan to your Pa and Ma, and give them the description, and I think they will feel that if we have "Eton Lodge" we shall be doing very wisely and well. I don't think there is anything further darling. Please give my love to all, and accept my whole true love for your dear self, and I wish I were with you to explain all this personally.

Jack was right to re-assure Beatrice that the house was "very healthy". Infection spread quickly and poor drainage, which led to infected water supplies and unhygienic conditions was common even in the late 1800s, although less so in middle class houses.

Ever your own devoted
Jack

$3\frac{3}{4}$ miles from New St; the house I mean, not myself.

By the way, there is a young lady Jennie knows, and her husband has gone wrong after about 2 years (and gone to Africa) and they had most of their furniture from Chamberlain King & Jones, being relatives of theirs. Their furniture is quite the best, and it is in a store and Jennie and Alec think some of it may suit us. They say they are sure we could not get anything better and that anything we liked to select, they are sure they would let us have it at a reasonable price. The man was a fool, he did too well and it spoilt him. He had everything of the best. Jennie promised to make enquiries. I am going up there tonight, to see if she has heard anything. Of course if you would like to have some of the furniture we must arrange with the people when you are

An advertisement for Chamberlain King & Jones, the large furniture store in Birmingham, well-known for its quality and wide range of items. (O)

*Jack's telegram to Beatrice to arrange for
Beatrice's visit to Birmingham. It had been
sent by Jack at 8.08 that morning and was
received at Streatham by 8.41 a.m. Jack
would have had to pay a half-pence for
every word after the first twelve for which
he paid sixpence. (A)*

*It was surprising that Beatrice didn't
jump at the opportunity to travel to
Birmingham at once to see the house – and
Jack. Even though she trusted his
judgement, she had very precise views
about what was acceptable and what was
not.*

*The Annual Bazaar at Immanuel Church,
Streatham Common, despite the fact that
"it rained a perfect deluge", made £568
that day from its annual sale of work.
Stall 9 was run by the Misses Morris,
Beatrice's friends' and despite the weather
it was considered a great success by
everybody.*

coming down, so that we can go and see it. I think it a very good opportunity myself, as the furniture was the best they could buy. Au revoir darling
mine.

Even if we never went in the house
there would be no difficulty in letting
it again, it is exceptionally good for
the money.

Ever your own

Jack

◇◇◇◇◇◇

I will write to Jennie tonight   "Roselea", December 9th 1898

My darling Jack

I don't know hardly what to say first, I seem to have such a lot to
say. Well dear, how good of you to take all that trouble in drawing the
plan of "Eton Lodge" and I quite see what a comfortable place it is and I
should think just the very thing to suit us. Of course I am sorry that you will
have to pay half a quarter's rent, but then it would be a pity to lose it, when it
seems so very convenient. Now dear I have thought it over, and I don't see that
it is really necessary for me to come down on tuesday. I am sure from your
splendid description that I could not do otherwise than like the house and I
shall leave it to you, perhaps Jennie would go with you and Alec and then see
what they think of it. I am glad the hall is tiled and so much stained glass in it.
What sort of shade is it over the incandescent light in the dining room, don't
take it if it shabby for I want a red silk shade, now about the venetian blinds,
if they are the tenants fixtures we are not obliged to have them are we? but of
course if the landlord put them in, we shall have to have 'em, but I do hope we
don't have to take them. If Jennie can have me later on, I would like to come
then but, I hardly see it is necessary after your grafic description. I can quite
picture the house and we two in it, I shall be most eager to get into it now, and
darling, I must choose the papers myself, *that* I feel I must do, for some papers
are so awful that landlords put on and perhaps by paying a little more, we
could have a good paper at least in the drawing and dining rooms. Now about
that furniture, of course it all depends on how it has been treated, I have a great
horror of having anything second-hand but perhaps we might get some things,
if they really are good. I hope you won't mind me not coming next tuesday, but
you see if I have to come later on, it will be double expense, and it would be
rather a rush if I had have come next tuesday. Of course, you know dear, how
much I should have enjoyed seeing you, for really it seems such ages since you
left me, and just fancy a fortnight more before we meet. Ernie has booked seats
to see *The Belle of New York* on the tuesday after Xmas, so I shall look forward
to that and shall hope to have a very jolly Xmas with you dearie. The whistle
has not turned up yet dear, I am afraid it has got lost in the post. Oh by the
way are the drains alright at Eton Lodge? I hope so.

I should hope you would not buy any furniture without me, for that I
certainly should like to have a voice in that matter. The bazaar was a great
success. Ma made her speech splendidly. They presented her with a nice
bouquet and the people made a tremendous fuss of us. Ma bought me ½doz
serviettes and ½doz tea cloths for my bottom drawer and an afternoon table-

cloth and a dressing jacket, a very pretty shawl for my head for evening wear, so I did not do badly. Granny is going on splendidly she has sat up for an hour today, and the doctor is not coming again after tomorrow and I expect the nurse will leave next thursday. Darling accept my warmest thanks for all your kindness in writing so full description and particulars of house and also that splendid plan. Heaps of love and do write again soon.

Yours most devotedly
Beatie

P.S. I do feel so excited won't it be lovely if we get to Eton Lodge.

<><><><><><>

Wylde Green, December 11th 1898

My darling Beatie

I was so glad to receive your dear letter yesterday and to find that you are so pleased with the idea of Eton Lodge.

I am so awfully excited over it I can tell you, and am glad to know that you are. I am always thinking of it, and fancying I can see ourselves in it. Jack Harrop came down to Gravelly Hill this morning so that he could go and see the house. We went over it, and he was quite pleased with it, and I was more than ever in love with it.

The venetian blinds are the property of the landlord, and I shall have them down for the first thing, for the rooms will look ever so much better without them, I am going to meet Holyoak the painter, there, tomorrow afternoon and go over it to get an estimate for doing it up, and on Tuesday I have to meet another man there, for the same purpose. Of course, I have not as yet definitely fixed the tenancy but shall do so as soon as the estimates are in, so that we can come to an understanding about the doing up. It will be a charming little place, darling, when we have got it done up, and our things are in, and you have been at work in it arranging things. You will be able to make it so pretty.

It does seem ages darling since last Sunday and however shall I get over the time till Dec 24th; it is such ages to look forward, but we must try and make up for it when we do meet. Mr. Harrop asks me if you are coming down for the Hooligan Dance, and I tell him I hope so. They are so anxious, all of them, to see you dearie, I did hope you would have been coming down on Tuesday for it would have been lovely. Fancy having you down here for nearly a week. Wouldn't we have enjoyed our little selves. But of course, as you feel that the house is sure to suit us there is really no necessity for you to have come on that account. Of course I would not think of buying the furniture, or selecting the papers, without you darling for of course that would not be proper. I expect the landlord will open his eyes when he knows what it will cost to do up the house. It is very dirty everywhere. We shall have it done all through though, before we go in. I am glad that you were able to go to the Bazaar, and that your Ma got on so well, it must have been very trying for her. It was good of her to buy you all those things, you did very well. I should think you are getting quite a large stock dearie, in that bottom drawer, and we shall be able to do with it, eh darling. When I was at Eton Lodge this morning there was a fine black cat came running up to me, when I went out at the back, and brushed herself up

Although Beatrice insisted on calling hers a "bottom 'box' not drawer", nearly all Victorian girls spent the time of their usually long engagements sewing and collecting items of table and bed linen for when they married. Such items were traditionally kept in a 'bottom drawer'.

Jack wrote this letter from the Harrops at Wylde Green having already persuaded Jack Harrop to see the house and gained his approval, although nothing was likely to put Jack off the house in his excitement about it.

Wallpaper was extremely fashionable in Beatrice's day and all the main living rooms and bedrooms would have been papered. There would have been many 'wallpaper houses' in Birmingham from which she could choose from a wide range of elaborate designs.

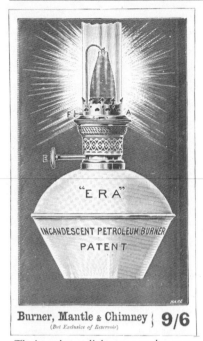

"ERA"

INCANDESCENT PETROLEUM BURNER
PATENT

Burner, Mantle & Chimney } **9/6**
(But Exclusive of Reservoir)

*The incandescent light was a modern way
of lighting by means of heating a mantle to
a white heat from a gas or petroleum flame.
Gas was expensive, as was petroleum and
many families still resorted to candles in
their bedrooms or hallways. An incandescent
pendant light hung from the ceiling with a
silk shade would have been very
sophisticated. (B)*

against me, that is for good luck I suppose. The red shade on the incandescent
light is very dirty, but that does not matter as the late tenant wants it. He is
leaving the light, and we can get a new shade. I am glad you were pleased with
the plan, but you know dearie I was so anxious to give you as full and plain a
description as possible. I shall go and see Jennie tomorrow night, and hope we
shall be able to arrange for you to come down with me at Xmas.

Cheer up darling and look out for
Dec. 24th and we will have a good old
time then. Au revoir, heaps of love
and a good old hug in imagination.

Excuse the black edge

your own devoted

Jack

"Roselea", December 12th 1898

My darling Jack

I expect you will think I have got "dotty" since you saw me last,
first saying one thing and now writing something different. Well dear,
I am coming down to Birmingham on wednesday and shall arrive at 4 o'clock
at New St. I refused for several reasons in the first place. You see Granny has
been a big expense during her illness and as you gave me such a graphic
description of the house, I thought I would bottle up my curiosity until later
on, but Pa like the good man he is says, it would be nicer for me to see the
house and advises me to come down. So I then jumped at it and at once
telegraphed to Jennie, I do hope it won't interfere with her arrangements at
all. I shall not mind her telling me if it does. I had a nice letter from Jennie this
morning, I think it is nice of her to have sympathy with us. I hope Jennie
won't mind but I told her I would stay until monday. It was cheek of me
wasn't it? but I feel sure she won't mind but I thought Sunday you could be
with me all day. Ma has asked nurse to stay another week from thursday next,
so I can very easily be spared. My train leaves Streatham Hill 12.51 and
Willesden at twenty minutes to 2 o'clock and arrives at Birmingham at
4 o'clock.

I have just received such a useful present from Aunt Renard, a work box full
of all the necessary articles and dusters, and almost something of everything, it
will be fine when I start housekeeping won't it dear? Do excuse this awful
scrawl, but I do feel so excited won't it be lovely being together a little while,
I am longing to see the house, and I think it is jolly that we shall have it all done
up and not those horrid venetian blinds. I am going out this afternoon for a
walk with nurse. Granny is down stairs today, so you see she is getting on
splendidly. She sends her love to you. Ethel goes home this thursday, so we
shall soon get quite into our old way. Excuse more now, but I must away.
Lots of love

yours ever

Beatie

*If expense had caused Beatrice's hesitancy
at first, having once decided to visit Eton
Lodge and take up Jennie's invitation to
stay with her, Beatrice had no intention of
making it just a quick overnight visit to
Birmingham!*

The Whistle has not yet turned up
Ernie asked me to enclose size of Laura's ring

Woodcock St. B'ham. December 13th 1898

My own darling Beatie

I can't tell you how glad I was to receive your dear letter this morning, with the exciting news that you are coming to Brum. It seems almost too good to be true, and I am almost beside myself at the thought of having you down here, and having a nice little time together before Xmas.

I could not help laughing at your expression, that you say you should think I should fancy you have "gone dotty". I don't think that darling, but I felt at first that the natural curiosity of your sex would prevail and that you would come down, you must allow me to tell you though, dearie, that you will not arrive in B'ham at 4 o'clock, as that train does not stop at Willesden. I thought this myself, but in order to be quite sure on the point, I sent up to New St. Stn. to a friend of mine there to ask him and enclose his reply, for your information. If you don't mind arriving in B'ham as late as 8.30 pm, the train from Streatham Hill at 4.52 would be best to come by, as it would not interfere with your lunch, and you would have time for a cup of tea before leaving home. If you think it too late though to reach here, come by the 11.11 and get here at 2.45. For goodness sake, don't come by the 12.51, or you will have to wait at Willesden, over an hour and a half. Let me have a wire in the morning, dearie, saying what train you are coming by and I shall meet it in. I went over "Eton Lodge" with the painter yesterday, and expect to receive his estimate in the morning.

It is nice of Aunt Renard to give you such a useful present; we shall be able to do with them all shan't we darling. Give my love to Granny, and tell her I am so pleased to hear that she is improving so nicely.

I am sorry to hear that that whistle has not turned up yet, and hope that three rings which I sent to Ernie, last night, have met with a better fate and reached

A photograph of the famous Bull Ring, Birmingham, in 1900 – only a few yards from New Street Station where Beatrice would arrive. St. Martin's Church still stands at the heart of this busy market area. (E)

The note Jack sent to his friend at New Street Station in order to check the train times Beatrice had suggested for her visit. His reply, written on the back confirmed that the 12.51 train from Streatham Hill to Willesden would mean a long wait, as the 1.30 p.m. train from Euston did not stop at Willesden. Jack scribbled a comment in pencil, "Fancy waiting at Willesden from 1.23 until 2.59". (A)

Greetings and sad partings were familiar scenes at stations such as this one depicted in the 1890s. For the majority of people trains, like the 'penny post', provided an essential link in their lives. (N)

It was a long time since Beatrice had been to Birmingham and it is unlikely that she would have imagined the last time that her next visit would be for such an exciting purpose. (N)

In such circumstances Beatrice was more disposed to like the Harrops, about whom previously she had been both cautious and disapproving.

him safely. It was a strange thing but the question of size never occurred to me until after I had posted them. I note you have sent me the size in your letter. If there is one of the rings, that Ernie would like to have, the size is not correct, we can have one made up like it, to the proper size. Give my love to your Ma and Pa, and tell them I will look after you alright while you are down here, and keep you in order. I am going up to Jennie's tonight and if necessary will write you another few lines, after I have seen her. The performance last night was quite a success, I believe. I enclose a programme. Well dearie, you must pray and excuse more now, don't forget to wire in the morning. Heaps of love.

Fancy, we shall be looking over "Eton Lodge" together on Thursday. Both trains on the card are L & NW through trains, Streatham Hill to Willesden.

Over your own devoted

Jack

"Roselea", December 20th 1898

My own darling Jack

Once more I am home again, but I have been wishing all the time, I was with you, I do wish the time was here for me to come to you, June seems further off than ever somehow. Well dear, I got home very comfortably. Ernie and Ma were at Streatham Hill station to meet me, I was so cold though and this morning we have had quite a sharp frost. I am longing for Xmas won't we have a time dear? I am afraid we shall not be very cold then eh darling? Granny seems quite herself, she sends her love to you. I did enjoy my visit to Jennie, she was so very kind and I did so appreciate it and Alec too spoke so nicely to me on Sunday night after you had gone. I have got to go to Miss Mann's tomorrow to be fitted with my new evening dress, if I had known I shouldn't have needed it, I would not have ordered one, for now I shall not use it at all for I know I shall not go to any dances here. Ethel is going home tomorrow and nurse goes on thursday, then a fresh batch comes in. Aunt Renard comes on thursday and my darling on saturday. I do hope you can get the house question settled before you come up, for I should be so disappointed if we were to miss it, for I feel we shall be able to make it so pretty. I am longing to get into it aren't you dear?

I have written to Jennie this morning to let her know I got home quite safely. Poor old Pa said he was glad to see me back again and he looked it. Well I hope to have a letter from you on thursday morning. I shall be so looking out for it, so please give me a nice long letter. If you see the Harrops please remember me very kindly to them all they made me so very welcome, and I liked Kitty so much. I must close now dear, as I want to catch the post. Lots of love and oceans of kisses, oh we will have a time at Xmas won't we?

Yours ever

Beatie

Woodcock St. B'ham. December 21st 1898

My own darling Beatie.

You cannot tell how anxiously I was awaiting your dear letter of this morning, for it seems such a long while since you went from me, and I was so anxious to hear from you.

I was so glad to know that you had reached home comfortably, but sorry you got so cold on the journey, however, I sincerely hope you will experience no ill effects from that. It was nice to have your Ma and Ernie to meet you at the station. I always think it makes one feel so much better, to have someone to meet them at the end of a journey. I know darling that you enjoyed your visit to Jennie's, and didn't I enjoy it too, but how soon it was all over. I know Jennie and Alec will always be nice towards us, and help us during the time which we have to get over, between now and our marriage, as much as lies in their power. There is no humbug about them, and their sympathy is genuine. Don't worry about the dress, dearie if you don't use it this season, it will come in very nicely for next, eh? I have felt ever so anxious since you left darling, over the house, lest we might lose it; but I don't think we shall. I received the further estimate on Monday night. Yesterday morning I went to see the Agent, but he would not be at his Office that day, they said, I then went off to see the Tenant, and he told me of another person who is after the house, she is a lady who has lived on the Main Road, opposite Jaffray Road, ever since we have been at Gravelly Hill, and she wants now a smaller house, and is very sweet on "Eton Lodge".

However, he has promised to keep it for me, until Saturday anyway, I have since left an offer at the Agents Office to the effect that if they will do the work as per estimates amounting to £14 = 16 = 0. I will take the house for three years. Of course he has to see the Trustees, about it. I will have a reply tomorrow, or Friday at latest. It will surely be settled this week, and I have no doubt I shall be able to tell you that it *is* our house when I come up on Saturday.

I sincerely hope so for I cannot bear to think of us missing it, and I am as anxious as your dear self for the time when we shall be in it, our little home, together. I have no doubt your poor Pa was glad to see you back again, but whatever he will think when you come to be with me always, I cannot imagine. However, you will need to make one or two more visits down here, again, before that time, and perhaps that will get them accustomed to it a bit more gradually. I have not seen any of the Harrops since you left, but will be sure and convey your message to them when I do. They were most pleased to see you there, and I know will make us both welcome at any time. They are good rough and ready straight forward people. Joe left here early yesterday morning for Manchester, and has been in Sheffield today, and I expect him at the works here about 7.20 tonight. I had to go over to Uncle John's on Monday night, as I told you, and attend to his ears, also Uncle Phillips! I went and the operations were successful in both cases. They both said they could hear very much better afterwards, and there was no wonder at that so far as Uncle John was concerned. On Monday afternoon, when I left New St. Station I went direct to the Solicitors and obtained the deeds relating to my Mortgage, so that I can now prove my title if occasion arises. I have decided that I had better have the whole of the Mortgage off, instead of reducing it, and have written a formal

Beatrice's family would have missed her while she was in Birmingham and have been excited on her return. It was rare that she travelled separately from them or went away alone, except to the Morris's. Jack rarely had anyone to meet him from the train on his return to Birmingham.

THE EAR AND THROAT HOSPITAL, EDMUND STREET.

Poor Jack, having to attend to the wax in the ears of the two old men! Perhaps he should have sent them to the Ear and Throat Hospital in Edmund Street, as shown above, instead. Uncle Phillips, was one of Jack's mother's three brothers. Her name was Jane Phillips before she married. (F)

Since the summer holiday in Folkestone, this would have been the first time that Jack and Beatrice had a chance to be alone together away from the parental roof for any length of time. They obviously took advantage of it.

notice, to my Mother, that I require it paid off next June 24th (six months notice) I have not yet handed it to her, but shall certainly do so, so that she may not be able to say that she has not had proper notice. Of course we should not be to a week or two, but it must be treated as a matter of business. We shall, of course, require money before June, to pay for our furniture, but then that will be able to be arranged for. I am so glad that poor Granny is so much improved, please give her my best love, and tell her I hope she will be quite her old self, when I come up for Xmas.

What a time we shall have, eh darling? You are right, I don't suppose we shall find it at all cold, we don't usually do we? Please give my love to your Pa and Ma, and dear Laura when you see her. Cheer up dearie, Saturday will soon be with you; heaps of love and lots of kisses and hugs (the latter in imagination until Saturday) Goodnight dearie.

Excuse note paper. I have had to make this from some plain sheets as I am just now without any of the proper kind.

Ever your own true

Jack

"Roselea", December 22nd 1898

My own darling Jack

It was nearly Christmas. Ernie's Laura was back for the school holidays and the seasonal invitations were beginning.

I have been so worried all the morning because I did not receive a letter from you, it has only just arrived and very thankful I was to receive it, for now these trying times I imagine all sorts of horrible things. Nurse has left this morning, we do miss her, I liked her so much. Ethel left yesterday and now Ma has just gone to meet Aunt Renard. Granny seems quite her old self, she sends her love to you. Laura came home yesterday and is coming here this afternoon. Yesterday I went to Kensington to have my dress fitted, it looks so nice dear, I feel sure you will like it. Coming back it turned out most awfully foggy, and so bitterly cold. This morning we have received invitations for Ma and Pa, you and I to Miss Lewcock's wedding, which is Jan 25th. I must talk that over when you come. It does seem a long time coming to saturday, but I suppose it will come if I have patience and wait. Oh by the way, we are all invited round to Ted's on saturday, the old ladies included, but I told Nellie you and I would not go, I don't want to go and I know you don't so we shall have a nice time together. I will come and meet the 7.16 train, whether you come or not, but I do hope you will manage to catch it. Now darling I do hope we don't miss the house, I shall be disappointed, do let me have a wire directly it is settled. I am afraid if the late tenant found someone to take the house from Xmas, he would naturally give preference to that person and we should have to take a back seat however, it might be an inducement to let us have it, if we take it for 3 yrs. I am glad you did that. I am so delighted you have got the deeds of your Mortgage and think you are doing quite right in taking it all off, but won't your Mother be wild. I had a nice letter from Jennie this morning. Your Mother went to see her on tuesday but did not mention my name at all, and it appears, she told Jennie, she couldn't have them at Gravelly Hill too long, as it would be imposing to Alice, what do you think of that? Jennie I

Jack had decided to take all his money in the business out in order to set up home. This, in addition to her many other reasons for feeling angry and bitter towards Jack, would make his mother even more resentful.

know is put out about it. I suppose the dear creature wants her Phelps up there. Well darling, I must dry up now, accept oceans of kisses and you know you have all my love.

Yours ever
Beatie

P.S. Let me have a letter saturday, won't you dearie

◇◇◇◇◇◇

Christmas was never to be quite the same again at Linwood Lodge. The arrival of Phelps and the departure of Jack made it a very different place.

Woodcock St. B'ham. December 22nd 1898

My own darling Beatie

    You will be wondering whatever has happened to bring this un-expected letter to you. Well, dearie, I had bad news to tell, I shall have to leave you for the day next Tuesday.

You no doubt remember me speaking sometimes of poor Bob Beeson, an old friend of mine who has been so ill for so long a time. Well, he died today poor fellow. His brother has just been in here to tell me, and ask if I will be one of the bearers. Poor chap he is fairly cut up over it, although of course he has expected it for a long long time. I do feel sorry for him; it was his only brother, and he has no father, mother, or sisters, I feel that I must come and pay the last tribute of respect to one who has been an old friend. His brother is fairly cast down, and I felt that even under the circumstances of being so far away I could not do otherwise than accede to his request, and so make his trouble a little lighter. The funeral leaves the house at 1.30, on Tuesday; and I propose to come down by the early train, and return by the four o'clock. Ernie could come up with you on Tuesday evening to the city and I can meet you at The Theatre.

I do hope darling that under these distressing circumstances, you won't mind very much, but poor Bob was such a nice fellow, and we have all been like a family of brothers together, I really must come dearie. Pray excuse more now darling, I am so upset about this, shall have your dear letter in the morning, and write you again tomorrow night. Au revoir. Heaps of my dearest love

Ever your own
Jack

Jack's friend, Robert Beeson, died at the age of only thirty-three years, his parents having both died some time earlier. Funerals were frequent and often grander occasions than weddings at that time, with processions of horse-drawn carriages following the hearse.

◇◇◇◇◇◇

"Roselea", December 23rd 1898

My own darling Jack

    Of course dear if you really think you would like to follow Mr. Beeson to his last resting place you must do so. I am sorry you have lost a friend but I really am unfeeling enough to wish he had waited another week before he died for it will be a muck up, and I don't like the idea of having a day short with you. Cannot you stay here until thursday to make up for it? We have just received a cable from David to say that he sails on Jan 8th in

Beatrice's brother David of the Royal Marines. David was to leave Hong Kong for Plymouth by way of Gibraltar, aboard H.M.S. Edgar. The ship was expected to dock in Plymouth in February. (H)

Jennie's Christmas Card to Ida in 1898, with a picture of herself and a greeting written on the back. (P)

the "Edgar" so we are all very excited and I guess he is too. Pa is ill in bed today I hope he will be alright by Xmas. Excuse more. Accept heaps of love and do try and give me an extra day.

Yours ever

Beatie

Suppose you have not heard about Eton Lodge

Woodcock St. B'ham. December 30th 1898

My own darling Beatie

I am so lost without you, and however I shall manage to get through these whole four weeks of enforced separation I really don't know. It was truly awful to me to part from you last night, and I did feel so troubled all the way.

I pictured my little dearie, and I know you must have felt so lonely, and anxious when I had gone from you. But we must try and cheer up dearie, and although that month of June seems yet so far off, we shall have so many things to think of in preparing our home that we must busy ourselves, and then perhaps the time will not seem so long. Darling, don't let any of those strange thoughts of me enter your mind. I am your true Jack as ever, and love you more dearly than ever I did, if that were possible. I never forget you darling, wherever I go and whatever I do you are always my first thought. When I got home last night Nin and Alec and Doris were there. It did seem awful to me, that every one seemed glad to see me back and greeted me, with one exception, my Mother, and she never said a word to me, and took an early opportunity of leaving the room. I could not help but feel it very much, but still I have got used to it now. I am going to the "Hooligan Dance" tonight but I shall be thinking of you dearie all the time. I had so looked forward to have taken you to it. I do wish you had been here to go. I do wish I were not going to this dance but having had so much to do with it, I feel I cannot back out now.

Please give my love to Pa and Ma and I hope Pa is better now, also dear old Granny. Cheer up my dearie, and accept my whole love and heaps of kisses for your dear self from

How bad of me darling I never wrote in your book before coming away, but I will mind and do it when I come next.

Your own devoted

Jack

destroy this letter "Roselea", December 31st 1898

My dear darling Jack

This separation is truly agonising, I feel as if I really cannot bear it, 'tis more than I can stand and the anxiety is simply wearing me out. Jack dear it is dreadful, if I only was sure of everything being well, but I

Beatrice instructed Jack to "destroy this letter" and several to follow. Although Beatrice destroyed Jack's letters, in response, comforting her in her panic, Jack did not do as Beatrice requested.

cannot help feeling miserable, and I do feel so dreadfully lonely, if only you were here to comfort me. I know darling I could not be loved more than I am by you, and I am so proud of your love, so true and honest, but I could not help my feelings the other day, and I had to let you know what was crossing through my mind, but I could have killed myself when I saw how I had hurt your dear feelings, it nearly broke my heart to see you, but forget it dear, for I do love you most devotedly, I almost wish it was not quite so strong for then I should not feel so bad as I do now, at you having to leave me. I really don't think I can bear this for 4 whole weeks from today, must it really be. I cannot settle to anything and all I can do is to cry and long for my darling Jack, my husband, how I wish I could come at once and be with you at Eton Lodge. June seems years off to me. Do write tomorrow dear so that I get a letter monday morning, or I shall quite collapse from this awful feeling.

Please excuse the paper, but I did not notice that Ma had started writing on that sheet and I feel too upset to write it again, I know you won't mind. I have felt very seedy since you left, such pain, but today I feel better of that, if only I could pop in and see you, I should feel happier, it is cruel that we must be parted isn't it dear? I am glad you went to the dance, it would do you good, did you enjoy it? We have heard that David has been given the Staff Officer's billet at Walmer in Kent and that is why he has been sent for to come home at once, so that he won't be able to go to America as he will only have 3 weeks leave, so I expect he will stay here. He expects to arrive in England about the end of February and Kitty and the children won't cross over until the end of March, because of the cold weather. David has a finished house provided for him and it is a 5 yrs appointment, so that he is very lucky to have been chosen for it. So many thanks for those lovely gloves, they fit beautifully, such a nice cut and so very comfortable. I was surprised that Jennie had not gone back, when does she go. Aunt Renard has gone this morning, Ma has gone to London Bridge with her. I have written to ask Aimée to come next saturday for a week, I thought it would take me out of myself a bit, and you remember what I told you about the end of next week, I only wish it has passed by, I should feel *perhaps* happier.

Darling I feel I could fill reams, telling you of my feelings, but I must think of you dear a bit, don't worry about me, I expect I shall toddle along alright soon. Now if your Mother had been alright with us, how jolly it would have been. I might have come up and stayed at Linwood Lodge a bit. Accept oceans of kisses and you know you have all my love and do write me a nice long letter and try to cheer me up pet.

Yours ever
Beatie

This was the end of an important year but an anxious time with an unexpected.. problem with which to face the next. Beatrice, who was so pre-occupied with her physical and emotional problems, barely remembered to thank Jack for his gift of a pair of gloves. (S)

⬦⬦⬦⬦⬦⬦

Linwood Lodge, Jan 1st 1899

My own darling Beatie

You can't tell how anxiously I was awaiting your dear letter of this morning. I have felt so worried and anxious for you darling ever since I left you. I am so sorry dearie to find that you are feeling the same, but cheer

A New Year for Jack and Beatrice whose relationship so far had been fraught with all kinds of hazards, although until this time few of them had been of their own making.

Jack and Beatrice's first tiff during their engagement came at a time of much anxiety for Beatrice. Jack, as always, was patient and re-assuring. This illustration was by R. Caton Woodville. (B)

up dearie, I do think all will be right, although I must say I have not been able to convince myself of that, try as I will. It is quite as hard to me darling, as to yourself, to be separated from you in this awful manner; but come what will darling we are one, and with such love as ours we can get over anything. I have quite forgiven your dearie, for that occurrence of the other day. But oh it was awful to me, to have you show such coolness to me, for I could not live without your love darling. I love you more than life itself, for without your love life would have no attraction for me. It was a mistake darling, and I will forget all about it. I wish I were with you today dearie to cheer you up, perhaps you will have the kiddies come round and they will perhaps liven you a bit. I went to the dance on Friday and it was supposed to have been an exceptional success. I had nine dances, but throughout the whole night I was never able to let myself go, and enjoy a dance, as one does as a rule. I was thinking of you the whole time dearie, in fact, I have been doing so ever since I left you. I went to Church this morning, feeling most miserable. There was to have been a visiting clergyman to preach, but for some reason or other he failed to put in an appearance, and Mr. Swindell had, unexpectedly to preach. He gave us a short address, and chose for his text the words "Let not your heart be troubled," I listened most intently, and must say that when I left I felt much more comfortable. Think of these words dearie, and perhaps you will feel better.

I am glad you have asked Aimée to come and stay with you for a time, for no doubt she will liven you up, but I hope that by the time she reaches you you will be able to tell me that you are feeling as bright and happy as ever. You will all be glad to know that David is coming home for a time, and I should think he will consider himself fortunate at securing the appointment, and appreciate it very much. I am glad to know dearie, that you received the gloves safely, and that they fit alright, and you like them. Jennie and Alec went home Friday

The invitation to Jack's Artillery Regiment's Annual Dinner, which he accepted. It shows a photograph of the Regiment's Annual Camp in Wales a previous year. (A)

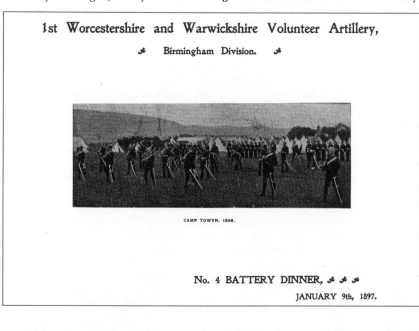

morning, and Doris went yesterday. I was amusing myself with Doris at Breakfast yesterday morning, teaching her the Philosopher's Conundrums. I asked her "who wore the biggest boots," and she told me "The Policeman". She seems to have a fair idea. You will feel quite strange with all your visitors gone away, but I suppose Ernie will have his dear Laura back tomorrow. She will cheer you up. Please give my love to her, and also to Aimèe when she comes if you can spare so much of it dearie. I do hope dearie that when I receive your letter on Tuesday morning, I shall find that you are feeling much brighter and happier. I shall have to try and cheer up myself as well, but I seem to have a big week to look forward to this week.

Monday. I have an appointment in the afternoon about "Eton Lodge" and in the evening Harrops usual New Year Dinner Party.

Wednesday. I have to attend Lodge at 5.30.

Thursday night we have a meeting to settle up over the "Hooligan Dance".

Friday the New Year Pantomime Party, but I think I shall get out of this.

Saturday, the Dinner of the Sergeant's Mess, to which I have received an invitation. It came this morning, and I have written accepting it.

What a round of pleasure you will say to look forward to, but darling there is pleasure in nothing for me without you and I am always thinking of you and longing to be with you, most especially at this time. Cheer up my dearie, all will be well, but come what may you know that I am ever

Your own true

Jack

I am going to walk up to Uncle John's to tea now. It is very wet though.

⬥⬥⬥⬥⬥⬥⬥

I hope you destroyed my last letter and do the same to this

"Roselea", Jan 2nd 1899

My own darling Jack

You cannot tell how eagerly I was watching for your dear letter this morning and of course the postman was later than usual. I cannot say that I am feeling any better dear, yesterday it was awful, I never had such an unhappy day for a long time. I went to Church in the morning, but my thoughts were with you all the time dear. I am so glad that you went to Church dear, and felt a bit comforted. I am afraid I did not. I shall not feel happy until next week, for I somehow feel so afraid, as I have been anything but well. The kiddies did not come round yesterday it was so wet, so I was all by myself in the dining room and I laid down on the floor in front of the fire, feeling most dejected. In the evening about 7 o'clock a cab drew up and two ladies got out, it turned out to be Nellie and Mrs. Morris. They came to wish us a happy New Year, I only hope and pray ours will be, they brought me a large bottle of lavender water. The first thing Mrs. Morris said to me, was "whatever have you been doing to yourself, how bad you look" and I must say I did look rather white, the worry is so trying. Have you thought how awful things will be if I am not better next week, I cannot bear it and with you so far away from me, it would cheer me up to be near you and have a loving embrace from my

Laura's family lived in Dulwich but she spent most of her holidays with Ernie at 'Roselea' and had almost become one of the family.

Jack's gay round of social activities held little pleasures for him without Beatrice, whereas previously he would have thrown himself wholeheartedly into such events.

Several Hughes generations had lived in Chester Road. Jack's grandfather, the original founder of the Albion Works, both lived and was buried there, in Boldmere Church. Jack's father was also buried there as was Uncle John eventually. (W)

darling, and we do know how to do that don't we dear? I am sure our love never could be greater than it is for each other, we do adore one another, what do you think? I am glad you went to the dance, it would do you good, what a gay young spark you are getting, don't get doing too much and knocking yourself up for your dear little wife wants you to be ever so well, and do try to get fatter. I shall not be able to find you if you get much thinner. I have just received a nice letter from Ida and one from dear little Doris. Hope you will enjoy your little self tonight, drink my health dear, and wish me luck – also the pantomime and dinner. We go to the pantomime on friday night, but I don't want to go one bit. I cannot believe that it is only a week today since we kept Xmas, it seems more like 7 months instead of days, doesn't it to you dear? I am going out this afternoon to get Ma a birthday present. I hardly know what to buy her. I think perhaps the walk will do me good. Accept a good old hug and many kisses

Yours ever

Beatie

Write soon dear to your poor miserable little girlie

✧✧✧✧✧✧

"Roselea", Jan 4th 1899

My own darling Jack

Don't worry too much dear, you will make yourself quite ill, never mind about me yet, forget about it for the present, and we will wait and see what next happens. I daren't think of the worst, it makes me bad to think of it, I shall have to decide in a great hurry if it comes to that and will let you know, but I don't think I can very well speak to Mrs. Morris or anyone else about it. Of course I shall be only too eager to let you know of my anxiety being over, I only hope it will be soon. I somehow feel that it is as we wish, for I don't see how it could have been any different do you dear? You must know. Cheer up darling, I am doing my best and I certainly feel brighter myself today. I only wish you were here to have a good old hug and some of your sweet kisses that would do me good. Laura is here for a few days, as we go to the pantomime on friday. Aimée is coming on saturday so I hope by then I shall be able to write to you and tell you I am quite well again. Don't think of anything else yet awhile.

I have bought a very pretty picture (print) called "disappointment". I feel sure you will like it, I am sending it to the shop to be framed in dark oak for the dining room. I am glad you are going to the pantomime it will do you good, what is the good of moping, it won't alter things will it? Poor Mrs. Grellet is buried today, poor thing she felt a pain in her chest and asked her husband to go down and get her some ginger, this was 8 o'clock in the morning, and when he got upstairs again she had fallen out of bed dead. Must not it have been a shock for her poor husband. I am going with Ma to buy my house linen next week and would you like me to get muslin for our curtains, so that I could make them before I come to "Brum". I could get them so much cheaper in the wholesale, you know dear and it would be much more comfortable to have them up when we go to Eton Lodge.

It was perhaps expressive of Beatrice's mood that the picture she bought to be framed was entitled 'Disappointment' – one of a series of sentimental Victorian engravings. The picture framer to whom she sent it was very likely to have been Fred Willis. (S)

Ma thanks you for your good wishes, she thinks it very kind of you. Laura sends her love, hopes you are not pining too much for me. I am pining for you dear, oh, so badly. Just fancy, 3 weeks more from saturday. This week seems as if it never would go. Heaps of love and oceans of kisses and try to convince me that you were cautious last thursday

Yours, ever
Beatie

"Roselea", Jan 6th 1899

My darling Jack

You don't know how I look forward to the day that I receive your dear letter, when I wake up, the first thing I think is, how lovely I shall get my letter this morning. I am so delighted if my letter gave you any comfort, I wish I could give you the good news but up to the present I cannot, we must have a little patience and I do hope that in my next letter I shall be able to do so, and shan't we be happy once more dear? I have hinted to Ma that you would like to be married next month, to see what she would say. She said "you must not be unreasonable", so I don't know what would happen if we were to, of course you know dear, I should only be too glad to, under any circumstances, but perhaps we shall think soon, that it would be better to do as at first arranged. I hope you will enjoy the pantomime tonight, which one are you going to? Don't forget *me* dear, I only wish I was with you to go also.

Ma has asked Laura to come here after I have gone. Laura thinks that her people will object, but she is going home tomorrow to talk it over with them and is going to let us know. You see if she is coming she will have to give notice to leave school at the end of next term. She wants to come very much, she says there is nothing she would like better. She sends her love to you and thanks you for your message. We are going to the pantomime tonight to see *Aladdin*. I don't care a bit about going but perhaps it will enliven me up a bit for I am beginning to get very dumpy again, but I must cheer up and look at the brightest side of things if I can. This week seems as if it never would go, just fancy only friday. I shall be thankful when Sunday has gone, at least I hope so, for if I don't feel alright then, I shall give up everything, but I hope to be able to tell you when next I write that I am feeling quite myself again. I hope you have destroyed my last 2 or 3 letters, I would rather that you did dear.

Aimèe comes tomorrow, I will then give her your message, but I cannot spare much for her, you know dear, I want all your dear love for myself, I have got it haven't I darling? Weren't you invited to the Blakemore's dance? Ida told me she was going. I suppose the Woodhill's dance was a great success, I rather liked Mrs. Woodhill. Well dear, I must away, time is going, and I must hurry up to catch this post, or you'll be worrying. Write soon dear a good cheery letter, perhaps I shall need it badly. All my love to me dearie

From his ever devoted
Beatie

Jack's letter in reply to Beatrice's request for re-assurance that he was "cautious last thursday" was destroyed by Beatrice, as were his other letters at this time. Jack did not destroy Beatrice's letters as she had requested, however.

Suddenly to have "to be married next month" would have been a shock to Beatrice's parents, whatever the reason. Jack and Beatrice's engagement was short enough, particularly when compared with Ernie and Laura's long romance.

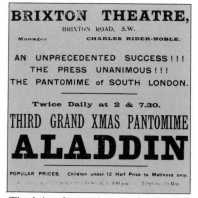

The choice of pantomimes in south London that Christmas was wide, there being several in Brixton and Streatham alone. (K)

This illustration for Aladdin, *the pantomime staged at the Brixton theatre for Christmas 1898, depicts the variety and fun of this annual theatrical extravagance. Pantomime flourished in the Victorian and Edwardian eras. Miss Jenny Owen played the principal 'boy' in this particular production of* Aladdin *"with a grace which wins everybody's imagination". (X)*

"Roselea", Jan 9th 1899

This was a joyful letter indeed. The relief Beatrice must have felt to discover she was no longer "unwell" must have been even greater than it would be for many modern girls in similar circumstances. Such a condition, though undesirable, would not be so appallingly unacceptable before marriage as it would have been for a middle-class Victorian girl.

My darling Jack

It seemed such a long time to wait for your letter from friday until monday. However, I was very delighted to receive it. What a crowd of you to go to the pantomime. I should think you must have had a real good time. I feel quite envious and only wish I was there to join in the fun, but that I hope will be later on eh dearie. You cannot think how bad I felt when saturday and Sunday came round and no good news. I felt I could not speak to anyone and was thinking the best to be done, when in the evening I got the joyful news, so I hope you will feel quite yourself now, I shall I hope. I almost feel as if I was treading on air, I only wish you were here, just fancy another 3 weeks to wait. We are going to have *the* dinner party on Jan 25th, so you must come by the 2 o'clock train. By the way dear, excuse me for asking, but what did you pay Harding's man for the cab when you went to Streatham Hill last, he has sent in the bill and has charged us 3/- then at the end he has put by cash 2/-. I only ask you incase he is trying to do us. The pantomime was not at all bad at Brixton, but I have seen funnier ones. I didn't enjoy it one bit. Funnily enough, Mr., Mrs. and Miss Woodward sat next to us, we were surprised to see them. I suppose the mortgage on Jennie's houses will be alright, if so you might just as well do that. Do you only intend to spend £250 on the furniture? Aimèe says she would like to send her love to you but she is a bit afraid to, but I tell her I don't mind. She is going to a dance this evening so she is going home this afternoon, but will come back tomorrow. She has had a proposal from a fellow in a fairly good position to be married in March, but she says she cannot care for him so has declined his offer. Her youngest sister has just become engaged so she will have to buck up. I am glad she is not going to be married in March for then she could not have been my bridesmaid. I have sent the coat and bonnet to Doris and I think Jennie is sure to like it, I thought they were lovely. I do hope they are just what she wanted. Write soon darling, I shall be looking out for your letter as you know. Lots of love and heaps of kisses and now don't you feel better?

Yours ever
Beatie

"Roselea", Jan 11th 1899

My darling Jack

Many thanks for your letter, which I was anxiously looking out for this morning. I also got one from Jennie, she likes the coat and bonnet very much, I am very glad, but I thought she would, as I think they are very sweet and she says they fit her very nicely, so that is alright. Just fancy your Mother offering one of her houses to Jennie, she will expect something now I should think as regards the Phelps affair, but I am so glad that Jennie will be nearer to us, it will be very nice for me, don't you think so dear?

Aimèe came back yesterday, she enjoyed the dance very much, but was very tired not having got to bed before 5 o'clock. She has made a list of the presents we could do with, not much of a cheek to put before people such a list as that – what do you think? I enclose it for you to see. I felt awfully seedy yesterday, so I laid down all the afternoon, but I feel a little better this morning. Aimèe and I are going out shopping this afternoon. If the mortgage is alright by all means have £750 on it, we must see when the time comes how our money goes for the furniture. It is very kind of your Uncle to take so much interest in you, there must be some good in him after all. I believe Ma and I are going up on monday to buy house-linen. Shan't I fancy myself eh! buying our things for *our* house. I do wish the 28th was here, what a time it seems to look forward to. Aimèe has chosen the 2nd best quality, £2 = 7 = 6 so I think it is very generous

The corner of Streatham Hill and Leigham Court Road as seen from Streatham Hill Station in the 1890s, showing the taxi cab rank from which Jack would have taken his cab. (D)

Aimée clearly felt that she knew as well as Jack and Beatrice did the things they needed to set up home. The list of wedding present requests that she compiled for them was not a modest one.

Jack and Beatrice's wedding present request list:

Fish Knives and Forks, Fish Carvers, Biscuit Box, Fruit Knives and Forks, Tea and Coffee Services, Claret Jug, Cake Basket, Preserve Stand, Napkin Rings, Salad Bowl and Servers, Toast Rack. Forks, Table Spoons, Dessert Spoons, Cutlery, Fruit Spoons, Salt Cellars and Spoons. Silver Muffineers. Gong. Jam Spoons, Pickle Forks and Butter Knives. Breakfast Service, Dinner Service, Dessert Service, Trinket Set, Toilet Service, Silver Egg Stand. Silver Hot Water Jug. Sets of Jugs. Standard Lamp. Pedestal and Pot (Large). Copper (must be) Coal Scuttle. Bronze figures (without drapery), Dish Covers, Crumb Tray and Brush, Kitchen Utensils, Oak Tea Trays. Hot Water Bottle. Piano. Cheques (gratefully received), Brass Ink Stand, Waste Paper Basket. Hearth Broom, Eider Down Quilt, Cut Glass Water Jug, Silver Candle Sticks. Brass Newspaper Rack. Silver Photo Frames. Silver Mounted Bread Trencher and Knife. Electro Soup Tureen, Cushions. Asparagus Service, Grape Scissors, Entrée Dishes, Nut Crackers, Silver Sauce Boat, Knife Rests. (A)

Jack was so meticulous himself that he would have been extremely irritated by Joe's slackness and lack of discipline. As Jack was younger than Joe he was prepared to "put up with" a good deal that he otherwise would not have tolerated.

Silver Hot Water Jug.
Sets of Jugs.
Standard Lamp.
Pedestal & Pot (Large).
Copper (must be) Coal Scuttle.
Bronze Figures (without drapery)
Dish Covers
Crumb Tray & Brush
Kitchen Utensils
Oak Tea Trays
Hot Water Bottle
Piano
Cheques (gratefully received)
Brass Inkstand
Davenport
Sugar Sifter & Tongs
Silver Back Brushes
Spirit Stand
Pickle Jars
Bread Fork

Soup Ladle
Cake Knife
Celery Glass
Glass Dishes
Ornaments
Pictures
Table Mats
Butter Dish
Brass Ink Stand
Waste Paper Basket
Hearth Broom
Eider Down Quilt
Cut Glass Water Jug
Silver Candle Sticks
Brass Newspaper Rack
Silver Photo Frames
Silver Mounted Bread Trencher & Knife
Electro Soup Tureen
Cushions

of her. I hope Huband is better, I should think he must have injured himself internally. Heaps of love and I would give something for a good old hug

Yours ever Beatie

Woodcock St. B'ham. Jan 12th 1899

My own darling Beatie

I was so glad to receive your dear letter this morning, for dearie it is the only thing that cheers me up. The penny post, and these little chats on paper are all very well, but it is your dear self I need darling, and like the proverbial boy and the soap, I "shan't be happy till I get it". I wish we could perform a miracle and find that tomorrow was June, and that we were married and settled in our dear little home. I suppose it is no use getting low spirited though, if one can help it but still it sometimes seems that one cannot avoid it. I have fairly had the hump today, for do you know Joe is so very trying. You know he goes out at nights and then can't get up in the morning, and instead of being here at 9 o'clock or soon after comes in at any time from 11 up to 1. (one o'clock today) Then when he finds the time gone and he has not sufficient time to do as he would have liked, he becomes very irritable and vents his feelings on other people. By the way, he seems to mark me out for the lion's share of it. He is awfully trying and it fairly gives me the hump, but I have to put up with it.

I went up to Jennie's the other night, and she shewed me the Coat and Bonnet. She liked them very much, and so did I. It will be nice darling if Jennie lives at Chester Road as proposed. In fact it is all settled I think. But my Mother has been to see a house which is situated in Chester Rd, and which is shortly being put up for Sale by Auction. It is a rather large house, and a lot of land to let I believe. "Chester Hall" I think it is called. Sounds big enough doesn't it. Whatever favor my Mother shews Jennie though I don't think she could ever buy her over so to speak, for Jennie is straight, I am sure.

I am glad Aimée enjoyed the dance. What a splendid list of presents she has made out. I don't think she has omitted many items. As a rule, when people are about to make a present to anyone they usually find it a hard matter to decide what form the present should take. To such people a list like you have sent me would be a boon. I like the remarks, in brackets, very much, especially as regards the Bronze Figures, what would be the use of such figures with drapery, there would be no charm about them whatever. Won't you feel proud on Monday, when you are out buying all the things for our home. I have not yet asked Harrops to take a Photo of "Eton Lodge" but I shall see Arthur tonight I think, and will ask him. No doubt they will do one for me at the end of the week. How good of Aunt Parker, to make us such a nice present. Please convey my best love, and thanks when writing to her. I have sent the Bracelet off today, addressed to your Ma, and trust it will reach her quite safely. They have made a good job of it, I think. I had all the other stones examined, in case perhaps there might soon be some more of them coming out. The charge was 14/-, I only mention this by the way, as I thought your Ma would be anxious to know. But pray don't think of sending it on. I think that was very reasonable. I am sorry dearie that you have been feeling so seedy, and do hope you are feeling quite well and bright now. It is so hard for me dearie without you, for when I go home there seems no comfort for me there. But I must try and cheer up and wait patiently and when June comes and I have my own little home and dear sweet wife to come home to, shan't we both be happy together.

There is to be a sort of evening party at Linwood Lodge next Thursday I understand. All the people are invited who took part in the Dramatic Entertainment. Phelps will be very much "en evidence" of course. Huband is very much better I am glad to say. For the present, dearie, Au revoir. All my love and a sweet kiss,

Your own devoted
Jack

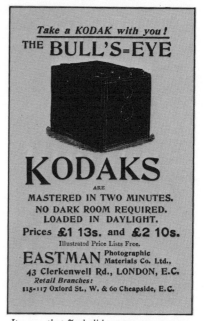

It seems that Jack did not possess a camera as he always relied on Jack Harrop to take the photographs he needed. It is likely that he would have used a Kodak Box Camera, such as the one illustrated, the prices advertised being those for February 1898. (B)

"Roselea", Jan 13th 1899

My own darling Jack

Your letter came this morning alright and I was so glad to get it, for I, like you, have been feeling very dumpy lately and I don't seem to be able to shake it off. It does seem such a long time since I saw you and such a time to look forward to before we meet again, it is hard isn't it dear? I have been feeling so very seedy the last day or two, especially today, but I hope to be better in a little while. I shall be glad to receive the photograph of the house, as

Beatrice suffered from many minor ailments which she rarely defined but which depressed her and restricted her activities considerably. She was frequently confined to bed for a day or two to recover.

Mrs. Mercer had proposed that Laura should come to live with the Mercers, in order to be with Ernie, once Beatrice had married and left home. It was not uncommon for a couple to live within the parental family until they could save enough to get married.

it will give them here a little idea what it is like. Ma received the bracelet alright and wishes me to thank you very much for getting it done for her, it does look nice dear, and how reasonable, we were surprised. Ma will settle with you when you come up, unless you would rather have it sent on. Aimee is here, she goes home tomorrow. Laura came over yesterday and will stay over Sunday. I don't believe her people will allow her to come here, they do not consider it would be proper. I am awfully sorry for I am sure she would be the nicest girl for Ma to have. Ernie says she must come and is going to try and get round Mrs. Wallers. Laura goes back to school on monday week, so they won't have much longer together. I am glad Huband is getting better, it seems frightful when one is in such pain. I am now, so I feel doubly sympathetic. It is too bad of Joe to behave so horridly but try and take no notice of it, and let him quiet down. Does your Mother think of living at Chester Rd. herself, if she bought Chester Hall or what is her idea? Have you seen "Eton Lodge" lately, I hope it is alright, have you the key?

I wish you could write so that I can get a letter on saturday night, and then I could write on Sunday, for it seems such a long time to wait until monday from now. Accept oceans of kisses and all my love

Yours ever
Beatie

⬦⬦⬦⬦⬦⬦

Linwood Lodge, Jan 14th 1899

My own darling Beatie

It was impossible for me to write that you might receive a letter tonight as I was so busy at the Works this morning, and again I did not receive your letter until about 12.30, as I went down on the first train this morning, and your letter was brought to me when the Carriage came to town. Perhaps it would be as well if, in future, you were to address my letters to the Works, (I am always first there) excepting of course, in case you post on a Saturday, then I should get it at home alright. I do feel so wretched dearie, for I have been so brooding. That Phelps affair fairly worries the life out of me. I do so wish I could have come to you today darling, for I should have been feeling so happy now. I don't believe I can go on like this until June for surely I shall be worried to death. That beast came up here tonight at 7.35, she had been upstairs for two hours getting ready to receive him. I have been in the Breakfast Room, all the night, on my lonesome, and first thing after Tea did three hours work at the "Stock Book" then had Supper, and now am writing to my dearie for I do need comforting. Miss Turner has been here, and Ida and Frank and Mother and the other thing have all been together in the Dining Room. I hear their shrieks of laughter, oh it grated on my nerves. I do believe darling, that if I were not engaged to your dear self, I should have shot that devil, or done something of the kind. Fancy a woman taking to a thing like him, and chucking over entirely her own child, just because he happens to venture an opinion. I have lost all love for her, she has never a word for me, and the whole thing so preys on me I shall be glad when I can get out of this altogether for I can't stand it. How strange, as soon as I write about getting out, here

A photograph of the 'dreaded' Phelps whom Jack hated so much that he could not bring himself to call him by his real name, 'the beast' or 'that thing' being more appropriate to his feelings then. (P)

comes Joe, he wants some supper laid in here so I must get out and finish my letter elsewhere. He has just come up on the 10.30. Phelps went at 10.30.

I went over to "Eton Lodge" this afternoon, to see if it had been blown away, but everything appears to be in its place, as before the gale. I think I shall have to get the work done and go and live in it for if I keep going on like I am at present there will be none of me left for you when June comes. I went all over the house today, and seemed as if I could not let myself come away from it and was picturing ourselves in it, as we shall be. If it is fine tomorrow morning I am going up to Wylde Green on the 9.13 train and shall walk down to "Eton Lodge" with Jack Harrop and he will take a photo of the house with a hand camera. I do hope it will be fine then I shall be able to get it, and enclose, in this letter. I am glad your Ma is pleased with the Bracelet. I am so sorry darling to hear that you have been still feeling so seedy, and do hope that you are now feeling quite alright. I hope you will be able to go and do your shopping alright on Monday. I was rather afraid that Laura's people would not quite like the idea of her coming to "Roselea" but still I hope Ernie will be able to prevail upon them for I should like Laura to be there, and how nice it would be for her Ernie. If my Mother buys that place at Chester Rd. she would go and live in it. "Verulum" is the name I find. I don't think it is very likely she will have it, for she has tried for so many one time and another, but she usually wants to beg them I notice. If I were only with you now darling we should be happy together, and I am so longing for you. I must be off to bed now dearie, all my love and a sweet goodnight kiss

ever your own true
Jack

Please give my love to Laura and Granny. I have got the keys. The gas and water is turned off.

❖❖❖❖❖❖

Sunday Jan 15th 1899

My Darling Beatie

I am feeling much better this morning, but it is such an awful morning there will be no taking a Photo today. It is very dull and pouring with rain. I am not going out at all today, but shall have a day's work at the Stock Book. I think I can pretty well finish it today and I am most

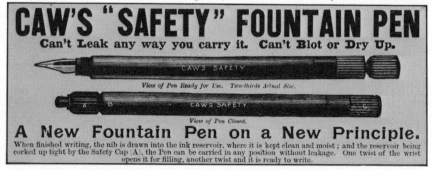
Jack was feeling so wretched at this time that he sought immense comfort from visiting Eton Lodge, which represented his only means of escape from the impossible situation he had got himself into at home.

An advertisement for a new kind of 'Safety' Fountain Pen guaranteed not to leak, which became available at this time. Perhaps Jack should have bought one for all his work on the Stock Book. (B)

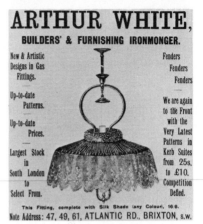

An advertisement showing a sketch of a pendant light with a silk shade like the one at Eton Lodge. (X)

anxious to get it done, so that we can get out the Balance Sheet and then we shall know whether I have got any money to pick up, and if so, how much.

I enclose an advertisement shewing a sketch of a pendant, like the one at "Eton Lodge". These are the people whom we must send to have the Pendant done up, and a new shade put on. Ida sends her love, and says she will write today.

Good bye for the present, and cheer up dearie. I am longing for the 28th. Heaps of love and kisses

Ever your own devoted Jack

✦✦✦✦✦✦✦

"Roselea", Jan 16th 1899

My darling Jack

I of course was disappointed not getting a letter on saturday night, but I knew it was because you were not able to write. I hope you will cheer up dear, I wouldn't let Phelps worry you, the beast, he isn't worth it. I must say, it is very hard for you to have to put up with, but bear it a little longer, I only wish we were going to be married sooner, for your sake, for I know how very uncomfortable it must be for you, your Mother never speaking to you. I shall be looking out for the photo of "Eton Lodge", no doubt you will be able to take one later on. I am glad the house was alright after the gale I presume you had it, as well as we. Aimèe went home on saturday, I am afraid she has not had much of a time, for two days I have had to go to bed. On friday I was very queer, I went to bed and did not get up until 7.30 at night, saturday I was almost as bad and yesterday I had a most awful headache, but I am pleased to say, that I am feeling so much better today. I have just finished making such a jolly fine large silk cushion, it looks so nice, I am getting on you see dear.

Beatrice's prescription from Day's, the Chemist, with her address handwritten on it. It is an elaborately printed and designed envelope which contained the written prescription inside it, with the addresses of the different retail pharmacies of the Company listed on the back. (A)

THE PRESCRIPTION.

92 Thrale Rd

DISPENSED BY

DAY'S METROPOLITAN DRUG COMPANY, LIMITED

IN CONNECTION WITH

DAY'S SOUTHERN DRUG CO LTD

DISPENSING CHEMISTS.

Copied Book, K4

No 456 4 5 — For addresses of Pharmacies see other side of Envelope.

Laura left here this morning. You see she goes back to school next monday so she is very busy. She is going to meet Ma and I tomorrow to go shopping with us. I am going to buy a lot of my things. David is on his way home and is expected about the middle of February.

They were talking last night how we should manage about putting the people up that come over night to the wedding, our only idea, which I think will be best is, to take rooms at "Thrale Hall". Nellie says she can put 2 gentlemen up, she suggested you and Joe. She says she would see that you got up in time etc. but you wouldn't want any looking after would you dear? we shall only be too glad to come to one another. I am longing for the 28th, it seems as if it never would come. The Lewcocks and Pattendens are coming that night to dinner. Accept oceans of kisses and all my love and do cheer up dearie.

Yours ever
Beatie

Ted and Nellie lived at Baldry Gardens, on the other side of Streatham High Road from Thrale Road. It would have been only a short distance for Jack to get to the church on time.

⋄⋄⋄⋄⋄⋄

Woodcock St. B'ham. Jan 17th 1899

My own darling Beatie

I received your dear letter in good time this morning, and it did me so much good. I am feeling in a much better state of mind than when I wrote you last, but really don't think I can stop at Linwood Lodge until June. You don't know what it is dearie. It is simply awful, and quite wears me down. Joe and I were at the Works last night until after 10 o'clock, and then I had to go up to town to post so could not get the 10.30. Joe caught that train, and when I got home by the 11.15 my Mother was nagging at him. Oh it was alright. Phelps had been up during the evening, I learned from Alice, to bring some Music for Ida, what a stall. There had been a gentleman there about the house at Chester Rd. and that was why he came. It seems a funny thing but he is present at all the interviews about the house. You must excuse the writing but Frank is working the Type-writer on the same table, and it shakes so. I know it is no use to trouble you dearie, all about this affair of my Mother's, but you are the only one I can open my heart to, and it does seem to give me some relief to tell you of it. I think dearie I shall have to get into "Eton Lodge" before June. If it is convenient to Jennie, do you think you could come down with me, next time I come, and select the papers and furniture, so that I could have the place done up, and go and live in it, for I can't stand five months of this. I am sorry darling, you have been so queer lately, for it does trouble me, when you are not well. I suppose you are like your poor old Jack and want comforting very badly.

Jack's mother was planning a new life for herself which necessitated a move from the house in which she had lived with Jack's father and brought up her family.

I am glad to see you have been again so busy, making such nice things for our home, shan't we be swagger. What a pity you have lost Aimèe and Laura, for you will be a little lonely I am afraid. Never mind dearie, cheer up, and don't get down in the dumps like I have been lately. Ida shewed me the letter she received from you the other day, she is quite frantic over the wedding, and most of all is anxious as to what form my presents to the Bridesmaids will take.

Ida was a fun-loving girl who enjoyed dressing up and special occasions. She would have been very excited at the prospect of being a bridesmaid to Beatrice.

The Bell Hotel in Birmingham where 'smoking concerts' were held. These provided a more middle-class rendezvous than the music halls, and were mostly for men. (F)

That seems a very important matter to her. You are right, dearie. I don't think I shall need calling on the morning of our Wedding. It wouldn't be very complimentary to you, if I did, would it darling. It will be a crowd I know, when we get all the people together. Do you know I made out a rough list, on Sunday, of people whom I thought I would like to be invited, and found I had got fifty down. Of course if they all had an invitation I don't suppose there would be above half of them accept.

I have not yet asked Joe about being best man, but suppose I must do so very soon. I shall have to have him I suppose, or the fat would be in the fire again. It is very kind of Nellie to offer to put us up there. I suppose that would be much the best thing for us to do. Well dearie, will you please excuse me now, for it is getting towards seven (seems like having half a day tonight) and I have an appointment to meet Harrops (Jack and Arthur) and Ned Hands outside Aston Theatre, at 7 o'clock. We have a Box there tonight, for the Pantomime. *Aladdin* I think it is. You know the theatre. It is that theatre where everyone smokes. I have told you about it. I don't know what it will be like, but if I am able to raise a laugh, well, that will be worth something these times.

I do hope, dearie, that you are now feeling quite alright, do cheer up, and let me know if you think you could manage to come back with me next time. Heaps of kisses and all my love

ever your own devoted Jack

Alice is about sick of it, and I feel sure we can have her. She would be getting married though in a year or two, but still she would give us a good start

◇◇◇◇◇◇◇

"Roselea", Jan 18th 1899

My darling Jack

Your dear letter came alright this morning, and I was very glad to get it. We went out shopping yesterday morning at 11 o'clock and we did not get back until 9 at night. I was dead tired but I have got some fine dresses etc. I met Mrs. Morris yesterday and she has asked me to go and spend the day with her today so I thought I would write to you before I go, so please excuse scrawl for I have not much time to spare. I have been mad almost with rheumatism again. I hardly slept at all last night I couldn't move for pain, Ma gave me a good rubbing so I hope it will soon be better. Now dear about yourself. I cannot bear the idea of you going to Eton Lodge, it won't do Jack dear. I should be perfectly miserable knowing you were there. Why don't you ask your Uncle John if you could go there, I don't blame you for wanting to leave home, but do go where you will have a little comfort, I believe your Uncle would only be too pleased to have you. Do think better of it dear, I don't want you to go to Eton Lodge without me.

How did you enjoy the pantomime, I hope you felt better for it. Jack dear, do cheer up, people will put it down to me, that you have lost your good spirits, and it isn't so is it dearie? Reg goes back to school tomorrow, we shall not be sorry. I should certainly ask Joe about being best man, to see what he

It was not surprising that Beatrice did not want Jack to go to live in Eton Lodge without her. Although her suggestion that he should live with Uncle John was a good one it would have been likely to have upset Jack's mother even more. His motives would have been sure to be misinterpreted, since everyone in the family was always conscious of the need to 'keep in' with Uncle John.

says, I hope he will though I must talk the matter over about Alice when we meet, I am rather undecided about it at present, but I will think it over.

Well dear write me a nice long letter and a cheery one. I shall be glad to know you feel better. Au revoir darling, heaps of love and oceans of kisses

Yours ever Beatie

✦✦✦✦✦✦

Woodcock St. Jan 20 1899

My own darling Beatie

I was so glad to receive your dear letter yesterday morning, but so grieved that I had not time to write you a proper letter last night. We are very anxious to have the Balance Sheet out, as early as possible, and consequently I have been having a very worrying time during the whole of this week, with the Accountants, and I think I shall polish them off today. I worked at home last Saturday night and Sunday and this is the second or third morning, this week that I have come down on the first train. I was obliged to come on it this morning, and now I have done what is absolutely necessary, before breakfast, am taking the opportunity to write to you dearie, for I don't suppose there will be another today, when once the ball begins rolling. What a big day you must have had on Tuesday. I hope you are not feeling knocked up after it, but I suppose you would willingly put up with it, if you were, after all the nice things you must have got. I do hope dearie, you are better of that Rheumatism, for I cannot bear to think of you being in such pain. Look after yourself darling, and mind and keep wearing your woollen underclothing. Have you been going without again. I shall have to see for myself, when I come up on the 28th.

Now dearie, since you can't resign yourself to the idea of my going to live in "Eton Lodge", before we are married, I must go on as I am and bear it; for if such a thing came about, as I went to live with Uncle John, for a time, the fat would be in the fire, I know. Joe seems to be as, well I don't know what to call it, jealous I think, of me as ever he can, and talks to me in such a style, as if he seems to want to make me feel that I have nothing but trouble before me in the future. But never mind, dearie, I don't despair, "Let 'em all come," and let them all do their best, and their worst if they like. We can't expect life to be all sunshine but whatever comes, we shall get through it all, alright, together I know darling. I think Uncle John would be pleased for me to go there, but it would not do, for I know, at the present, Joe and my Mother are so embittered against me, that if I only go to Uncle's on business they think I have been there trying to make trouble, and do them harm. Goodness knows, I don't want to make trouble, there is enough already, and it is not to my interest to always parade it in front of Uncle, for I don't want him to get disgusted, and leave the business. If he did I am afraid it would be a bad thing for me. As long as he remains in it, I know I shall be alright, but I feel that my Mother and Joe would not mind doing anything they could to upset me altogether, as far as Joe is concerned he has as good as told me so. But it is no use meeting trouble half way, but when it does come I think we can stand up against it.

Alice, the Hughes' servant at Linwood Lodge, had observed the goings on and disruptions in the family for some time and with some irritation. Although already engaged to be married and therefore unlikely to be able to work for Jack and Beatrice for more than two years, she was likely to welcome the change.

Dr. Jaeger's woollen underwear was not proving very effective for Beatrice as she was still suffering great pain from her rheumatism. Needless to say, Jack looked forward to checking for himself that she was still wearing it, on his next visit to see her.

The private and working lives of the Hughes family, all living together and working for the business, were so intertwined that jealousy, mistrust and insecurity was inevitable as a result of the new relationships and developments of the past months.

*An advertisement for the Midland Cycle
and Motor Show which was held at
Bingley Hall – the large exhibition centre
in Birmingham. (O)*

*David was to take up the post of Staff
Officer, Royal Marines Depot, Walmer,
near Deal in Kent. It was there also that
he died in 1920, during a return visit,
then as Major-General Sir David
Mercer, K.C.B.*

The Pantomime was pretty good the other night, but of course it is a small place, a small stage, and a small company. I hope the "Edgar" is getting along alright and that David will reach home safely. I shall be looking forward to seeing him, my second visit from now. Will he and Kitty be able to be at our wedding now, I wonder. I hope so. The B'ham Cycle Show opened yesterday, at Bingley Hall, and remains open until the 28th. I shall be here until about 8 o'clock tonight, and then I am going to the Show. Now dearie, for the present, Au revoir, heaps of love and kisses,

your own devoted

Jack

◇◇◇◇◇◇◇

"Roselea", Jan 20th 1899

My darling Jack

I have just got your second letter and delighted I was to get it. Of course I was a little disappointed this morning as I was so looking out for it. I am sorry you are working so hard, is it quite necessary, and do you know how much you are likely to have for your share? I cannot make out why Joe and your Mother think you have nothing but trouble before you, unless they mean to do you harm, for I am sure we shall be alright together, what say you dear? If your Uncle ever talks of resigning again, I should let him know then how you have been treated and ask him to stay on, if only for your sake, for surely he could not do better with his money. They are a set of brutes, but take no notice dear, the time is slipping by, a month less to wait before I am your wife, and I will cheer you up, or at least try to, do you think I shall succeed darling? Do you think you would have had all this to put with, if you had not been engaged to me, I feel so honoured, to know you are putting up with all this for poor little me. Never mind dear, I will do all in my power to make up for it. My rheumatism is much better, in fact almost well. Ma has rubbed it every night with embrocation. No dear I am not quite so silly as to leave all my woollen thing off they are still all on, as you can see if you like, when you come. Another week, oh dear, I am so pining for you, I really cannot be so long without you again, don't do it dear, it is awful. I went to Morris' for the day on wednesday, and did a lot more shopping. I have such a lot of things in my bottom box (not drawer) I hardly know what to do with them, but we can do with them can't we? I brought my 2 pictures home from being framed, the print ("disappointment") I have had done in dark oak, the other is a little one I did myself, I think they both look very nice. I don't know whether David will be at our wedding or not. We cannot quite make out whether he intends going to America or not. I must tell you about it when you come. Don't forget to let me know what train you are coming by next saturday. I have not heard from Ida yet, I wish she would write and let me know if she likes the suggestion for the bridesmaids, the others are waiting to know, for there is a great bargain at Jones & Higgins (drapers) in chiffon, which they want sashes of, and would like to get that now at least. Granny sends her love, she says she is very sorry for you, but you must buck up and not worry. Don't do that dear, for there won't be any of you left, if you get much thinner, then what should I do?

Ernie and Laura have gone to the theatre tonight to see Alexander in the *The Ambassador*, she goes back on monday so you bet, they are making the best of their time. I hope you will enjoy the Cycle Show tonight but don't burn the candle at both ends. Surely you are not obliged to go to the Works so early in the morning. Has Alice said any more to you about coming to live with us?

Well dear, I have given you an epistle tonight, I hope you will send me a nice long letter in return and I hope to hear better news and to know things are going on a little smoother. When does Jennie move? Accept oceans of kisses and you know you have all my love,

Yours, ever
Beatie

An advertisement for the 1899 winter sale at Jones and Higgins, to which Beatrice went for her bridesmaids' chiffon. (K)

Linwood Lodge, Jan 22nd 1899

My own darling Beatie

It was indeed quite a pleasant surprise to me to receive your dear letter yesterday morning, for I hardly expected to hear until today. I got your letter about 11.30. I am so glad dearie, to know that you are better of that horrid Rheumatism. I expect it is the damp weather we have been having lately, which has brought it out. I do wish I were with you today dearie, for I have been so down in the dumps, and want you so badly. It has become quite the regular thing for that devil Phelps to come here on a Saturday. He was here again yesterday. I was at the Works until about 3.30, and then took the train at 4.15 to Wylde Green. It was an awful day raining and blowing a gale. We had some Billiards and I came home on the last train. They wanted me to stay very badly and I wish now I had, for as I came up the road from the Station I met Phelps and have done nothing but think of him since. It does prey on my mind. It gave me quite a turn, when I saw him coming down the road, and I felt I could have done anything to him. He will be quite big here I suppose tomorrow, it is the dinner party you know, for all those who took part in the Dramatic Entertainment. What a lovely stall, for honouring him, eh? I have been asked to go to The Empire, and think I shall do so, for I cannot come here and mix up with him and there are none of the people who are friends of mine. I shall never be able to stay here for nearly five months, it would wear me out I am sure, for I have never felt in such a state all my life. Uncle knows all about it, and he knows and in fact has told me that I must look out for myself, as he feels Joe and my Mother will try and do me harm, and work me out of the business. He is quite alive to that and so am I. We shall be alright together dearie, I know, if we have fair play; and if we don't have fair play I suppose we must make the best of it, and we can do that for when I have got you I shan't care for anybody. Uncle will be a friend to us I know.

I did not go to Church today for I was so tired that I did not get up until 12.30, and I have had such a fit of the blues all day. I have not been out at all yet today, so when I have finished this shall walk up to post, and on as far as Uncle's. You are right I have had a big week of it this week, but I am so anxious to know what my share of the profits is, if any, that I have not spared a moment and have worked as hard as I could, to get our Stock Book finished.

An illustration by Walter Wilson R.I. Billiards with the Harrops at Wylde Green was a pleasurable relaxation for Jack at weekends and a means of escape from Linwood Lodge. (B)

An engraving of Bingley Hall which was erected in 1850, for the cost of £6000. It boasted an exhibition area of "Width within walls 212 ft., Depth 224 ft., 10 entrance doors". Bingley Hall in Birmingham town centre is still used as an exhibition hall today. (F)

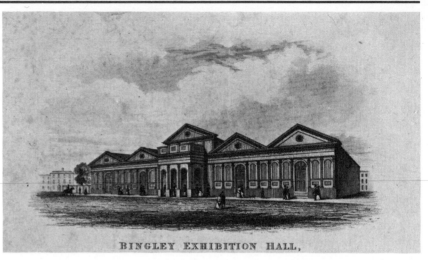

BINGLEY EXHIBITION HALL,

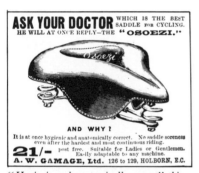

"Hygienic and anatomically correct" this saddle would have satisfied the need of the "many recruits to cycling often greatly discouraged from persevering in this pastime" owing to discomfort. (B)

The Cycle Show was very slow, not so many exhibitors as previously and very few people in. A very good band playing and nobody to listen to it. Alice has not said anything further to me, about coming to live with us. We must have a talk about that when I come up. Shan't we have a lot to talk about. Jennie is moving at end of March I believe. Ida has written you a short note, and as we have only one stamp, I am enclosing it with mine. Next Friday is the Yeomanry Ball, Joe and my Mother are going, I believe. I am *not*. Please give a little of my love to everybody, that is, as much as you can spare, and tell them I shall be with you next Saturday, all that is left of me. Fancy poor old Ernie got to lose his dear Laura, after today. They have had a good long time though haven't they. I suppose I must try to cheer up and make the best of it, but it wants a lot of doing. I am glad there is only a week between us now, for then I shall be happy with you my dearie.

It is perfect misery to be here. Don't worry about me darling. I expect I shall live through it. Heaps of love and ever so many of our sweet kisses,

Ever your own devoted

Jack

"Roselea", Jan 23rd 1899

Ida's silence in reply to Beatrice's letter to her request for arrangements for her bridesmaid's dress was now explained. This was yet another attempt by Jack's mother to sabotage their wedding arrangements.

My own darling Jack

Your letter has so worried me, do try and buck up, and I am beginning to think you make too much of it you know what I mean dear, don't take any notice of it. Of course, as far as Phelps going up to Linwood Lodge, your Mother has every right to have him and of course marry who she likes, so I don't see the good of you kicking against it, it won't alter matters and only makes things look blacker to you, so constantly giving way to your feelings. Now this morning I have had another knife thrust in Ida's letter. Your Mother is sending Ida to Brussels to school and of course she chooses

April as the time, so that she will be unable to be my bridesmaid. Oh, I do feel enraged, she is a beast. I never wish to see nor hear from her again and I now know if she felt inclined to speak to me I could not, for her behaviour to me is beyond a joke. What difference would it really make if Ida went to school the next term? I am just off up to the wholesale to buy our house linen etc. but really I don't seem as if I had got heart enough for it, these goings on are truly awful, nothing to help brighten one.

I went to Church yesterday morning all on my own, a new window was dedicated and an appropriate sermon preached. Isn't this weather awful? it has been blowing a terrific gale for the last week and raining continuously. We had quite a little crowd here yesterday. Jim and May were here, Arthur Salter, Ted and Nellie and the two kiddies, they are getting little monkeys, you know I haven't seen them for some time, young Leo said to me, "I am very angry with you". I asked him why? he replied, "Because you are going away". We had a letter from David this morning, he says why not have the wedding earlier, and then he could be here. I wish we could and then Ida could have no excuse. Really, I shall be truly thankful when all is over and we are settled in Eton Lodge, and I know you will be won't you dear? This continual rubbing up the wrong way sort of thing, really makes me feel quite ill. Well dearie, au revoir, write me a nice cheery letter, I sorely need it. How I am looking for saturday, but the worst of it is it will so soon be over.

your own Beatie

Linwood Lodge, Gravelly Hill. Jan 24th 1899

My own darling Beatie

I received your dear letter this morning, and am so sorry my last letter put you about so much, but you can't tell how I felt on Sunday. It was something awful, but I am going to try and act on your good advice and see if I can manage to take no notice of it all. Of course I have nothing to say to my Mother about it now, for she never speaks to me, and even if she did I should not mention that matter, but what I can't get over is the manner in which she treats me, and your dear self, just because I told her what I thought, when the matter first came about. But there it is no use to go over all that again. What a nice thing, for a Mother though to shirk her responsibility and send her young daughter away to school, because she can't awhile to look after her. Another thing I know she is spiteful enough to try and get her away so that she shall not take part at our Wedding. How horrible of her; Ida tells me tonight that they will allow her to leave her present school at Easter, so of course that means I suppose that she will go to Brussels in April. Won't it be a piece of petty spite, if my Mother does that. You are quite right darling, it really seems as if there is nothing to brighten one, but we must cheer up and laugh at it all. You know nothing can ever alter my love for you darling, and we love each other so perfectly that we shall be able to get over any trouble. I am glad you have heard again from David, and need hardly tell you that I quite like his suggestion of the wedding taking place before June, and I know you will too

For Ida to be sent to school in Brussels was an exciting venture at the age of fifteen, although she did not fully realize the motives for it. She was disappointed at not being able to be a bridesmaid but it was an experience that was to effect her future considerably.

Jack was now in a more philosophical mood despite the worsening situation at home and at the Works. An additional reason for Ida to be sent abroad to school was, as Jack realized, that this would make things easier for the new life their mother was planning for herself.

A photograph of Joe Hughes taken as a younger man. He was engaged to be married at the age of twenty-two when Jack would have been only eighteen. Joe had since become a rather aimless figure and showed his jealousy for Jack and his own insecurity by cruelly siding with his mother against Jack. (M)

dearie, but what would your dear old Pa and Ma think about it. If they would approve of it, we could get our house done and get married before March was out, or even in April, before Ida went away.

Wouldn't that be fine. We must talk it all over with your Pa and Ma when I come up and I do hope we shall be able to bring them to see things in the same light as we do. They will no doubt think I am very unreasonable, to wish to take you from them as they would think so soon, but here I am, always feeling so miserable, and you the dear girl who is going to make me so happy, waiting to come to me. I have asked Joe if he will be the best man for me, and told him I would like him to. He says he will be very pleased to. How gracious of him, don't you think. Fancy he was engaged about ten years ago, and I had never dreamt of such a thing myself, and now here he is drifting about like a ship without a rudder, and going to be best man for me. Rather good isn't it. What a big family you must have been on Sunday. I am so sorry dearie you have got into Leo's bad books, that is rather serious. I hope he won't take a dislike to me again. The weather here has improved, it is quite nice and frosty and such a lovely night. I shall enjoy the walk up to the village to post this. You will notice I am writing from home tonight, of course you understand Tuesday is the night out for my Mother, so it is nice and quiet here at present. I saw the Accountant today, and he promises to let me know, how the Balance Sheet comes out before the end of the week. I told him I was very anxious to know by Friday at latest. I do hope there will be a decent sum for me to pick up, for we can do with it, eh? I hope you had a fine day dearie, for your shopping yesterday. Please give a little of my love to your Pa and Ma and Granny. Sympathise with Ernie for me, he will miss his dear Laura. Cheer up dearie, for "now we shan't be long" it quite does me good to feel Saturday is so near. "Au revoir". Heaps of kisses and all my love,

Your own devoted Jack

❖❖❖❖❖❖

"Roselea", Jan 25th 1899

My own darling Jack

Many thanks for your nice letter it has done me ever so much good to feel that you will try to cheer up. I am dead tired, all my things came this morning so I have been unpacking them and they were so heavy to move about. Ma and Pa have gone to Lewcock's wedding, haven't they got a lovely day. I only hope we get as good. I wish it was ours don't you dear, but there I know you do. Wouldn't it be lovely if we could be married before June. I really don't think I could be ready by March, but by the middle of April I could. I really think if you do want it sooner, say April, my people could be persuaded if you put it nicely to them, for I hinted it to Ma this morning and she did not say anything, what is there to wait for dear? We have got the house and it could soon be done up and we should not be long getting the furniture. However we must have a good talk about it when we meet, which will not be long now, will it dear? My won't our tongues go eh?

I have got a lovely lot of house linen dear, sheets, pillow cases, tablecloths,

For Jack and Beatrice to bring the wedding earlier to April would certainly mean a lot of work and panic at 'Roselea', in order to have everything for such a large wedding prepared in time.

serviettes, tray cloths, glass cloths, toilet covers, quilts, etc. and I also got a piece of muslin to make curtains frilled, and so cheap, of course dear that is your department but it was so much cheaper than we could have bought in the retail, that I think it was wise to get it now.

I shall have plenty of work now, shan't I darling? I do feel so put out about Ida going to school, before the wedding. I feel it is done out of spite but if we could be married by April before she went, it would be lovely. Granny sends her love, supposes you are love sick, are you dear? I had such a horrible dream about you dear last night, it made me so miserable for a time, I must tell you about it on saturday.

Ernie has got such a long face he does so miss his Laura, I tell him what about me? but he says he does not see Laura for about 3 months. Well dearie, I am looking forward to seeing you on saturday, won't we have a time? Lots of love

Yours ever

Beatie

This is what I saw last night, was it you?

A postcard from a lovesick lady — expressing perhaps the sentiments and fears resulting from Beatrice's dream about Jack the previous night. (E)

❖❖❖❖❖❖

Woodcock St. B'ham. Jan 26th 1899

My own darling Beatie

Here we are again. I was so glad to get your dear letter this morning and know that you are feeling so much brighter. I am I can tell you. I suppose it is the nearing of Saturday that accounts for it, although I can tell you I am not letting these things here trouble me quite so much. The fact is I had worked myself into a very low way, but I am going now to try and not care so much about what they all do and say.

I am glad your Ma and Pa had such a nice day for the Wedding, and like your dear self wish it had been ours, but we must be patient, eh dearie, for we shan't be very long now, although the weeks certainly do seem to pass very slowly. Now what do you think? Uncle John came to the office this morning, and told me he was going up to London on Monday and stay until Thursday. I took the liberty of telling him that you would all be very pleased to see him down at "Roselea". He thinks of coming up by the 2.10, Arr. Euston 4.40 pm, and I suggested that after driving to his Hotel and making arrangements he should come down to "Roselea" for a few hours and stay until the early train Tuesday instead of returning Monday night.

I hope I have not exceeded my sphere in any way, I think not. He told me he would come in tomorrow and tell me more about it then, but he is such a queer customer you know, that we must not be surprised if he does not come but I do hope he will myself. It does seem so hard doesn't it to think no one from my friends has yet been to see you and your Pa and Ma and say something nice about our engagement, but there never mind. I do hope he will come to "Roselea", and then your Pa and he and I can have a good long talk about our Wedding taking place earlier, I do hope we can have it in April before Ida goes away, so as to get even with my Mother on that point, for I know she is doing her utmost to disappoint us. My word, you have got a lot of nice things for *our* house. I wish I knew when you were coming down to choose the papers,

Both Uncle John and Joe travelled to London quite frequently on business and though Joe previously visited 'Roselea', neither of them had called in to see Beatrice's family since their engagement.

The news from the accountants was anxiously awaited by Jack as it would determine his financial status. This was critical for Jack if he was to be able to marry and meet all the additional expenses marriage would commit him to.

etc. for I am longing to see the work started on, and get it finished, and find ourselves settled down there. Give my love to Granny and thank her for her message. I hope that dream was not quite so horrible, as you would have one think, but tell me all about it when I come, if it is not too bad.

I do hope to hear from those Accountants tomorrow, but in any case shall hear before I leave on Saturday. It is Harrison's Concert next Monday. Joe and Mother and Phelps are going, how nice, don't you think? I don't know what Joe can be thinking of to take that on. Well dearie pray excuse me further tonight, it is now 8.30 and unfortunately I have arranged to meet some gentlemen at the Cycle Show at that time, so must now be off as I am already late. All my love dearie, and heaps of kisses wishing that tomorrow were Saturday instead of only Friday.

Cheer up dearie, I am doing so.

Your own devoted

Jack

Jack's large gold pocket watch which Beatrice kept and which has been handed down through her family, kept in the box in which it was originally bought. (A)

"Roselea", Jan 27th 1899

My darling Jack

Just fancy dear, I am going to see you tomorrow, it has come at at last, how I am longing for you, it seems months since we were together last, I only hope the next few months will go a little quicker. I was glad to read you had asked your Uncle to come and see us and Ma and Pa will be delighted to make his acquaintance. I have been so busy all the morning. I have made 25 towels, so I have not been idle have I? There is a cupboard full of work for me now, I am delighted with all my linen and I am sure you will be, everything is of the best and I have not been stinted at all. I shall not be able to meet your dearie tomorrow as I shall be too busy. Ma and Pa had a very good time at Lewcock's wedding, they had a full choral service and the bells rung and I don't know what. They were awfully lucky, they had 200 wedding presents. Isn't this weather lovely, but awfully cold. I am sorry not to be able to send you a time card, I enquired for one at Streatham the other day, and they were out of them, but I asked both Reg and Ernie to get me one and of course they forgot it, but no doubt you will manage alright.

What a sneak that Joe is, just fancy he going with Phelps, is Phelps going to the Yeomanry tonight? What Hotel does your Uncle usually stay at? Don't forget he can come to Streatham from Ludgate Hill as well as London Bridge. Well dear excuse a short letter this time, but I must tell you all I have to tell when I see you. Ma says it is a pity your Uncle was not coming to London tomorrow and then he could have come to the dinner party tomorrow. Accept oceans of kisses and all my love

Yours ever

Beatie

So Much To Be Done

FEBRUARY & MARCH

News of Jack's entitlement to the company profits reveals a cunning scheme and a disappointing amount with which to start a marriage. Jack is determined he can stay no longer at home. An earlier wedding date of April is finally agreed. Now there is so much to be done to get ready in time but Mrs. Hughes manages to marry her Phelps before them.

Woodstock St. B'ham. Feb 1st 1899

My own darling Beatie

I have just finished dinner, so am now stealing a few minutes to write to my dearie. I got down here this morning at 7.15, and have been hard at work ever since and shall have all my work cut out to manage to to get to Lodge today, but I must go this month, as I missed last meeting, and if I were to be away today, am afraid they would begin to think something was wrong.

Of course dearie, the first thing I got when I reached home last night was an official wigging from Joe, for staying away yesterday, but I didn't take very much notice of that. I know very well I ought to have come home, first train Tuesday morning, but then I felt on Monday that I could not do that, and then on Monday night I had such a poor night and felt so miserable on Tuesday morning, that I really could not leave you. I quite expected to be pulled over the coals for it, but then I don't care for that a bit. What a time we had, didn't we darling, and how soon it is all passed away. I think I must come and see you again before a month as suggested though, for I don't think I can wait.

Joe has just come down into the office and as he sees I am writing, is trying to make a bother so I have adjourned upstairs. Uncle John did not come to London at all, as expected. He caught a bit of a cold, and the weather frightened him. It didn't take him long to catch the cold, for I saw him on Friday night at his house, and he seemed alright then. I have not yet seen him since I came back, for he has not been to the Office today. Joe has not yet told me as to what my share of the Profits will be, and I am not going to ask him, as I feel there would only be a bother, but I shall get to know for myself, and tell you in my next. I have not yet seen Ida, as she had gone to bed when I reached home last night and I left before any one else got up this morning. I had a chat to Alice last night, and feel sure that she will like to come to us when we are ready. I wish we were ready now, but we are, so far as we are concerned personally, aren't we dearie? I shall have to think over that letter I am going

Jack wearing his masonic regalia. He was initiated in Lechmere Volunteer Lodge, No. 1874 in October 1895. He became Master in 1907 and Charity Steward in 1911. (M)

Jack had hoped to hear from the accountants before he left for London but it seems he was the last to have the news.

Jack and Beatrice had decided over their weekend together that they would seek Mr. Mercer's permission to marry earlier than originally planned. It was going to need a tactful and careful letter from Jack to get the permission they wanted.

to write to your Pa, for if I paint the picture of my present troubles and worries too black, it may frighten him and make him hesitate about letting you come to me at all. Still I think I shall have judgement enough for that. I know your Pa will miss you very much darling, when you come to me and does not want to lose you any sooner than he can help; but still I am missing you now, and waiting for you to come, and as you are quite as anxious dearie to come to me, I am sure we cannot wait until June. Well darling, I really have not time for any more today. I hope you are feeling first rate, and will continue so. Cheer up, and be as bright as ever you can. I am going to be. Heaps of love and kisses for your own dear self, and love to Pa and Ma and Granny.

Your own devoted

Jack

"Roselea", Feb 2nd 1899

My own darling Jack

How I was longing for your dear letter this morning, for I have been so awfully dull since I left you dear, time goes so slowly without you, but does not it go all too quickly when we are together? I quite expected that Joe would be rusty about you not going back earlier, but never mind dear, you can put up with that can't you? I had a long talk with Ma yesterday about our marriage taking place earlier she is not half bad about it, she said she would rather that it had taken place as first arranged, but of course the present circumstances alter cases. I asked her if she would talk it over with Pa, she said she would, but she felt sure he would object, however I do hope he will not.

I went over to Norwood to see Mrs. Sutton with Ma, she has met your Mother here and she has not seen me since my engagement. She said she supposed Mrs. Hughes was delighted and she was so surprised when I told her how she was behaving. She said why not get married at once, and everybody is of the same opinion. Be sure and write a nice letter to Pa, he may come round, oh, I do so hope it will be alright. It is Ma's at home day today. I do hate it for I don't feel as if I could be very entertaining. I am going to be busy with my needlework. I must buck up and get my things done in case we want them in April. There are lots of things to settle when we know about the date, for instance, my pew rent is due, and I am waiting to see if I am to give notice to leave in the March or June quarter, then I must see to getting my dresses made if it is in April etc, etc, so something must be said one way or another. Of course dear I shall be delighted if you come on saturday week and then in case things are settled I think if I come to Jennie's I had better come alone and you bring me back, what do you think? Give Ida a hint about the probability of our wedding being earlier and see what your Mother says to that. I expect she will make some excuse even then. How did you enjoy your Lodge Meeting. I hope you had an enjoyable evening. Well dear au revoir, accept oceans of kisses, some of the real good old sort and all my love

For Beatrice, marrying Jack did not only mean a busy time preparing for the wedding itself but also all that was involved in leaving Streatham in order to go to live in Birmingham. (A)

Yours most devotedly Beatie

Woodcock St. B'ham. Feb 3rd 1899

My own darling Beatie

I was so glad to receive your dear letter this morning and was awaiting it most anxiously. It does seem quite a long time, to me, since I left you dearie, but you must try and cheer up, and not get dull, for it won't be long until Feb 11th, and I must really come and see you then. I am glad darling, that you have been talking to your Ma, about our Wedding taking place in April, and that she seems more to favour the idea. I will do my very best you may be sure when writing to your Pa, to put the matter in such a way, as to cause him to give us his approval. I am trying to arrange for a sweep to go to "Eton Lodge" tomorrow, to sweep all the chimneys, and next week shall start having some fires in to keep the place dry. I thought of seeing the Painter early next week, and asking him how long he will take over the work, when I give him the order, so that I shall know how much time we have got; and then when I come up next week, I can arrange about you coming down to select the papers and furniture. It was a great surprise to Mrs. Sutton, I have no doubt, when she heard of my Mother's conduct towards you, and not very pleasant for you to have to tell people of. Not at all complimentary to you, her behaviour; but then dearie, any one who knows you, knows, that if she were honest in her opinion she cannot help but admire you, and ought to be proud of you. Never mind dearie, I am proud of you and of your dear love, you know all about that, don't you darling? I am going up to Nin's tonight, and shall speak to her about our wanting to be married earlier, and ask when it would be most convenient for you to come down. I think myself, that as far as we, personally, are concerned it would be best for you to come back with me on Monday the 13th. However I will let you know all about that later. I shall tell Ida tonight, if I see her, about our idea of April, and shall be very anxious then, to hear what my Mother's next move will be.

Now for a bit of business, over which I feel very sore. I told you dearie you should know, in my lext letter, as to what was my share in the profits. Well dearie, according to the general agreement, which we will call it, I am entitled to £333=0=0, and of course this will be paid over to me by the firm; but according to that agreement of my Mother's I have to refund to her between £216 and £217, leaving for myself only a sum of between £116 and 117. Of course Uncle John will think that I have had the full amount for myself and I shall appear in a false position to him. Of course my Mother is supposed to receive the same amount from Joe, and if she does, she will be about £433 better off than Uncle, on the year's trading. Of course the idea of the agreement, originally, was, that Joe and I should do this in order to equalise benefits in a measure, with Jennie, and Frank and Ida, by allowing my Mother to save money for them. Of course on the face of it that looks alright, but with all these later developments, such as the Phelps affair, and Joe's general bearing towards myself, it all rather tends to shake one's confidence. Again it is all very well to share, what you happen to get, with others, but when it comes to giving £217 nearly, out of £333, I think it is very much off. However there it is, that is the agreement; so we can't get past it, all I can say is, that when this year is out, there will have to be something very different to suit me. I may say that our Balance Sheet came out much better than antici-

For Jack, marrying Beatrice would be his salvation, and he did not mind how busy he would be to get the house ready in time for an earlier wedding.

A marble tablet in Erdington Parish Church, dedicated to Jack's father by Uncle John, his brother. It includes the words: "His kindness of disposition endeared him to his family and his honesty of character inspired universal esteem". The Hughes family moved from Castle Bromwich, which also has a stained glass window in the church dedicated to him by his wife, because he found the uphill walk from the station too much for his weak heart. (T)

A photograph of Joe Hughes, Jack's father. For Jack it was a tragedy that his dear father was not alive at this time, as he would never have allowed such an unfair agreement to have been signed for the share his sons had in the business profits. (T)

pated, and that if our profits had been only two thirds of what they were, I should have had exactly the same for myself as now; for you see where my Mother gets the pull, is that over a certain amount she takes her own share, and ours as well. She has been so hard on us though. I am going to study this agreement, to see if there is not some way of getting past it. Joe was very hard on me, in the first instance, and I must say that I signed the agreement under very great pressure. He is not overpleased with it now. Never mind dearie, it is no use to worry over spilt milk, but doesn't it shew you what a cunning devil she is, and how deep she is. I have not told Uncle about it, and think that perhaps it would be best not to, for I think, if he knew, he would chuck up the whole bag of tricks, and a nice thing that would be for me. I went up to Uncle's last night, and he tells me he is coming up to London on Monday next, and returning Thursday. I have told him he must come down to Streatham one day.

We had rather a small meeting at Lodge on Wednesday, and I was very disappointed myself that I was late getting there, as I was so busy. I came down on the 6.52 this morning, and it was bitter cold, such a sharp frost. Well dearie for the present "Au Revoir" heaps of kisses and all my love *ever your own devoted Jack*

◇◇◇◇◇◇

"Roselea", Feb 4th 1899

Beatrice certainly had little reason to feel at all charitable towards Jack's mother and must have found her greed incomprehensible compared with the generosity of her own parents.

My own darling Jack

I don't seem as if I could throw off this awful fit of depression I have on me, and then getting your letter this morning has made me feel worse than ever. The more I think of your Mother the less I think of her, how

A view of Thrale Road from the corner of Penwortham Road, looking north west where 'Roselea' still stands, some yards along on the right hand side of the road. (D)

she can be so mean as to take that money from you I cannot think and you her son too. What a greedy thing she is, to want to cut you down like that, ah well, it strikes me it won't do her much good for all her cunning. But really I think if it was me, I should feel inclined to tell your Uncle for he must keep to his agreement for another year, and surely he would stick by you. Why not keep the whole amount of the cheque she couldn't make you give it her, for it would be exposing herself. I do feel indignant about it. We went to Lewcock's yesterday to see the presents, they have got a lovely lot, I only hope we get as many, but they had such a crocky lot of people there, I could hardly help laughing at some of them. I told Mrs. Morris how much we wanted to go to Jersey, she says we ought to go, it is so lovely, and she says we could go to Southampton for the night and cross over by the following night's boat. I do hope Pa will give in, but I am not at all hopeful. Ma was talking to him again about it and he says we have made our arrangements to be married in June and we must abide by it, but I am hoping that your letter will have some effect, do it nicely dearie, for I am so longing to come and try to cheer you up and then when you are yourself again, I shall be so happy. If you come next saturday, I think it would be rather soon for me to come back with you to choose the furniture, of course it would not be for the papers. Why don't you wait until the following saturday Feb 18th and then you need not go back until monday evening. Of course dear, don't think for one minute that I don't want you to come, for you know different, don't you dear? but it seems such a pity to come so far and have to go back by the early train on monday. However it is for you to decide but I don't think I had better come back with you if you do, but wait until the week following that will be sat 18th. I have got the spoons from the Stores, they are nice, I feel sure you will like them. I shall be looking out for your dear letter on monday also Pa's copy, don't forget dear. Aimèe has just written to say she may come over tomorrow. Cheer up darling and accept oceans of kisses

Yours ever
Beatie

◇◇◇◇◇◇◇

Copy   Linwood Lodge, Gravelly Hill. Feb 5th 1899

My dear Mr Mercer

    You will remember that when I was last at "Roselea", I hinted to you that Beatie and I would much like our Wedding to take place in April, instead of June, as originally intended. I have been thinking over this matter, all the week, and have now decided to write and ask if you will please give your consent to this. I quite know and feel that in this I am asking much of you, for it must surely be a great trial for you and your dear wife, to lose your only daughter, one who has always been so loving and thoughtful for you; and I know you will not wish her to leave you any earlier than you can help. But be assured that I will always be good and kind to dear Beatie, for I do love her so.

    Here am I with absolutely no comfort at home, for my Mother seems so bitter against me, and my dear Beatie, who is going to make me so happy is as anxious to come to me, as I am longing for her to come. For another reason, we

For Jack to be able to retain only £116 from his total share of £333 from the annual profits of the business was poor indeed. As during many crisis points, Beatrice suggested Uncle John as the solution and confidant.

It was unlike Beatrice to try to persuade Jack to delay his next visit – it was usually the opposite.

Another difficult letter that Jack had to write – this time in desperation. Jack laboriously copied it all out again for Beatrice so that she would be able to see what he wrote to her father. It did not seem too hopeful that Mr. Mercer would give the permission he requested.

are anxious to be married in April, so that my sister Ida may be one of the Bridesmaids, for my Mother is sending her to Brussels to School, end of April, so that she may not be at our Wedding in June.

I have the house, and all the arrangements are made for the necessary work to be done and if Beatie could now come down and stay with my sister Mrs. Hawkes for a time, and select the papers etc. it could be proceeded with at once. We could also at the same time, purchase our furniture etc.

I do sincerely hope that Mrs. Mercer and yourself, will see your way to grant what I ask, and that when June comes round, instead of me coming to claim my Bride, my dear Beatie and I may be honoured with a visit from yourself and Mrs. Mercer, to see us in our new home, where we shall be so happy together.

With my best love to you all,

I think of coming up next Saturday

Ever your own devoted

Jack

David Dixon Mercer, Beatrice's father, in his masonic regalia as Grand Pursuivant in 1890. He was initiated in the Sphinx Lodge No. 1392 of which he became Master in 1889, as well as holding several other Grand Ranks and honoured positions. (M)

Linwood Lodge, Feb 5th 1899

My own darling Beatie

Pray excuse the pencil but I have such a brute of a pen, that after writing the letter to your dear Pa, and the copy for yourself which I enclose herewith, I cannot really use it any longer. Well dearie I went up to Wylde Green yesterday evening, and stayed the night, and I walked down home this morning.

I received your dear letter, but darling I am grieved to know that you are feeling so depressed. Do try and cheer up dearie, or you will make yourself quite ill. Don't worry darling over my Mother and that sharing of the profits business. It is too bad, but then we can't alter it. I half wish I had not told you all of it, but then dear you know I tell you everything, don't I. When you are writing to Jennie or Ida please don't say anything about that business at all. I think it would be better not.

I am glad you all managed the journey down to Lewcock's alright. I don't know dearie what you will think of my letter to your Pa, whether you will think I have done it alright or not; but then I have tried to express to him, my feelings on the matter, and oh I do hope it will have the desired effect. I hope you will feel first class in the morning dearie, and be down to Breakfast; and that your Pa will have had a good night and be feeling in a very good humour. He will surely give way, at least I hope so sincerely. Won't it be jolly, Jersey on our Honeymoon in April. I should have liked it on Thursday the 20th, Ida's Birthday, but really as far as business is concerned, Wednesday the 12th would be most convenient, (if you were fixed up for that date dearie). I met the painter in the Village this morning, and he says he would not be much above a week doing the work. So if we reckon a fortnight, as I said at first, I think that will be ample. He gave me the names of two firms in town, and says we can go there to either of them, any time as soon as we are ready, and choose our papers. They are the two best houses and he deals with both of them. I will let you know later about whether I come Saturday the 11th or 18th, but at present I feel I

The geniality for which Mr. Mercer was known in his official positions was needed now by Jack in his attitude towards their hurried marriage. Jack was by this time more optimistic.

must come on the 11th. I will see Jennie soon, and then let you know definitely. I am glad darling to know you have received the spoons. I shall be sure to like them. I do wish we were together this afternoon dearie, we shouldn't need much fire should we. By the way, there is snow on the ground here, we had a lot down yesterday. I met Uncle John and his nurse this morning. He asked me to go up this afternoon, so I am going now. He was to have come up to London tomorrow, but I am much afraid that this weather will put him off it. I shall try to persuade him to go, and to have a run down to "Roselea". I will let you know if he is coming. Phelps will soon be leaving the Works, so I suppose he will then be at Linwood Lodge more than ever.

Oh I must get away from here I can't bear it simply. I do hope your Pa will do as we wish, and that we may be married and happy together in April. Won't it be awful if we have to wait till June.

Well dearie cheer up and throw off that depression, just be as bright as ever you can. Au revoir. All my love and heaps of kisses,

*Yours ever
Jack*

Jack was still determined to persuade one member of his family to visit the Mercers at 'Roselea', but the chances of Uncle John travelling to London diminished with the arrival of the snow.

❖❖❖❖❖❖

"Roselea", Feb 6th 1899

My own darling Jack

Your letter was brought up to me in bed, where I have been since saturday. I think I took a chill at the Lewcock's for I have not been well since, all day yesterday I was very bad and I don't feel much better today. I don't seem to be able to fancy anything to eat, they have got some beef tea for me now, so I think I shall be able to take some of that. I have got up so as to write this to you, but I shall not be long before I get back to bed again. Many thanks for your nice letter, which you wrote to Pa, Ma says he did not say a word, when he had read it, but passed it on to her, after she had read it she said "a nice letter isn't it?" but he never answered. I do hope he will give his consent something will have to be settled very shortly one way or another, because of hurrying things on. I have sent notice to give up my sittings in March and he knows that and did not make any remark. I shall look forward to seeing you on saturday dear, I am so longing for you to cheer me up and I think it would be better for you to come and settle things definitely. If it makes no difference to Jennie, I think if I came down on the following week Feb 20th (monday) for it seems so early to buy the furniture now, even if we get married in April and if I came on the 20th it would make a fortnight's difference nearly. But of course it really does not matter, as far as I am concerned when I come, you must choose the most convenient time for Jennie. David expects to arrive at Plymouth on saturday. He won't know until he gets there, whether he has to go onto Portsmouth or not, but he says, until the paying off is done, which takes about a fortnight, he will only be able to run up for a couple of days to see us. He wants to go to America as early in March as he can, he says they have had a lovely trip, not a bit rough, he was at Port Said when he wrote. We have not had any snow, but it has been bitterly cold and now it is raining. Don't forget dear, to let a man go and see to the rose trees in the garden, and if you

Beef tea which Beatrice was given, was one of the many old-fashioned remedies for colds and chills and provided a warming and nourishing drink in the cold winter months. (B)

There was no talk of presents from Jack's mother as she was not even prepared to send them her good wishes for their marriage. A gift of £10 from Mrs. Mercer alone was an extremely generous amount.

can manage it have a few standard trees put in. Last night Ma said I was to look in the Store Book and choose things to the amount of £10 as a present from her, so I have chosen

    1 doz fish eaters and carvers to match in case
    1 doz large forks
    1 ,, small   ,,
    1 doz dessert spoons

and I have asked Ernie to give me 6 table spoons to match, so that will be a lovely present, won't it dear, and things we must have, they are all of the best quality and I think we are lucky not to have to buy that sort of thing. It was such a wretched day yesterday, that the children could not come round, neither did Aimée come. Have you told Ida about the wedding being in April?

Well I have given you an epistle today, but it seems nice to have a little chat with you, even if it is only on paper. Accept all my love and oceans of kisses

What is Phelps going to do?

Yours ever
Beatie

◇◇◇◇◇◇

Woodcock St. B'ham. Feb 8th 1899

My own darling Beatie

I was so sorry I had not time to write you a nice letter last night, for I know you must need something to cheer you. It does grieve one darling to hear of you being so unwell again, and I do sincerely hope you are quite feeling yourself again. I am glad dearie that you liked the letter I wrote to your Pa, and goodness knows I hope it will have the desired effect. Of course I quite anticipated that your Pa would be somewhat reluctant. I am sure Beatie he will miss you more than your Ma will when you leave them. Well I shall hope that when I come on Saturday, we shall settle it one way or another, and you know which way I wish, don't you darling.

Joe has to go to Glasgow today, and will not be back until Saturday evening, so that I cannot come before the 4 o'clock on Saturday, and I shall have to come back on the early train Monday. But still we shall get a whole clear day on Sunday, and it will be so nice to be together, won't it darling. Jennie says she will be glad for you to come and stay with them, as soon as you are ready to come and see about our papers, furniture etc. I told her I thought Monday 20th would suit you very well, and she says any time will suit her, she only wants to know what day you would be coming. She said she would be writing to you today. She says as far as she herself is concerned, it would suit her much better if our Wedding took place in June, but we can't hear of that can we dearie? You see April is the first in my thoughts, I even wrote it when I should have written June. I am glad to hear David has been having a good passage, and is getting so near home. I shall be anxious to meet him. I have had some coal sent to "Eton Lodge" and arranged to have some fires going in the place to keep it dry. When the ground clears of snow, I must have a gardener, to go over there, and have a look around, and see what there is in the garden, and what we can have put in to make it look a bit nice and pleasing. It is so good of

A photograph outside a Birmingham coal merchant. Coal merchants had a thriving trade at this time and coal fires at Eton Lodge would have been the only means of airing the house, which it would have needed after standing empty. (F)

your Ma to give you that present; and I think you have done very wisely in your selection. I told Ida all about it, that I thought we might be married in April, and she was very pleased with the idea. But what do you think now. I hear that she is likely now to go to Brussels before March is out. I don't say that is done for our own especial benefit, but doesn't it look very much like it. Well dearie, don't trouble and worry yourself over that, for that would do no good. I have quite done troubling over those things now. Well darling I am sorry but I must close now, so that you can get this this afternoon. All my love, and heaps of kisses.

I am going to enquire today as to when we can view that lot of furniture I told you of some time ago.

Ever your own devoted

Jack

A photograph of Ida taken in 1906 and by then a sophisticated young woman. She attended the Royal Academy of Dramatic Art from September 1906 to July 1907, leaving after three terms 'due to ill health'. Early the following year, however she married a German, Hugo von Grundherr. (P)

"Roselea", Feb 8th 1899

My darling Jack

Have just got your letter and thought that as I am writing to Alice, I would write to you and enclose it for you to give to her, did you know she was going to write to me, I think she is a bit of a humbug myself, and I don't believe she ever meant to come to us. I have left her letter unsealed for you to read, will you read it and seal it down and give it to her for if your Mother saw my writing she would think I was trying to get Alice away, and from her letter, really one would think that was the case. However we must look out for somebody else. I am feeling a bit better dear, but still far from well, for one thing I think I have stuck to the machine a bit too long today, and I feel so done up tonight. I have made 10 sheets today, but then I am anxious to get my work forward. I do hope we meet with a nice servant. Pa won't give a decisive answer except that he very much objects to it, but you must talk pretty to him on saturday when you come. David left Gib yesterday and arrives at Plymouth on saturday. I don't suppose he will get home yet awhile though. I am glad you have had fires put in Eton Lodge for I expect it will be a bit damp. I feel now that I shall be so thankful when all is over and we are settled down for we have had some ups and downs haven't we dear? What is the idea of Ida going in March, the term is not then? I have had such a lovely picture sent to me from Amy Sellers, she has painted it most beautifully, the design is Tulips and Wallflowers in a bunch. Aimée was here last night she did not stay all night as she was going out this morning. She brought back the wedding presents that Ma and I gave her, I didn't want mine back because it had got her initials on it but Ma said she could give hers to me if she liked, and so she did, a lovely solid silver sugar tongs and sifter in a case. Just fancy the fellow she was engaged to is married what do you think of that? isn't he a brute? Well dear I shall look forward to seeing you on saturday, even if is only for a short time, it will be better than nothing won't it

Ever yours

Beatie

Aimée must have felt very envious of Beatrice marrying so soon after meeting Jack, after her own unfortunate long engagement. She sadly gave her own somewhat premature wedding presents back.

*To Beatrice it must have seemed that even
Alice was shunning her in addition to all
the Hughes family, except for Jennie. For
Alice to have left Mrs. Hughes to come
to be their servant would, however, have
caused all kinds of problems.*

Woodcock St, Feb 10th 1899

My own darling Beatie

    I know you will feel somewhat disappointed at not receiving a letter
from me this morning, but I had such a day yesterday that really there
was no opportunity for writing, that you might hear from me this morning.
However I have come down on the first train, and am seizing the opportunity
of writing you before the bustle of the day commences and you will receive this,
this afternoon. I received your dear letter alright yesterday morning, and it
was quite a surprise to me, to learn that Alice had written you, I can assure you
darling. You must shew me her letter when I come up, as I should like to know
what she said. I don't know why she should write to you. I think that at first she
was really quite serious about coming to us, but has since felt that my Mother
would think she was treating her shabbily, if she were to leave her at the mercy
of a strange girl during her moving. I speak of the moving as if it were all
decided upon, however, I think it is. Don't think dearie that I am trying to
defend Alice at all, and don't let this trouble you, for if we don't have Alice no
doubt we can get some-one else. I did not see her last night, so I sealed down
her letter, and left it on the kitchen table for her this morning. No doubt she
will have something to say about it tonight. I saw Alec yesterday and he tells
me he believes Jennie has suggested next Monday for your coming, now really
if this would suit Jennie (and she said any time would suit her) it would be best
for me, as I could better spare time from here next week, than later.

    Now dearie, about your dear little self. I am so glad to know you are about
again, but don't knock yourself up again with that machine. You are of course
anxious to get all your things forward, and I am so glad to know it, but mind
not over do it. I do hope your Pa will have come round to our idea a bit before
Saturday. More presents eh, how jolly. We can do with them, can't we darling.
Let them all come. The Artillery Ball takes place tonight dearie, but I have no
time for that. I must get off home tonight and turn out early again in the
morning. I would find time though dearie, if you were down here for it, as last
year. Well dearie it is close on Post
time so I must away. I am longing
to be with you again, mind 7.16   *Ever your own devoted*
tomorrow and I hope we shall meet   *Jack*
this time. Well then, Au revoir,
All my love and heaps of kisses.

◇◇◇◇◇◇

Woodcock St. B'ham. Feb 14th 1899

My own darling Beatie

    Here we are again. You will begin to feel a little bit neglected, I am
afraid dearie, as you did not hear from me this afternoon, but I had
quite intended being down here by the first train this morning, and writing
you then; but I was so tired I could not get up in time, and there has been no
opportunity all day until now, and I am embracing it, I wish I were embracing
you though darling.

*Valentine's Day 1899 was an extremely
happy one for Jack and Beatrice, who
were able to greet it with the knowledge
that they were very soon to be married. (R)*

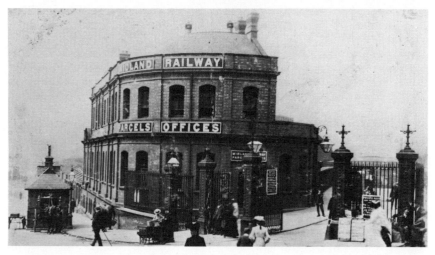

I got back to B'ham quite safely yesterday, and met a gentleman from B'ham at Willesden, whom I knew, so that made the journey a little more pleasant. I am looking forward to next Monday dearie, to have you down here for a time, and go out together buying our furniture etc. Your Pa was good to give way so nicely as he did, and I do hope that he and your Ma will be able to make all their arrangements without any of those little unpleasantnesses (How do you like that word). We have all got a lot to do in the time, but dearie, I am glad we have not got to wait until June. I went up to Jennie's last night, and she said it would be quite convenient for you to come next Monday. Jennie tells me that my Mother has arranged for Ida to go Brussels on March 30th. Mrs. Archer is going over then to see her daughter and has promised to take Ida with her. How horrid isn't it. I think if we had arranged our Wedding for March, that my Mother would have got Ida off in February. I must speed to Uncle about drawing my share of the profits, for we shall need it now, eh darling? I am afraid we shall make it look very sick. I have been consulting the Calendar, and find there are eight Sundays between now and our Wedding, I think that perhaps the best time to have the Banns published would be March 12, 19 and 26, then if I came up on March the 4th, (Saturday) I could make the necessary arrangements on the Monday. Jennie says she would much rather that we were married in June, as far as she is concerned, for it will be rather inconvenient to her, but then she laughed and said "ah well when we were married we suited ourselves", she said she knew it was all my doing. I am annoyed darling to think that even now Ida will not be at our Wedding. Whatever will you do. It will seem so strange to have to ask someone else now, won't it. I will get out a proper list of people I should like invited, and when you are down we can go through it and complete it. I must also think as to what present I will give the Bridesmaids, and have some suggestions for you when you come, and then that can be decided. It was too bad of me to have you up so early yesterday, and take you out in such a rough morning, but dearie, I do hope that you don't feel any ill effects from it. I hope you had a good rest, to try and make up for what you lost. You will be ever so busy now, I know darling, but pray mind and not overdo it. Won't we be proud next week, eh? when we

It seems as if Jack's visit in person to plead with Mr. Mercer did the trick to get permission to marry in April instead of June, though Jack's letter in advance to prepare him for the shock was obviously necessary.

With less than eight weeks to go until the wedding there was plenty to be done if they were to be ready in time for the kind of wedding Beatrice's parents wanted her to have.

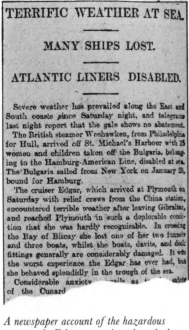

*A newspaper account of the hazardous
passage the* Edgar *experienced on the last
stages of her voyage from Hong Kong. She
had encountered terrible gales off Cape
Finisterre and docked at Plymouth
"according to her itinerary" but "with
only one funnel". (O)*

*Messrs. Paul and Collard were Streatham
caterers and it was typical of Mr. Mercer's
generosity that he should insist on a more
formal, and expensive, wedding breakfast,
than allow Mrs. Mercer to cater for a
reception herself.*

are getting all the things for our dear home. I wish I were going home to my
dear little wife at "Eton Lodge" tonight, don't you darling. But never mind,
we must be patient, for we have already hastened it by two months. I suppose
David has not managed to get up to "Roselea" yet. I read the accounts of the
passage of the "Edgar", the damage she sustained and how well she behaved,
in the morning's paper, coming down yesterday. Alec tells me he thinks my
Mother has made up her mind to have that house in Chester Rd. If she does I
expect Uncle John would be moving away. There is no reason why he should,
but then he is so funny. I feel sure if she marries Phelps and they live there, that
he would move away. Please give my love to your Pa and Ma, and tell them I
am ever so glad that they are allowing us to be married in April. Jennie speaks
well of the place at Bournemouth, "Devon Towers", but she lays stress on the
fact that the people are Roman Catholics, and cater principally for their own
class. I don't see that that would
make any difference though. She says
it is well managed, and everything
good and clean. Now dearie I hope
you are quite well and will keep so.
All my love and heaps of kisses

your own devoted
Jack

◇◇◇◇◇◇◇◇

"Roselea", Feb 15th 1899

My own darling Jack

I got so anxious when the last post came in last night and brought
no news from you, of course I fancied all sorts of things, but I at last
consoled myself with "no news, is good news". However I was very glad to see
your letter waiting for me when I got down this morning. On monday morning, I got very wet about the head and face, not being able to hold the umbrella
up, then in the afternoon I washed 21 muslin curtains, and in the evening I took
Ma's umbrella to be mended, it was a lovely night when I started, but coming
back it rained in torrents and I got drenched again. Now since then, I have had
Rheumatics so bad, in my neck and hands and arms it makes my hand ache to
write. I am going to rub them well with embrocation and I hope they will be
better. No more washing for me, if that is how it is going to serve me. Old Chief
has just jumped up on the table and is sitting close to me, in fact almost on this
letter. I had a letter from Ida this morning, telling me that she is going to
school on March 30th so I can see plainly now that this has been done on
purpose as well! never mind. Yesterday we had a book of invitation wedding
cards, and cards for us to be sent out when we are married, such a lovely
selection but we have not decided yet. Then Pa asked Ma if she would go to
Paul's and ask for a estimate for a wedding breakfast, she did not wish to give
it to a caterer, and she is mad to have a reception, but I am glad to say, Pa still
sticks out for the breakfast, which she very much resents. Pa said, he would
have nothing to do with it, if she attempted to do it herself and that he wished
the thing done well, not made a hash of. Well this morning Ma went to Paul's
and they are going to send estimates. We have made a list of our friends to be
invited, so far they number 130. I shall have to talk to Jennie and ask her about
"Devon Towers" and whether she would recommend us to go there.

Nellie went up to a specialist on monday, and he says she must be operated on, he is coming down on Sunday morning and bringing a nurse with him, his fee is £50. Ted explained to him, he was not a rich man, so he said he would do it for a reduced fee, but I expect it will cost a tremendous lot with one thing and the other. We heard last night that they won't let Laura come, she is awfully down about it, and so is Ern of course. Pa is going over to see her people to-night to see if he cannot persuade them, I think it is very unkind of them, and Ma promised to give her the same money that she is getting at school. Mrs. Morris wants me to go over to dinner on friday to talk the matter over with regard the bridesmaids' dresses, I mean ordering them. Well dear. I shall soon be with you, and won't we enjoy our little selves, excuse this scrawl but I can hardly hold the pen. Heaps of love and oceans of kisses

Yours devotedly Beatie

David is coming tomorrow, he is now at Walmer

For the poorer classes doctors were far too expensive and many doctors took advantage of the richer families – charging whatever fee they thought they could get. For Beatrice's brother Ted to find £50 for Nellie's operation was a great deal of money indeed.

◇◇◇◇◇◇◇

Woodcock St. B'ham. Feb 16th 1899

My own darling Beatie

I was so delighted to receive your dear letter this morning, but am so grieved to hear that you are suffering again from that horrid Rheumatism. You must certainly leave the washing part of the business severely alone, that is so far as curtains, clothing etc. is concerned. How delightful to have Chief so near to you. I hope he behaved himself properly. Of course dearie, it is most unfortunate, about Ida going away at March 30th, but then don't let it worry you. You remember what the Palmist told you dearie, at Folkestone about the woman who was trying to prevent our wedding. It looks as if it is to be kept up until the end of the chapter, doesn't it. Never mind, she has done her best, but we don't care do we darling. I am not surprised darling, to hear that you have not yet finally decided about the cards, for I suppose there is such endless variety, that it becomes a very hard matter. I am sorry there is still the difference of opinion between your Pa and Ma as to the Breakfast or Reception, the former course I say for choice, but certainly it would be very costly, but then as your Pa is anxious to have it, why should he not. Stick up for it Beatie, and your Ma will come to alright. It is a pretty favourable sign seeing she has been for the estimate.

I had such a pleasant surprise at tea this evening, Frank told me he is going to give us a clock for the Hall, for a Wedding Present. Fancy poor old Frank. It is quite his own idea. He has not a big lot of money to spend, and I was naturally surprised when he told me. I shall appreciate it very much I can assure you, and you can't tell dearie how much it touched me, and how deeply it makes me feel for him in his affliction. He is so good natured. Simmy came to see me yesterday morning, about doing the garden, but I had not time to see him and have arranged for him to come down on Sunday morning. I thought that would be the best time, as I should then be at liberty to go over with him. I called to see Mr. Sanderson today, but he informs me that his sister is going to start housekeeping again, and consequently there is none of the furniture

Frank Hughes, Jack's brother with the 'affliction'. He was slow and rather simple but, unlike the rest of his family, was determined not to miss out on the celebration of such an important occasion for Jack, of whom he was very fond. (M)

An evening of cards was a popular way of spending the long winter evenings and provided a pleasant social or family activity. It was hardly what Jack needed at this point in time, however, as he could not afford to play for money and risk losing it.

for sale. I went up to Uncle John's last night to supper, and afterwards we had a game at Nap. I lost 5^s/7½^d, fancy. That game won't do will it. He asked me up to meet a young gentleman, but it strikes me they were a bit too clever for me. I am looking out for next Monday, dearie, and have told Joe that I am coming down early all next week, as I want to have all the afternoons off. We shall have all our work cut out I know. I think we had better choose the papers on Tuesday. I went up in the train with Mr. Harrop on Tuesday evening, and he was so pleased to hear the date is fixed and that you are coming down. He says I must be sure and take you over and that if it would be more convenient to you for getting to Eton Lodge, he would be very pleased for you to stay at "Stafford House" for a few days. Of course we shall not be going to Eton Lodge much during your visit shall we darling, only about once I expect. They are all looking forward to see you again at Wylde Green I know, perhaps we may find time to pay them a visit when you come, they will feel disappointed if we don't, I know. Shan't we be happy together next week. It won't be very long now. Cheer up dearie, and I do hope you have moved those horrid Rheumatics. All my love and a sweet good night kiss, and a good old hug.

Ever your own devoted
Jack

"Roselea", Feb 17th 1899

My darling Jack

Jennie's refusal of the wedding invitation was the last straw for Beatrice. What she did not know by this time on Friday was that Jennie was also about to telegraph her to cancel Beatrice's visit to her on Monday due to illness.

    I hope you will forgive me for not writing this afternoon but you know dear I had quite a rush to get off to Morris' this morning, so really I had not the time. David has just arrived, so there is great excitement just now, and I have only just got back from Dulwich. I have been finally to decide about the bridesmaids' dresses. Jack dear, do you know that Jennie says she is not coming to the wedding. Now I think this beats all, there only wants one more thing, that is for Joe to refuse and then perhaps your Mother would be satisfied. Ernie says you will be the next to back out of it, but I know different to that, if I had not implicit trust in you I could not bear all this. Jennie makes some excuse that she cannot leave a strange girl in the house, but I know she could manage it if she liked. I feel most hurt about it, but I must not worry for I feel quite queer already. Nellie is very queer indeed and very low spirited, the operation takes place on Sunday, it will be a good thing over. David leaves for America tomorrow week for 3 months, so he will have a fine time up there, I know. I am longing to see you. The Caterer has been down today, he wants £60 for the Marquee alone, but of course we won't pay that, he has not settled the price of the breakfast. I suppose you will meet me on monday at 2.45, I hope Jennie will be alright to me, for somehow, I feel so slighted now. Excuse more dear in haste, it is just upon 11 o'clock. How good of poor old Frank, tell him I much appreciate his kindness. I went to Miss Mann's and ordered my wedding dress, it will be elegant dear. Lots of love

With Beatrice about to leave for Birmingham on Monday following the coming weekend, everything seemed to be happening at once at 'Roselea' so that it was perhaps just as well that she later received Jennie's news delaying her. In order not to disappoint her, Jack made a flying visit up to London on Saturday the 18th, as a result of which he too "was quite knocked up".

Yours ever Beatie

Woodcock St. B'ham. Feb 21st 1899

My own darling Beatie

I received your dear letter last evening at 8.15 and must confess that I was feeling quite knocked up after my Saturday night's experience, and that I felt quite relieved when you asked me to let you have a letter by the last delivery tonight, instead of having to write straight away, for this enabled me to get off home and get to bed. I am very glad to say that Jennie is much better and she hopes to get back to her own home before the end of the week. If she does we will go up and see her there, and she will explain this matter to you fully, and why she is afraid she may not be at our wedding. I expect you heard from Harrops this morning but you must please excuse the business envelope. Thinking perhaps they might be going out last evening, I did not wait until evening to go to Wylde Green, but went and saw Mr. Harrop and Mrs. Darby at their works. Mr. Harrop was very sorry to hear of poor Jennie being knocked up, and said he would be very pleased for you to come and stay with them, and told Mrs. Darby to write and tell you so. They were all going to the Grand Theatre in the evening, so Mrs. Darby said she would write from their Works, first thing after tea, and I addressed the envelope, as of course you would notice. I shall be at New St. to meet you at 2.45 Wednesday and hope you will have a comfortable journey and be feeling quite well for we shall have a busy time while you are down here, shan't we darling. I called at the Bedstead Works yesterday, but Mr. Hoadly is in London until about Thursday. Uncle John went to London yesterday and is returning Thursday. Well dearie I am dying for tomorrow to come, and bring you to me. Heaps of kisses and all my love.

Ever your own devoted
Jack

Alfred Hoadly or 'Uncle' Ben as he became known. He was a great friend of the family, and a bachelor. He sent this photograph of himself to Ida some years later and remained connected with the family. His brother ran the Bedstead Works. (P)

❖❖❖❖❖❖❖

"Roselea", March 1st 1899

My own darling Jack

You see I am safe at home once more, but I don't like it one bit, I do want you dear. I shall be longing to see you once more. I had a very comfortable journey but was alone from Weedon. I found the rug most acceptable, it was good of you to think of it. They all think I look better and I feel it too. I have told them all about the furniture and they are delighted. Mr. and Mrs. Pattenden came last night and he is going to provide the marquee and awning from the front door to the gate but what do you think? Ma has actually written to Cousin Ted to stop printing cards until she writes again, as she is trying her hardest to get the Reception after all, but I put my foot down and was most angry about it, as we ought to have them by now. However I am going to write to him this morning and ask him to let us have them at once. The teapot that David has given is awfully nice, so good, but I wish it was a little larger, he said the next size was bigger than ours and was £7 = 10 = 0, he thought that would be too big and they had nothing between. Darling, I

Beatrice had returned to London from her delayed trip to Birmingham to choose furniture for Eton Lodge. Her stay with the Harrops proved an enjoyable one but she had returned to 'Roselea' to continued squabbles and fraught wedding arrangements.

Beatrice was extremely strong-willed and liked everything to be as she wanted it, and so it was a good thing that Jack had chosen a house to please her as much as Eton Lodge did.

must thank you for those lovely grapes, they were delicious. I am proud of my future home, I only wish I was in it. You are good to provide me such a pretty home. Excuse more dear I must be off. Heaps and heaps of kisses and all my love

Yours ever

Beatie

❖❖❖❖❖❖

Woodcock St. B'ham. March 2nd 1899

My own darling Beatie

I went to Lodge last night, and when I reached home, your dear letter was waiting for me as anticipated. I need not tell you how eagerly I devoured it; for I was feeling so anxious to hear from you dear. I am so glad dearie, that you managed the journey so comfortably, and have reached home safely, also that they think you are looking better for the change. It did me good to have you down here I am sure, and I do so miss you, but never mind dearie, you will soon come to your own little home now. Shan't I be glad when all the things are done, and our dear home is quite ready. Won't it be lovely. I am so sorry your Ma has taken that idea of the reception into her head again, and do hope you will be able to cure her of it. We must have a Breakfast, if I can say anything in the matter, eh dear? You stick out for it, and back up your Pa, and it will come off alright. I am glad you have received David's teapot, and like it, never mind it being small, we must be thankful for small mercies I suppose.

Shall I have the Banns published at Erdington this Sunday, or would you like them to wait a week and be asked the same days as at Streatham. If you will tell me this, I will communicate with Holyoak, the clerk, if necessary to have it altered. Holyoak the painter has started to work today, I shall try and go over in the morning and take down the pendant. The material for curtains has arrived this afternoon. I will bring it up with me on Saturday week if I don't hear to the contrary. I called at Giles' this morning and selected a postal handle for our front door. I think it is a very nice one myself, and that you will like it, however if not we can easily change it. I have also got the bolts I told you of for the drawing room window, and when they are on they will make a very neat job. I am all the while thinking of our dear little home, and do hope the time will fly until April 12th, afterwards I am afraid it will fly only too quickly. I will get out the full list of people I would like to be invited to the wedding and enclose in my next. Joe has been awfully bad tempered. I suppose it is on account of me having lost so much time just lately. Never mind dearie he will get over it. We have done pretty well all, and done it well too I think don't you.

I gave the furniture people my Cheque for £50=0=0 today, and they are to deliver the Goods on Wed April the 5th and receive the balance on delivery. The dining room furniture and second bedroom suite have been made up some time and are thoroughly seasoned, but the best bedroom suite has to be made, and they say that if after a time it needs attention, drawers sticking or any such matters, they will of course see to it free of charge, upon hearing from us. I paid

Jack was certainly right in that they should be glad for wedding presents at all considering the hazards the wedding plans had gone through – and a small silver teapot was certainly better than no teapot!

A photograph of Jack and Beatrice with their dog, happily together some years later in their married life. Time certainly did "fly by only too quickly" for them, but quicker than even Jack expected. (A)

for the pictures today and am going to let the cart call for them when passing that way. What do you think? I have sent in a proposal today, to take out a policy in the Rock Life Co. to provide against accidents. I think it will be money well spent: £5 per year. I don't know whether they will take me on yet though, for I had to tell them about my left ear being destroyed, and perhaps they might not take me on as they might think that would be conducive to getting into an accident some time. Harrops were so glad you made yourself quite comfortable with them, they tell me I looked ever so much better after you came down, and I am sure I felt better darling. Well dearie, all my love and heaps of kisses

Your own devoted
Jack

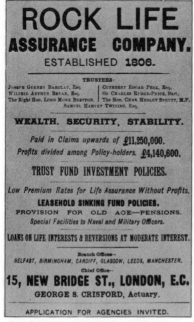
An advertisement for the Rock Life Assurance Company which was current at the time that Jack decided to take out his policy, which at £5 per annum was considerably cheaper than he would have bought one today. (S)

"Roselea", March 3rd 1899

My own darling Jack

I was delighted to receive your dear letter this morning for it seems ages since I left you. I am so glad they have started the work at Eton Lodge, for now it looks like business doesn't it dear? Aimèe has been for the last two days, she has just gone home as she is going to see *The Belle of New York* tonight. Do you know dear, that the night before last I had such a bad attack in the middle of the night and I don't know what I should have done if Aimèe had not been with me, she said I frightened her to death for I went just like a corpse. She fortunately thought of the brandy and rushed downstairs and got it, she found I was coming round, or else she was going to fetch Ma in, it seemed too bad for only the day before, I was saying I had not felt so well for a long time, I am afraid I felt too well. However, I stayed in bed until late in the morning and now today, I feel quite myself again.

I received the photo from the Harrops of you and I, and very good it is, it makes quite a pretty picture, and the dogs have come out very well. They all think it is exceedingly good here, and they would all like one, do you think you could get a few for me, I do not like to ask and Aimèe says if you could ask for them unpolished, and then she can touch them up for me and mount them. I have told Aimèe that we chose brooches for their presents, she seemed disappointed that it was not a bangle, as she already has 5 gold brooches, so Ma says she does not see it would matter if you gave her a bangle with the same pearl initials on it and the other two the brooches. I am going to get several estimates for theirs and my bouquets, when I go up to town and I will let you know. What about the blankets dear? I should leave it to your Cousin, he will know what quality. I expect we should want 2 prs good ones, 1 pr single ones for servants bed and under blankets for the 3 bedsteads. Don't forget to bring the curtains with you. I have just finished making the last tablecloth. If I were you, I should let the banns be published at Erdington on Sunday, I don't see that it matters but be sure and bring the certificate that the banns have been published at Erdington, or else they won't marry us and that would be sad, wouldn't it dear? Well it is to be a breakfast, I am glad to say, and I hope to get all the invitations out next week. I have fixed the time for 12.30 and Mr.

Mrs. Mercer had suggested that they would do better to buy their blankets in Birmingham — and it seems as if they were to come from Mr. Hoadly's Bedstead Works.

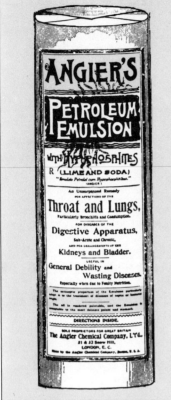

Jack should have taken some Angier's Petroleum Emulsion for his sore throat and chest cold. This was one of many proprietary brands available from the chemists at that time, in addition to the many home remedies that were so popular. (B)

Aston Villa finished the 1898–99 football season top of the First Division, as they had done the previous year. In the last game of the season they beat Liverpool at their new home ground at Villa Park, before a crowd of 41,000 fans.

Pattenden is going to provide the marquee. They are going to give us either a silver cake basket or a silver trinity dish. I told them I did not much mind which. Well darling, I have given you an epistle. Accept oceans of kisses and heaps of love

Yours ever
Beatie

◆◇◆◇◆◇◆

Linwood Lodge, March 5th 1899

My own darling Beatie

I was so glad to receive your dear letter yesterday, but am so grieved to hear of that bad turn you had the other night. I do hope you are feeling quite well now dearie. You see I am writing from home today. It has been quite peaceful here today. Mother is *away*! She is still in London, and is returning on Tuesday, I think. I have not been feeling quite up to the mark today, for I rode to town and back on my bike yesterday, and it turned out a cold and wet day and I have now got a sore throat and cold on my chest. I could scarcely speak this morning. Nin and Alec and I, went over to Eton Lodge yesterday afternoon. Alec likes the place very much. I went over again this afternoon to shew Joe round. I have seen the ceiling papers and admire them very much. The one for the Drawing Room is very choice. I might say, in the language of the man at the warehouse, that "They are two clinkers". Well dearie, I did not go to Church this morning, but every one else went and of course heard our Banns read out. We had it all to ourselves, there were no others published. It appears there was not anyone, who knew "any just cause or impediment etc." so that is alright darling. I have so wished I were with you today dearie, and so longed for you, but that is a treat in store for next Sunday. Won't we have a nice little time together. I am so glad dearie that it is quite settled that it is to be a Breakfast after all, but quite thought all along that your Pa would carry his own idea through. I shall be glad to know as to the cost of the Bouquets.

I met Arthur Harrop on Friday night and he told me that had sent one of the Photos on to you. He shewed me one but I could not have that as his father had not seen it. He only came home from London on Friday night. I thought the photo was very good indeed and am glad you like it. I think all the Brides-maids had better have a bangle and so be all alike, but I can't yet make up my mind what to give you my dear little wife. I must be quick and decide though mustn't I dearie. What do you think? Jack Harrop is going up to London next Saturday, to see the Aston Villa team play. He will stay with their friends at Norwood, and has told me he shall come over to Streatham and look us up on Sunday. Rather cool! We don't want anyone to look us up when we are together do we dearie, but I suppose we must put up with it. Doris is such a nuisance, she keeps coming and interrupting me. I have just asked what she wants and she says "A little bit off the top". I taught her that this morning. Nin doesn't like her saying such things. They have got all the paper off the walls at "Eton Lodge" and those horrid venetians are removed, so I can now see how pretty our windows will look when we have got them done as we intend. I do

The photograph of Jack and Beatrice and the dogs which Jack Harrop took during Beatrice's visit to Birmingham. She was staying with the Harrops at the time and this picture was taken at Stafford House, Wylde Green. (A)

hope with time will fly past until April 12th, and then won't we be happy darling? Ida says "fancy me in a convent. I won't do any work the day of the wedding." Well my dearie I do hope you are quite well, and cheer up until I come to you on Saturday and then we will have a sweet little time together. All my love and heaps of kisses.

Ever your own devoted

Jack

Poor Ida, as exciting as the prospects of her new school in Brussels might have been, she knew she would have much more fun as a bridesmaid on April 12th than she was likely to have on that day at school.

Jack and Beatrice's romance began in April the previous year – the date this advertisement appeared, and though they did not meet this way, train journeys played an important part in their lives. (B)

"Would you object to my smoking a cigarette?"

"Certainly not, providing they are OGDEN'S GUINEA GOLD"

"Roselea", March 6th 1899

My own darling Jack

It did seem an age waiting for your letter, but I was delighted to get it this morning. I thought you would have enclosed your list, but be sure and do so in your next as we are going to send out the invitations this week. I went to Church yesterday morning, 3 couples' banns were published. I thought of ours being called at Erdington and here next Sunday. I am so longing to have you with me once more, won't we have a time. I presume you are going to stop until monday night, you really must dear, for there will be such a lot to talk about. Ma says she will be very pleased to see Jack Harrop next Sunday and will you ask him to come to dinner and you and I could meet him at the Station. There is a train from Norwood Junction on Sunday morning at 10.59 reaching Streatham Hill at 11.17, so if he comes ask him to come by that train as the next train will be too late for dinner. I find the last train back would be best from Streatham Common to Norwood Junction, leaves Streatham Common at 9.23 reaching Norwood 9.37, so now you have it all.

Ted and Nellie were here yesterday, she went back in Granny's bath chair, she is getting on splendidly she sent her love. Mrs. Morris and Aimèe have gone today to buy the bridesmaids' dresses, they wanted me to go, but I am a bit off colour so thought I was best at home. I am going over tomorrow to spend the day with Morris', she is going with me to do some shopping. Your Mother is having quite a stay I wonder she can leave her dear Harry for so long. Just fancy, Joe condescending to look over Eton Lodge, how did he like it? I am

There was no chance of Jack's mother calling in at 'Roselea' during her unusual visit to London, and little did they suspect her real reasons for that visit, or who she was with.

glad Alec liked it. Please give my love to him and Jennie by the way, how is Jennie, I hope better. David arrived at New York last friday night, so he must have had a good trip. So glad you like the ceiling papers, isn't the drawing room one fine? Don't forget the brass finger plates. What about a brass umbrella stand, will you get that? and dearie I think you will have to ask "Grey" to send 3 common forks (table) for the kitchen as Ma has not got any to spare and I don't care about letting the girl use our best ones. Ma is giving us those you know. If anyone up your way wants to give you anything, we want a dinner service badly, perhaps your Uncle would give you that, and it would save repacking from here. Now with regard to the bridesmaids' presents I don't see why you could not give them different, for I know the other two would rather have brooches. Everybody that sees it, is delighted with the teapot, and I feel sure you would like it. Well dear don't forget the list in your next letter. Heaps of love and oceans of kisses

Yours most devotedly
Beatie

PS. Only 5 weeks on wednesday. What ho!

"Roselea", March 8th 1899

My own darling

How are you? I do hope quite well by now, it worries me so to hear that you are not well, be sure and take great care of yourself and I do hope you won't take a fresh cold after the Turkish, I am glad you liked it I never could muster up enough courage to be slapped about like a lot of fish. Well, I went to Morris' yesterday for the day, they had got the bridesmaids dresses for me to see, and they are perfectly sweet and I feel sure they will look very nice indeed. I have not been about the bouquets yet, I was going on monday night, but I was so queer I had to go to bed instead, but I am going tomorrow. Aimèe and I are going out on the spree today, I am going to meet her at Victoria at 12 o'clock and we are going to see Alexander in *The Ambassador*. She is coming back with me to help get the invitations out, as we hope the cards will arrive tomorrow morning. Laura is coming up on friday week to have her dress fitted, she will go back first thing on monday morning. Just fancy old Phelps being with your Mother, did he stay at Adams? When does he leave the Works? Don't you think you might write to Folkestone for a tariff, the address is Avenue Mansion, the Leas, Folkestone. Maggie Harrop sent me their photographs you know, the four taken together, I also heard from Kitty. Be sure and send your list as soon as possible, time is getting on, isn't it dear? I wish today was saturday, for I do want a good hug from my darling and I don't feel very grand myself. How are they getting on with the work at Eton Lodge, I am longing to know how the papers look when they are hung. Don't forget the muslin when you come. Well dear, au revoir. I must be off. Lots of kisses and all my love.

Yours most devotedly
Beatie

It was not likely that many guests would face the long journey from Birmingham to London for a wedding even in the best of circumstances, and even less likely when the wedding was one which had caused such a rift in the family and which even the bridegroom's mother was unlikely to attend.

Phelps had been employed at the Works for some time which had added to the embarrassment of Mrs. Hughes' affair with him. Jack was still not facing up to the reality of the relationship and therefore had an even bigger surprise to come. (M)

Although the cost of a wedding in another century provides a sharp contrast, many of the pressures and problems of pleasing everybody and doing the right thing are ones with which every modern bride can identify.

Woodcock St. B'ham. March 9th 1899

My own darling Beatie

    I hope you are not quite scared by the official looking envelope which brings this to you. My dearie, I was so glad to hear from you this morning and especially to know that you are better. I am feeling more like myself again, but have had a very rocky time the last few days. Well now I have actually made out my lists at last, but don't be afraid dearie, there will not be very many acceptances I am afraid on account of the distance. I am so glad you are so pleased with the dresses for the Bridesmaids, I know when you say they are perfectly sweet, that they must be lovely indeed. Give my love to Aimée and tell her to get on with the writing as fast as ever she can, and you shall come and help her send hers out some day. Ern is in for a treat I see, he must be counting the days now to Friday week. I am looking out dearie and longing for Saturday that I can come to you again. I do want you so badly darling. I hope you enjoyed the Theatre today, rather yesterday. They are getting on rather slowly with the work at "Eton Lodge", and will not be finished this week, but don't worry about that dearie, I shall see that everything is ready in time for I am only too anxious like your dear self. I don't know where Phelps stayed in London, but they both returned together on Tuesday. He was stuck up at Gravelly Hill last night. He leaves here on Saturday, I believe. I am sure our home will look ever so nice dearie, when it is finished, and I am so longing to be there with you darling, but then it won't be very long now will it? It is getting very late now dearie so I must away. I shall get the 10.30 train now. Pray excuse the brevity tonight. Heaps of kisses and all my love to my darling

Ever your own devoted.

Jack

"Roselea", March 11th 1899

My darling Jack

    I received your letter and lists this morning, but do you know that Cousin Ted has not sent the cards yet, isn't it too bad? I am going to telegraph this afternoon, Aimée is here waiting to do them. I had a letter from Jennie this morning and she says that she thinks that they will be able to come to the Wedding after all. I am glad, I don't feel quite so snubbed as before. I have asked them to come here, as we shall be able to give them a shake down of some sort. Aimée and I went about the flowers yesterday and the nice shop opposite the Town Hall will do the bridesmaids' bouquets for 7/6 each. Mine they say would be 21/-, but I don't want such a big one, so I think they would do one for about 12/6 or 15/- if I asked them. They say you must have a white carnation for your buttonhole not *pink*. Now I have to tell you that Mrs. Tory bought Haidée a robe like the bridesmaids, so I thought it over and as she had got the dress and 4 bridesmaids would look better than 3, I wrote and asked her to take Ida's place. She wrote me an awfully nice letter, and accepted with much pleasure, so I feel very glad about it, as 3 would have looked rather odd, wouldn't it? I am glad you have written to Avenue Mansion and we shall then know how much it will cost us. I suppose you will come by the 4 o'clock train tomorrow and I will meet you at Streatham Hill 7.16. Aimèe and I enjoyed our little outing immensely, Alexander is perfect as you know, and Miss Fay Davis is sweet. Well, I cannot stay longer, it is tub day, so au revoir

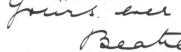

Yours ever
Beatie

We went to 2 other shops about the flowers, one wanted 17/6 for the brides-maids and 2 guineas for mine, what do you think of that, and the other; brides-maids 14/6 and mine 25/-, so I think the shop opposite the Town Hall is very reasonable and I know we can depend on them.

❖❖❖❖❖❖

Woodcock St. March 14th 1899

My own darling Beatie

You will see I have managed to get back here safely once more, and thank goodness I shall not have to leave you many more times like this. Fancy the next time (Easter) will be the last, and then the time after when I come, you will really be my wife. How delightful isn't it dearie to think of, but it will be ever so much better to realise. I am ever so anxious for the time to fly past, so that we shall have April the 12th here. I met Jack Harrop last night at Willesden, as arranged and we had a very comfortable journey up here in the Dining Car. The train was late getting to Willesden, but still we were just in time for the main line train. It came dashing in just as I stepped from the Croydon Train. I have seen and heard of one or two of the people down here already who have received invitations. Alice says when my Mother received hers, she smuggled it away into her pocket and did not open it. I saw Joe's this morning and that had been opened. Frank knows he is invited on the same card as Joe, but I don't know if my Mother has told Ida that she (Ida) is invited, but I shall see her tonight or tomorrow morning and will ask her. I went over to "Eton Lodge" this morning, and find there are no papers hung yet, so I immediately went off to the painter and blew him up finely about it. There was no one at work there, but he has promised faithfully to start paper-ing tomorrow. He has been ill in bed for a week with influenza himself, and that accounts for the delay. I left the portmanteau in the Cloak Room last night, and have not been able to get it away today, so have not yet been to see about the Madras. You will have lots to do between now and April the 12th, and cheer up dearie and be as bright as ever you can, and your Jackie will be looking out and longing for the time to go that he may be with you again. You must please excuse me further tonight dearie, for I have a letter yet to write in connection with Masonry, and have also promised to go and see poor old Hands tonight, and as it is getting somewhat late I must be off. All my love to my dearie. Heaps of kisses

Ever your own devoted
Jack

George Alexander, another of the great theatre actor-managers of the time, played in The Ambassador *by John Oliver Hobbes. It was described at the time as 'a delicate, effective and successful comedy'.*

THE ORPHANAGE AT ERDINGTON. (See page X.)

An orphanage founded by local freemasons, at Erdington. The Lechmere Volunteer Lodge was the craft Lodge to which Jack belonged. (F)

The Vane's were already aware of Jack's habit of speaking his mind for the sake of principle and their news, though partly incorrect, should have come as no surprise.

Jennie and Alec, some time before their marriage by the Revd. Davies, in 1895. Alec spoke fluent Spanish and for some time worked in a merchant's office. (M)

"Roselea", March 14th 1899

My darling Jack

So glad you had such a comfortable journey home. I did miss you so, and wish I had got you with me now. The answers to the invitations are rolling in now, and so far 13 have refused and 13 accepted. Medlicott and Burgess are coming. Your Uncle and Aunt Cooper has refused. Ma met Mrs. Vane and your Mother is going to be married from the Adam's in Easter week and some parson from Birmingham is coming up to marry them. She told Mrs. Vane, that she was very upset at the way that you had treated her. She told Mrs. Vane that she liked me very much or she should not have invited me, but she said you had so insulted her over the Phelps affair and when you apologised, she was coming round and felt all would be well, but that you so hurt her feelings by saying that you were not sorry for what you had said, and by telling her she ought to be ashamed of herself as it was disgusting, she said that made her say a lot of things she did not really mean, hence this awful breach. Now Jack dear, I really think it is a good deal of your fault, I know she has insulted me in her temper, but I don't believe she meant it. She says she is not committing a crime by marrying and she has a right to have whom she likes. Of course she is right dear. She says she wants some one to look after her and be a companion after her children have left her. I believe Joe is going to the wedding and Mrs. Vane and one of the girls as well. The rest of the cards have come and we have sent out 17 more invitations making 215 in all. Don't forget to write to Mr. E. W. Bayly, his address is:

Wetherby, Thrale Rd. Streatham Park

Mrs. Morris is coming over for the day and tomorrow we are going to buy my trousseau. Aimèe goes home today and Laura comes on friday, so I shall not be long alone. A month today dear, won't it be lovely? but I wish it was over for I know I shall be awfully nervous. Well dear excuse more. Accept all my love and heaps of kisses

Yours ever

Beatie

I am writing Mr Bayly by this post

Woodcock St. B'ham. March 17th 1899

My own darling Beatie

I am so sorry I have been unable to write to you earlier, for I know dearie how anxiously you would be looking out for a letter, but really there has been no opportunity until now. I was glad to receive your dear letter, and to hear something of the arrangements for the *other* wedding. You have been misinformed dear, I am afraid as to the date for it takes place next Wednesday the 22nd and at a Church at Hackney. The clergyman who is marrying them is the Revd. Davies from Wolverhampton. Jennie and Alec feel rather sore on that point, for Mr. Davies is a personal friend of theirs, and performed the ceremony at their wedding, and Jennie thinks it rather a presumption to have asked him to officiate in this case. However, don't let us trouble about that, for the whole affair simply makes me sick. But don't try to win me over to her dearie for that can never be. Let us not trouble about her any further, she has got someone to care for her now, and I hope he will do it alright. I have ordered Aimée's bangle, and the four brooches, also the Wedding Ring and shall have them with me when I come up at Easter. When I went to Eton Lodge this morning, I found they were about to paper the ceilings, and find that Holyoak had not selected any friezes, so I have been to the Warehouse this afternoon and selected them. He had intended to use the same papers for them as the walls. I have sent on the Madras by Parcel post tonight, and hope it will reach you safely, and not share the fate of the Whistle. I told the man to put 22 yds and 3 inches that is the exact measure required, and hope he has done so. I have ordered a cast iron curb, for the Dining Room today, and Jennie and Alec are giving us Copper and Iron Dogs and Brasses (if one can call them so, seeing they are made of copper and iron).

A most important building in Victorian Birmingham – the main G.P.O. building in the centre of the city, photographed in 1895. (F)

I received a very nice letter from Mr. Daffarn yesterday morning. He says they were not aware of our engagement, until they received the invite to the Wedding. He says they have always held a good impression of you as being a very sensible girl and are so glad to know that it is you who is to become my wife. I had a nice letter from John Burgess today, he regrets he will be unable to attend the Wedding, but sends us every good wish for our future happiness. I hope dearie you are quite well and have not knocked yourself up this last day or two while you have been out shopping. What do you think? Uncle John has made up his mind to come to the Wedding. I hope he won't alter it again. He thinks of going to London on the 11th and stay at the Temple, Arundel St, come to the Wedding and leave London for a stay at Bournemouth on the 13th. I should like him to be at our wedding and do hope he won't change his mind. Laura is with you by this time, of course, please give my love to her, and tell her I am simply dying to see her again for then I shall know that April 12th is not far off. I enclose a supplementary list for Invites etc., will you please add it on to the original. I met Uncle and Aunt Phillips at Chester Rd. last night. Aunt told me she had written to your Ma in response to the invite. She said the distance would preclude them from being present, but they wished us every good wish, and would most certainly come and visit us in our new home. I wish we were in it now dearie, but then time is slipping away, it will not be very long now, so we must be patient I suppose. Forgive me dearie for not letting you hear from me this morning, but you understand how it is. Heaps of kisses, and all my love to your dearie

Ever your own devoted

Jack

❖❖❖❖❖

"Roselea", March 18th 1899

My own darling Jack

I could not make it out not getting a letter yesterday I thought something must be wrong, so I was delighted to get your dear letter this morning. Well the presents are coming in now. I have just got Ted's tea

Both Jack and Beatrice were so preoccupied with their own wedding plans that the eventual news of Jack's mother's wedding came as less of a shock for them to brood about. Beatrice still fretted if a day went by without a letter from Jack.

At least Beatrice was honest about her
disappointing present of a tea service from
her brother Ted – perhaps Aimée's present
list should have been more specific in terms
of make and design. Beatrice chose the
cutlery from her mother herself so it was
not surprising she liked it.

service. I hope you will like it I don't so it is no use saying I do. Then Ma's
present is simply lovely. 1 doz dessert forks, 1 doz table forks, 1 doz dessert
spoons, 1 doz fish eaters and carvers in case to match, and Ernie has given me
6 tablespoons to match the forks etc. Our two servants have given me a glass
and plated salad bowl and servers, isn't it good of them? I have sent the other
invitations off that you wished but I hope Mr. and Mrs. Hawgood will not
come. We heard from the Daffarns and your Aunt Phillips, they as you know
have declined. The Rev. and Mrs. Bayly have accepted. Don't forget dear to
get me that little pin for Leo. I am glad you are having the friezes put on the
wall, it would have looked horrid with the ordinary paper. Just fancy your
Mother marrying so soon, well I wish them luck, hope they won't be disappointed with each other. Write me a nice long letter tomorrow dear, won't
you? Please thank Jennie and Alec for their kindness, I shall like their present
immensely, I know. I wish you were coming up today, I do so want you. Laura
sends her love, we went to the dressmaker this morning to have her dress fitted.
Up to now 30 have refused and 59 accepted. I have got all my trousseau on
view now in the billiard room, I have got a lovely lot, and everybody that has
seen them say they are fit for a princess. I am afraid it will take your eyesight
away when you see them. Have you heard from Avenue Mansion? I received
the curtains this morning, many thanks for sending it, I will start on monday.
Well dear, heaps of love and oceans of kisses

Yours ever Beatie

Mrs. Morris is giving us a pair of entrée dishes.

◇◇◇◇◇◇

Love to Laura, Granny   Stafford House, Wylde Green. March 19th 1899
and in fact to all.

My own darling Beatie

I was so glad to receive your dear letter this morning. It was
brought up to me, in bed just after 8 o'clock, together with one from
Mr. Bayly. Mr. Bayly says he will have much pleasure in officiating at our
wedding and is most particular in his note to state the exact time, date and
place. It would be rather awkward certainly, if there were any misunderstanding, and he or we turned up at the wrong time, wouldn't it dearie. However, there is no fear of that, at any rate so far as we are concerned. I have got
the wedding ring dearie, and oh it does look so sweet. I am simply dying to see
you with it on. It is 22 carat, and made a quarter of an inch wide. You liked
your engagement ring much, but although this is a plain one I venture to think
you will like it even better. To tell you the truth, I quite forgot Leo's pin, when
ordering the brooches etc, but thought of it since, and ordered it yesterday. I
have also spoken about two brooches for your two servants. I feel I ought to
make them some little present, and that they would much appreciate some
small souvenir of the occasion. However, perhaps you might not think the
same; or think a present to them should take some other form, so I will not do
anything definite until I hear from you again. I am glad the tea service has
turned up, but it is a pity you don't like it, perhaps though you might like it

*Pearsall's, jewellers on the corner of High
Street and New Street, a short walk for
Jack from the Woodcock Street Works.
The windows above have the hated
Venetian blinds. (F)*

better on further acquaintance, dearie, like you did me, eh! Your Ma's is a very handsome and useful present, and it is very good of Ernie too, to give us the spoons to match. How good too, of the servants to think of us. I see you have got more people writing to accept, than to decline, at present. Won't it be a big crowd of people, and shan't we be proud of each other that day, dearie.

Mr. Harrop and Jack are sitting here snoring, as I write. Jack is very tired. He and I had quite a big morning. We went to Aston this morning to see Ned Hands, and walked back here to dinner. There was such a cold wind blowing in our eyes, it was simply awful. Poor Hands is very ill indeed. He was getting better the end of last week, but has since had two relapses and has been much worse each time. The Doctor seems to think he will get through alright, but I don't like the look of him at all. I do wish you were here today darling, for I have been so longing for you. How sweet if we could only have one of our sweet Sunday afternoons now, eh dearie. I am so lost without you, and quite wish with you that I had been coming up to you yesterday. I have now decided what to give you for a wedding present, and am sure you will like it very much, but am not going to tell you what it is. That is to be a surprise, and a pleasant one. I think Harrops are writing today in answer to the Invites. The order is placed for our Brass Curb. I hear also Dogs, Brasses and Screen. We shall be quite swagger. Well dearie, Au revoir, and I do wish the 12th was here. All my love dearie

Over your own devoted
Jack

The Hughes and Mercer families had met through a masonic connection and Beatrice and Jack had been 'acquainted' for some time before they realized their love for each other.

Fireside implements – whether brass or not, were essential items for every Victorian household where coal fires were the only form of heating, and were not used simply as decoration as in many cases today. The screen Jack ordered was a wrought iron and copper fire screen.

"Roselea", March 20th 1899

My darling Jack

So delighted to get your dear letter this morning, we had quite 12 letters this morning, I had 2. The people are mostly accepting, so we shall have a good old crowd. I am most curious to know what you have got for me, you might tell me, I cannot wait all that time without knowing. Of course I shall like it I know, your choice of things is always so sweet and what a lovely wedding ring, I shall be proud when I get that on. I have cut the curtains off to the lengths you said and I have got a yard left, so I think they must have given you 23 yds. I have made 2 and am going to start again today. I am going to the tailors this morning with Nellie, so I thought I had better write your letter before I go and so make sure of the time. I had better give you a list of your friends, who wrote this morning.

coming A. Beeson, Butcher, A. L. Harrop, J. Harrop, J. Brettell
not coming Mr. and Mrs. Green, D. Rock

We are very curious to know whether the screen you mention is a fire screen or what, as you mention Jennie is giving us one and one with the brass curb. I have got no end of people coming this week to see my things, isn't it strange how people are always curious to see trousseaux. Is Mr. Harrop or any of the girls coming? I am very glad that Mr. Bayly can officiate at the wedding, it is so much nicer, having a man that you know. I think it is very good of you to want to give the girls a little gift, I am sure they would appreciate a brooch very much, but don't give too much for it, just a small one will do. I wish you were

Beatrice would have known the Revd. Bayly, then curate of St. Alban's Church, very well as she was a regular attender and he lived, as was the church, only yards away from 'Roselea'.

A photograph of Jack's mother – now Mrs. Phelps, after her marriage to Phelps, 'the old buck' in London. Harry Phelps looks obviously delighted with the event though Jack's mother looks somewhat sheepish. (M)

coming this thursday it seems such a long time to wait until Easter, but when it does come we shall not have long to wait, shall we dear? Have you heard from Avenue Mansion yet? Has Jennie gone to Chester Rd. yet? and when does your Mother return from her honeymoon. Well dear, I must be off now, so please excuse me, accept oceans of kisses and all my love and do write me a nice long letter

Jars most devotedly
Beatie

Woodcock St. B'ham. March 22nd 1899

My own darling Beatie

Here we are again! At last I have a comfortable moment to write to my dear little wife. I have had two harassing days and scarcely a moment to call my own. Joe left for town by the 7 o'clock train last night, to give the Lady away , (if that were necessary, for I think she has already done that for herself) and I expect that by now, the lady whom you used to know as Mrs. Hughes will be known by another name, and you are quite aware what that is. But no matter, we must not trouble about that. She has got her dear Phelps, so that is enough for her. Now dearie about your present. Of course I can quite understand your curiosity, but then you know darling you would not satisfy mine when I was anxious to know what you were going to give me. But still I know there is no curiosity so great as a woman's, so I feel almost

Jack wrote many of his letters from the Works in Woodcock Street in the centre of Birmingham. The business had moved to Aston Street in the mid-1850s. Following Jack's grandfather's death and the move to Woodcock Street it became better known as Messrs. J. & J. Hughes. (T)

JOSEPH HUGHES,
BRASS AND GUN METAL CASTER
IN GENERAL,
MILL BRASSES AND RAILWAY CARRIAGE AXLE BRASSES, &c.
Axletree Manufacturers supplied with Caps, Nuts, and Collets.
DEALER IN METALS, AND MANUFACTURER OF INGOT BRASS AND GUN METAL.
76, ASTON STREET, BIRMINGHAM.
J. H. HAS ALWAYS FOR SALE PIG AND BAR LEAD, **OLD TAPS AND MILL BRASSES.**

inclined to satisfy yours. In fact I will, and what I have made up my mind to give you is a ring with sapphires and diamonds in. Don't tell anyone else though dearie, it must come as a surprise to you. I leave it to you entirely whether you tell me or not, what you are going to give to me. You are giving your dearself to me, and that is what I want and what will satisfy me. I do hope you will like the ring, dearie, when you get it, and it took me ever so long to decide what to get, but now I have decided at last.

The curtain man said he would give me long measure, and I should think he had if he sent a yard over. Still better over than under. You surprise me dearie, when you speak of going to the Tailors with Nellie. I thought she was still away, but am ever so pleased to know she is back for I know she must be better. Please give my love to her, when you next see her. I had to go out today and so thought while I was out, I would call at my Tailors. Oh my word he shewed me so many things that it was a hard matter to know what to choose, however I think I chose some very nice things. I am glad Joe Brettell is coming up for our wedding dearie. Uncle John has quite made up his mind to come, and intends coming up on the 11th by the 2.10 and see *The Musketeers* that evening. Gay old spark. Kitty and Maggie Harrop will come, but not Mrs. Darby or Gertie or Mr. Harrop Senr. Mr. Harrop and Mrs. Darby will be at the business, and Gertie remain in charge of the house. The screen I mentioned to you dearie is as you suppose, a fire screen, we shall have one to match the curb etc, in each of the Rooms. The papering is all done now except the kitchen, and that has not been done yet, because the "Bilers bust", of course you understand what that means. The Agent has given instructions to Holyoak to put in a new one. Of course it is no expense to me, but it is a very great nuisance. The rooms look very nice, especially our bedroom, the windows will all look charming I know and oh I am anxious to be married darling and settled in our dear little home. I shall get the brooches for the girls and hope they will like them. I think they will. What do you think, Joe is going to Brussels with Ida next week, and I don't think he will be back until after Easter. In that case I could not come up until Saturday. I am writing to Avenue Mansion tomorrow. I have got the tariff. Jennie is in residence now at Chester Rd. I don't know when the honeymooners return. I wonder how they are getting on duckie, never mind our turn soon. "What ho". All my love dearie, and a sweet kiss

ever your own devoted
Jack

This view of Woodcock Street shows Messrs. Cooper and Goodman, Gunmakers. (F)

"Roselea", March 23rd 1899

My darling Jack

The presents have begun to appear now so the excitement is running very high. Mr. and Mrs. Barclay from Glasgow have sent a pair of lovely cut glass scent bottles with silver tops, they will of course not be able to come. I wrote at once and thanked them. I have also received a pair of ivory glove stretchers with silver handles, very nice, from Mrs. Posnett, they are not coming. We heard from Hoadley this morning, he is unable to come.

Now dear, how good you are, to give me such a lovely present. Do you know,

While Jack was dealing with burst boilers and unreliable decorators, Beatrice was enjoying the presents she was receiving — one advantage of a large wedding which Jack's mother and Phelps would not have shared.

The sapphire and diamond ring that Jack gave Beatrice has since been split into two rings, now owned by her great grand-daughters.

I will tell you a secret, that is just what I wanted, but I could not tell you for I never thought you would care to spend so much money under these circumstances, but I shall love it I know and I do so appreciate all your goodness to me, which I hope to prove to you in the future. I should so love to see our house, I am sure it must look lovely and when we get that beautiful furniture in, shan't we fancy ourselves dear, being there together? Time is going now dear, only a fortnight next wednesday. I am sorry that you won't be able to come until saturday, for I do so want you dearie. I am disgusted with Joe for going to the wedding, what a sneak. Where have the giddy young things gone for their honeymoon? Have you engaged a room at the Avenue Mansion? What are their prices this time of the year? Don't forget the blankets dear, for this cold weather we shall want something warm to cover us shan't we? What about Frank, is he coming up for the wedding? I am afraid we shall be very full up with people sleeping here, but if he did not mind, Nellie could make up a bed for him on the sofa in the same room with you. I had a letter from Ida this morning, she seems very upset about your Mother marrying Phelps, but I don't think they are worth it. I am not going to trouble myself, and I hope you won't, and only think of our future happiness. Well dear I do hope you will like what I have got for you, I have chosen a pair of gold links, torpedo shape, I couldn't think of anything else. Have you bought the kitchen furniture yet? 97 people have accepted up to now. Don't disappoint me next time of writing, and write me a lovely long letter for I do so long for you dear. Heaps of love and I wish I could tell you how much I think of you and love you so

Yours ever Beati

Beatrice was not nearly so excited about the present she had chosen for Jack and was almost apologetic about not being able to think of anything other than cuff links.

❖❖❖❖❖❖

Woodcock St. B'ham. March 24th 1899

My own darling Beatie

I was so glad to receive your dear letter this morning, for I do miss you so my dearie, and want you to be with me very much, and when I get a dear letter from you to read it quite puts fresh life into me. It must as you say, be quite exciting at "Roselea", just now, especially with the presents arriving. Of course, I did not for a moment expect that Mr. and Mrs. Barclay would be able to come to the wedding, but they were anxious to know all about it, and I think it is so nice of them to have sent us a present. I am glad dearie, that you are so pleased with the present I have decided to give you. Truly it will be expensive, but then I felt you would like it, and that I should like to see you with it, so there you are. I am sure it will be very nice, and you will be proud of it. You are right dearie, our house is lovely, and when the furniture is in it will only want your own dear self down here to complete the picture. The men have come to put in the new boiler today; and this afternoon the blinds and carpets will be delivered, and tomorrow they will be fixed, except the carpet on the stairs. That is being left for a time, so that I can get the furniture into the rooms, and then have the Hall and Staircase papered and the stairs stained. Then when the stair carpets are down it will be complete. I have arranged it that way so that the papering and staining should not be knocked

The planning and timing of the work to be done at Eton Lodge and the organization of its complete furnishing, well ahead of their residence there, was typical of Jack's meticulous and ordered approach to things.

about when the furniture went in. When they go to do the Hall and Staircase, I shall have all the rooms locked so the furniture will be alright. The furniture will be delivered on Monday, also the beds and crockery ware, and I shall have a day off from here, so as to be up at the house to take them in, and see them put properly in their places. I have got the goods from Gray's there, also the two pictures. I think you said you had one or two pictures for the dining room, if so, I think it would be better for me to bring them down at Easter, and put them up in their places.

Joe came back last night by the 7 o'clock train. He told me he called upon your Pa, yesterday morning. I suppose you have heard of that by this time. The newly wedded pair went to Bournemouth I believe. Joe has not told me, and I have not asked him. I wrote to Avenue Mansion yesterday, and shall no doubt hear tomorrow. I told them we should arrive there on the 12th and leave on the 26th, and should like to know if they could accommodate us for that time and what their terms would be. I also said we should require a good large Bedroom, with a sea view if possible, and not higher than the second floor. I do hope they can take us for the time, and the terms will be alright. On their Tariff they say July 1st and during Season from 2½ Guineas according to position and size of bedroom. Other months at lower rates. I shall see about the blankets alright. This is just the sort of weather to be married. Not too hot. I heard of a couple who once went to Bournemouth for their honeymoon, and it was so hot they couldn't stay in bed, and got out and sat on two chairs laughing at one another. Still that is frivolous talking like that. Frank will come to the wedding, and I think he must come with us on the 11th, it would never do to leave him to come up on the 12th. Ida had a box of wedding cake come yesterday, and she played football with it, to shew her contempt for the beauty. There was not any sent to me of course. I am sure dearie I shall like the links very much, and it is really too good of you to buy them. I have not yet got the kitchen table and chairs, but that won't take long. Well dearie for the present Au revoir and I do want the time to go by fast. Heaps of kisses and all my love to my darling

Ever your own devoted
Jack

Our pendant and shade had arrived. I see the announcement is in today's B'ham Post

◆◇◆◇◆◇◆

My new trunk has come marked B.C.H.

"Roselea", March 25th 1899

My darling Jack

I was looking out for your letter most eagerly this morning, many thanks for it. I have just had two more presents, a copper flower pot and a lovely hand made lace and linen tablecloth, so I have been just acknowledging them. We are getting quite alarmed, for so far 104 people have accepted and have not all replied. You see Pa did not want to exceed 105 as we should then have to have the next size marquee to hold 160, this Pa does not want to do, for the expense would be so much greater.

Seaside resorts were popular honeymoon places and it was not surprising that Jack and Beatrice should choose Folkestone again after their romantic and happy summer holiday there. Jack's frequent and coy hint that they knew how to keep each other 'hot' would insure that an out of season honeymoon would not matter to them.

MARRIED.

LEIGH—UNDERHILL.—On the 29th ult., at St. Augustine's Church, Edgbaston (by the Rev. J. C. Blissard, M.A., vicar), Alfred Broughton, youngest son of the late Zebulun Leigh, of Edgbaston, to Florence Beatrice, eldest daughter of the late Edward Underhill and of Mrs. Underhill, The Highfields, Edgbaston. At home, Glenesk, City Road, Edgbaston, May 9 and 10.

PERKINS—WILSON.—On the 29th ult., at St. James's Church, Ashted (by the Rev. W. Chapman, M.A., assisted by the Rev. W. Hunter, M.A.), Charles Briton Perkins, second son of J. Perkins, of Penzance, to Rose Annie Wilson, second daughter of Councillor Thomas Wilson, of Nechells.

PHELPS—HUGHES.—On the 22nd ult., at the Church of St. John-at-Hackney, by the Rev. John H. Davies, M.A., late Colonial Chaplain Gold Coast Colony, assisted by the Hon. and Rev. A. G. Lawley, M.A., rector), Harry James Phelps to Jane Hughes. At home April 18, 19, and 20, Linwood Lodge, Gravelly Hill, Birmingham.

WOODALL—NETTLEFOLD.—On the 23rd ult., at the Church of the Messiah, Birmingham (by the Rev. L. P. Jacks), Henry, son of Corbett Woodall, Esq., 69, Fitzjohn's Avenue, Hampstead, to Bertha, daughter of the late C. J. Nettlefold, Esq., The Grove, Highgate, and of Mrs. Nettlefold, Hallfield, Edgbaston, Birmingham.

The wedding announcement of Jack's mother, now Mrs. Phelps. She had got her way, despite so much family opposition and general disapproval and was prepared to announce it publicly. (I)

Whereas Beatrice was now prepared to adopt a rational acceptance of the Phelps affair, Jack was still bitter and unforgiving. Similarly, now that his mother had got what she wanted, despite everybody, the likelihood of her giving her blessing to Jack's marriage was no less remote.

Why, dearie do you want the furniture sent in so early, I hope it won't get stolen or damaged, don't you think you had better insure against burglary? Joe called at Pa's office, but was in a great hurry and did not stay many minutes. He told Pa that he was as much opposed to your Mother's marriage as anybody, but said that made no difference, as she was quite justified in marrying whom she liked, he made the best of a bad job. Now Jack dear, you know he is right, he said you had not been at all diplomatic and I am afraid you have not been. Just fancy the giddy old thing sending cake, I wonder if she will send us any? I have now done all the ordering I have to do and have got all home except my hats and dresses, and of course I shall not have those, until quite the last thing. It will be jolly to have a nice large bedroom at Avenue Mansion, for we can sit there, instead of going to the drawing room, when we wanted although I don't suppose there will be many people there. I do hope the weather gets a little warmer, for it is bitter here. Nellie Morris is coming this afternoon to spend Sunday with us. I wish it was you instead. You must be having quite a fine time at home, all by yourselves. Millard is coming to the wedding and Mr. and Mrs. Ashwin. Ma has written to our organist and he is able to preside at the organ on the 12th. I shall be looking out for your dear letter on monday morning, so do write a nice long cheery letter, for I do so want you my darling. Don't forget to order some coals dear. Pa is having my visiting cards printed for me, and he will get the plate and I can then have them done anywhere. I wrote my new name for the first time on some things I was marking "B. Hughes" it does look funny doesn't it dear? Well dear I think I must go, I have a lot to see to. Accept my most devoted love and heaps of thanks for your kindness and trouble you are taking to make me happy and comfortable in my new home

Yours most devotedly
Beatie

Is Alice going to stay with your Mother?

<><><><><><>

Wylde Green, March 26th 1899

My own darling Beatie

I was up here yesterday and went down to Linwood Lodge this morning to get your dear letter. Of course you know I was not disappointed. There was also a letter from Avenue Mansion and they can accommodate us at the required time, and give us a good large room with sea view, for $2\frac{1}{2}$ guineas each a week. I have written tonight and accepted it so that is alright. The presents are still arriving I see, I found one at home this morning, and when I opened it, found a pair of pictures, from Bert While, one of my old Sergeant chums. They are small but very nice. One is fruit and the other flowers painted in oil, and mounted in deep gold frames. What a crowd of people there will be on the 12th, well I hope it will not prove too many, but still you know the saying, "Let em all come". I went to Eton Lodge this morning, and found all the blinds and carpets fixed, and the furniture and beds will be delivered tomorrow, as I told you. You are surprised I know to hear this, but then I am so anxious dearie, to get our home all ready, and feel that I must

The two oil paintings from Bert While – a valuable gift. They are by the artist Oliver Clare and were sold recently to someone who, by sheer coincidence, had lived at Linwood Lodge for several years. (U)

have it all in form before I come up for the wedding. I shall see the furniture is not damaged, and I don't think we need fear burglary, for there will be no small valuables to remove. I quite wish with you dearie, that I had been coming to be with you this week, but then we have only another week to wait. Really it does seem ages since I left you; and wouldn't I give something for a sweet embrace with my darling. Shan't I be busy tomorrow. I shall enjoy it though and I do wish you could be there with me, but then you will see it when it is all done and I know you will be pleased with it. The carpets look lovely and the one in the Dining Room treads beautifully soft. I shall put up the pictures tomorrow. Arthur and I walked through Sutton Park this afternoon, and it was very enjoyable. I thought so dearie of the Sunday afternoon you and I went up there. I loved you then dearie, but had never told you for I did not feel you could have loved me, but I have since found differently eh darling. We shall often go to Sutton Park I have no doubt when we are settled down in our home. I am glad the organist is able to preside at the Organ on the 12th, it will liven things up a bit.

I have got the brooches and Bangle and very nice indeed they look. I feel sure they will be much liked. Aimèe will be pleased with hers I know. I had two tons of coal delivered last Monday, so we shall do for a time. Alice says she doesn't know if she will stay on with Mrs. Phelps, but will not if he interferes with her, she says she can't stand the sight of him at all. As I write they are joking and say they don't know whatever I can find to say, to be writing all this while. Arthur wishes me to give his love, to you. Gertie wants to know if I have finished as she wants to come here and write, so my dearie I must wish you Au revoir. Think of me tomorrow putting our little home straight. Au revoir again, All my love and a sweet kiss

Your own for ever
Jack

❖❖❖❖❖❖❖

"Roselea", March 27th 1899

My own darling Jack

I do hope the furniture will be perfectly safe and I really don't think it ought to be left for I have heard of burglars taking a pantechnicon and taking all the things off at night. If you wish it I dare say the servant would come sooner, she is at home. I know you will be sorry to hear, but I am so queer dear, I had a horrible faint yesterday morning, and consequently feel very shaky today. I have made up my mind to go and see the doctor, I shall never go through the wedding excitement if I do not feel stronger. Nellie Morris and I were having our breakfast in bed, and I was so bad, I got out of bed and sat on the floor and put my head between my knees, having been advised to do that when I felt faint, but I rolled over and fainted, with my head under the bed, and Nellie had quite a job to get me from underneath. I stayed in bed until dinner time. Then Nellie Morris fainted in the bath chair on her way home, she looked fearfully bad while she was here. Ernie and Ma went with them and they were with her until 12 o'clock. The Tory's are here today to see my things, I have had such a lot of people to see them and some are

Beatrice had her own very positive views about how she liked things to be done and it was surprising Jack was so confident that she would like the way he was to arrange everything, without her being there.

The wedding excitement and so many things to be done had been too much for Beatrice, who was prone to fainting and feeling 'queer' at the best of times. Both she and Nellie Morris fainting on the same day must have made the family wonder if all the excitement was worth it. (B)

The motives for sending Ida off to school abroad were all too obvious for most of the family, although Ida herself would not have realized it at the time. Her mother and Phelps needed her out of the way for their own sakes in addition to them not wanting her to be able to be a bridesmaid.

coming every day this week. I wish you were coming on thursday but I suppose it will have to be saturday. Give my love to Ida, wish her goodbye for me and tell her I hope she will like the school, I will write to her before she goes, if I have time. It is good of you to give me that ring dear, I am longing to see it, but I know I shall like it. My darling, I think you are paying too much at Avenue Mansion, especially being out of the season, but no doubt it will be a lovely room, it ought to be. I know a girl who has just come back from Folkestone, she said it was delightful, so we ought to get fine weather later on. Well dearie, write soon and cheer me up, I feel so down. All my love

Yours ever
Beatie

Linwood Lodge, March 28th 1899

My own darling Beatie

I am so grieved dearie to hear that you have had one of those horrid fainting turns again, and are feeling so queer. It is doubly unfortunate that you should be ailing just now, when you have so very much to see after. I do hope dearie that by this time you are feeling more like your self again. Don't worry about me and the house, and the safety of the furniture etc, for I don't think there is any need to do so. Leave it to me and I think it will be alright but I know you are so anxious my darling. All the furniture is now in, (with the exception of the pedestal for back room, and the servant's towel rail) and very nice it looks too. I have fixed the pendant in Dining Room, and very swagger it looks with the Terra Cotta shade. The two small pictures which Bert While gave us, I have put up on either side of the sideboard. The two we bought in New St. I have put on the wall over the Couch, and although they are supposed to be a pair, one is a bit larger than the other. The difference is not very noticeable though. The room will look very nice indeed when quite finished off, and the table when at its smallest suits admirably, and when at its fullest length the room takes it well. Fancy, I was at Eton Lodge all day yesterday until about 9 o'clock and have had another day today until about 8pm. The painter's men are coming tomorrow to do the kitchen and staircase wall, and will be finished by Thursday night with the exception of the staining which of course must remain until the stairs are scoured down after them. I am sure dearie we shall have ever such a pretty home when it is finished. I am going over tomorrow morning early to fix the wire mattresses up. The Bedsteads are up and the bolsters and pillows and felt covers are there, but the hair mattresses have not yet arrived, they will be there soon though. There is no occasion dearie, for the servant to come earlier than originally arranged, but I hope she won't fail to turn up then. I gave Ida her brooch last night and she likes it very much indeed. I will bring the others up on Saturday.

Jack had enjoyed himself arranging their new home and was in good spirits now that the wedding was so close and the chance to get away from Linwood Lodge at last looked certain.

Avenue Mansion was a small private hotel on the corner of Clifton Crescent and Earl's Avenue in Folkestone. With a large room with a sea view for two and a half guineas a week, it was more than they had paid at the Victoria Hotel in the summer, but Jack clearly decided that this special occasion warranted it.

I am sorry indeed to hear that Nellie is still so poorly, please give my love to her when next you see her, and say I hope she will be better by this time. I am sorry you think we are paying too much at Avenue Mansion; of course if we had a small bedroom up in the top we could no doubt get in for less, but you wouldn't like that dearie, would you? We shall want plenty of breathing space, and not too many stairs to climb. Well my dearie buck up, and try and be ever so well. Whatever would we do if you are like this on the 12th. I do hope the excitement will not be too much for you my darling. Keep cool.

Well dearie I have to go to town tonight to post, so you must please excuse anything further this time. All my love and a sweet kiss, and I do hope you are now quite well. Au revoir.

Your own devoted
Jack

"Roselea", March 29th 1899

My own darling Jack

How busy you have been, I do wish I could have come and helped. Have you put the brass curtain rods up and brass finger plates on the doors? How does the furniture in our bedroom do? and how and where have you put the dressing table? Excuse all these questions, but you know darling how anxious I am. Well dearie, Granny is very ill indeed again in bed and we have had the doctor to her. I do hope all will go well, it is a worry, I don't know what we should do if anything happens to her. I have had a bottle of medicine from the Dr. He says I am very run down but that the change is what I want and will do me a lot of good, the medicine is filthy and really I felt a great deal worse this morning than I have done for a long time, but I am feeling better again now. Nellie is much better, she and Ted are going away tomorrow until tuesday, then they have taken a house at Herne Bay from April 19th to the end of May, so that ought to set her up. I shall be longing to see my ring and the bridesmaids presents, so do bring them dear. I have had a letter from Mrs. Proud asking me to go over tomorrow morning to see one of the Chippendale chairs that is finished polishing and upholstered, as she and Mr. Proud will be away over Easter tuesday. She says she has got several patterns of brocade that if we bought the chairs she would get them all finished and sent direct to us, so dear I think I will go over and see it and then write you full particulars. I suppose you will still like me to see them, however there will be no harm done my going to see it. Mrs. Weston sent us a brass table gong yesterday. Well darling excuse more as we have got a lot of visitors coming again this afternoon

Yours ever
Beatie

For Grannie to have been dangerously ill again at this important time would have caused a family crisis indeed. She was determined to live to see her grand-daughter married. It seemed as if the wedding excitement was effecting everybody. (B)

Excuse envelope, it is the only plain one I can find

Woodcock St. B'ham. March 31st 1899

My own darling Beatie

You are quite right I have been busy, so busy in fact that I could not write to you last night, but then that doesn't matter, for I suppose there would be no delivery today, being Good Friday. The whole of the paint-

It was the Easter weekend and a whole year since Jack had stayed for the first time with the Mercers. Following that weekend, a year before, Beatrice wrote to Jack politely: "I am glad you enjoyed your short stay with us and hope next time you will try and stay longer, I enjoyed your company and did miss you". She then invited him again for Whitsun . . .

ing work will be finished today, and shan't I be glad. I have not put the curtain rods up yet, but shall do so before I leave on the 11th. It won't be long now will it, tomorrow is the first. The furniture in our bedroom looks very nice indeed, but there is not room to place the tables across the corners, as I had thought; the dressing chest is between the two windows, at the foot of the bed and there is plenty of room to get by, and to open the drawers. The washstand is in the corner between the far window and fireplace (at present). I think that is about the best way to arrange it, as then there is a good lot of clear floor space on the door side of the bed, all clear in front of wardrobe, right up to the window. I bought a copper and wrought Iron lamp for the hall yesterday afternoon, and fixed it last night, and think it looks very nice indeed.

I have got the gas connected, so, when I had put up the lamp, had an illumination for the first time. The pendant in the Dining Room looks very pretty. In fact the entire place looks well, and I am quite pleased with it. I am so sorry dearie, to hear of Granny being so ill again, please give my love to her and tell her she must try and get quite alright for the 12th, so must you darling. I am glad you have been to the Doctor at last. I think he is right too dearie, about the change doing you good, I hope so anyhow. You must try and not get too excited and then I think you will be alright. I shall hope to bring your ring with me tomorrow although I have not got it at present.

I was in a fancy metal workers' place, with whom we do business, the other day, and he was shewing me one or two special orders he was just executing, one was a small grandfather clock, and he informed me it was going to London for a Wedding present, early in April. How strange if it should come to us. But there will be no such luck, I suppose. I hope you liked the chairs, and found them good and reasonable in price. I am annoyed dearie, that I am unable to be with you today as anticipated. Do you remember last Good Friday, and the walk to Dulwich, I do. What a change in a year, eh dearie. I saw Brettell the other night, and he asked me if we had a Salad Bowl given us yet. I told him yes, about five or six, so he said he had thought of giving us one, but under the circumstances must try and think of something else. Joe and Ida left on Wednesday, and I don't expect Joe back again until about Thursday night, and as the Works re-open on Tuesday, that means I shall have to come down by the early train on Tuesday morning, or at latest the one about 11 o'clock. Isn't it a beastly nuisance. Oh I know there is something else to tell you. Yesterday I insured the household goods against loss by fire, or burglary. So now you need not feel anxious for their safety. Of course it would be a great annoyance if anything was stolen, but still we shall be alright. I have not yet got the policy, but the receipt for the premium covers in the meantime. Well

A photograph of Joe taken in Brussels. Joe accompanied Ida to her new school there and spent most of the Easter week in Belgium, once again leaving Jack to have to cope at the Works. (V)

dearie I am anxiously waiting to come to you, and shall hope to see you at Streatham Hill tomorrow 7.16 if you are well enough and I hope you will be. All my love and a sweet kiss.

ever your own devoted
Jack

Jack & Beatrice Are Married

APRIL

Jack puts his thoughts to 'conjure up a speech' while Beatrice makes final preparations for her trousseau and the wedding day. Jack, while trying not to worry too much that Beatrice might faint during the ceremony, or whether his mother will eventually turn up, sets off for London and their wedding day at last . . .

Love to Aimèe   Woodcock St. B'ham. April 4th 1899

My own darling Beatie

You will see by this that I have arrived safely in B'ham once more, and I know you will be anxiously waiting to hear from me. I did feel so down in the dumps when leaving you this morning dearie, for I was so sorry to have to come from you so soon, but I must cheer up I know for the 12th will soon be here now, and then we shall be alright. I can't help continually thinking of all the handsome presents, and especially of the one from Lord Rothschild. It was so good of him, and so utterly unexpected. We used to think at one time dearie, that the world was against us; but now I feel differently, and

At one time everything had seemed to conspire against the chances of Jack and Beatrice marrying, but now Jack knew that he had made his last weekend visit and that the next journey up to London would be to be married.

St. Alban's Church, Streatham Park in 1900, where Jack and Beatrice were married. The church still stands on the corner of Fayland Avenue which leads off from Thrale Road and it was only a short distance from 'Roselea' for the family and guests to walk. (D)

Lord Rothschild, with whose company the Mercers had worked for generations, gave Jack and Beatrice a gift of £100 – a handsome present indeed. In order to be able to display it among the wedding presents without fear of it being stolen, this photograph of it was taken, to which a gift tag was attached. (A)

Jack was quite a shy and modest man and the prospect of a speech was daunting for him. He certainly would not have gone into it unprepared or left anything to chance.

Beatrice's parents had wanted a seven year engagement but Jack had courted Beatrice for only one year before they were to marry. Beatrice's father was to miss her dearly.

think what a lucky couple we are to have such an array of beautiful and useful presents. I shall have to rack my brains during the next week, and see what I can conjure up in the way of a speech. I don't feel afraid but that I can make up a very nice reply to the toast, but the trouble will be in delivering it. I do hope I shan't be very nervous, but still I must make up my mind not to be, for your sake darling. I find I have got the Wedding Ring alright dearie, and have just tried it on and it does look so fine with the other one in front of it. Won't you be proud of them both, eh darling, and shan't I be proud of you. I am sorry I didn't see Granny before I came away today. Please give my love to her, and tell her to get as well as ever she can by the 12th, and you must do the same yourself dearie. I do hope you are feeling more like yourself when you receive this, for darling it does so grieve me to find you so poorly as you have been lately. Never mind, you can't help it can you dearie, you are not poorly because you like it.

I do wish we could have one of our good old embraces now dearie, but fancy we can't have one for a whole week. I expect this week will go more quickly though, than the weeks have done of late, for everyone will have so much to think about, and do. It is good of your dear Pa, to go to so much trouble and expense, to entertain such a great number of guests, so handsomely, but then my darling you deserve it all. Won't your poor Pa miss you when I take you away. I know it will be a big trial for him.

Well dearie I have to go off about your ring tonight so please excuse more this time. Mind not knock yourself up with all your work this week. Au revoir. All my love to you dearie, and a sweet kiss.

ever your own devoted

Jack

"Roselea", April 5th 1899

My darling Jack

Glad to hear you arrived safely. It was a shame you were not able to stay longer, but never mind, we shall soon be always together, shan't we dearie? I had to wait 20 minutes for Ma and Aimèe and it came on to rain so fast, we did our shopping and then came home, we got so wet, we had to change our dresses. Well dear, I wrote to the servant and asked her to let us know within the next few days, whether she thought she would really come. Then I wrote to the chair people, and offered them £10 = 10 = 0. Ted says if they are really genuine, £12 would be dirt cheap, so we must wait and hear what they think of our offer. This morning I have ordered the bouquets and they will send a buttonhole for you and Joe to the vestry of the Church, so it will save you calling. They are going to send you a white carnation and Joe a pink one to match the bridesmaids' bouquets. Then we went to the photographer and he will come down and we also hired a piano so weren't we busy? This afternoon Aimèe and I are going to shampoo our heads, ready for the wedding. Tomorrow both dressmakers have sent for me at once, so I am going to one in the morning, and from there up to Kensington to the other, shan't I be tired? Mr. and Mrs. Raby sent us a very nice crumb scoop, silver and ivory. I wrote and acknowledged it at once. This afternoon, I have just received an eider down quilt, such a nice satin one, but I don't know who it is from, I believe it is from Mr. and Mrs. King but I must wait and see. Have you heard when Joe is coming back? Take care of the furniture on saturday dear. I hope you will have a very enjoyable evening don't overdo it and make yourself bad for wednesday. Well darling, ta ta. Heaps of love

Yours ever
Beatie

Aimèe sends her love

❖❖❖❖❖❖

"Roselea", April 7th 1899

Darling Jack

I do hope all is well with you, do write and let me know how you are, I am so anxious not having had a letter today. I heard from Proud this morning, and he says he cannot take less than £11 for the 3 chairs so will you wire to me whether you will have them or not. If you decide on them he will send you pattern of brocade to choose from. Oh darling the lovely presents we are having, it really is too much for me. Mr. and Mrs. Lane have sent a lovely silver and glass fruit dish, Mr. Raby a crumb scoop and Mr. Daffarn a silver cheese, butter and biscuit dish but unfortunately I have one already but never mind that, it is the first duplicate I have had. Excuse me now dear, I want to catch the post. Lots of love

Yours ever
Beatie

Mr. Alfred Rothschild has sent me £50 isn't it generous, I don't know where I am.

The prevalent hair style of that time, which Beatrice also wore, was hair swept up to a coil or bun with a curly fringe and tiny curls on the forehead. She did not wash her hair very often it seems and she would probably have used ordinary soap.

By this time Beatrice was in a complete daze, though still ever anxious at not having received a letter from Jack, even though she knew there was no real reason to panic.

This was a significant letter in that it was the first Jack was to write from Eton Lodge. It was to be hoped that his last 'bachelor' evening the next night would not undo all Jack's careful preparation of the house.

"Eton Lodge", April 7th 1899

My own darling Peakie

I was so awfully sorry that I was unable to write to you last night, dearie, for I know you would be anxiously awaiting a letter this morning, and would be much disappointed. There is no need to tell you the reason I did not write, for of course, you will quite understand how my time is so fully occupied just now. However, here I am at last having a peaceful time, and so am sitting in our Dining Room, and writing to you. This is the first time I have written from "Eton Lodge". The Dining Room looks lovely dearie, ever so nice and cosy but oh it just wants you here, and then it would be alright. When we have got the curtains up, it will be ever so nice. I have got a nice fire, and the place looks quite cheerful. The Gardener was here today, but he had a very wet day to work in, so could not do so much as I should have liked. I wanted the grass all cutting, to look smart for tomorrow, but as it was so wet, it had to be left. I am sorry you got so wet the other day dearie, and hope you have not got any ill effects from it. I had a letter from Raby this morning, and he is ever so sorry that they are unable to come. Joe Brettell has come out handsomely. He has sent us a lovely liquor stand. Oak with silver mounts, with places for liqueur glasses, cigars and a drawer fitted with two packs of playing cards and a cribbage board. It looks fine on our sideboard.

I hope the chair people will accept our offer, but am rather afraid not. I am glad you have ordered the bouquets, but dearie, will you please ask them to send three buttonholes to the vestry; so that there will be one for Frank. Frank has been in having a look round, and has just gone. He thinks the house looks very nice. I was very surprised yesterday morning, on reaching Woodcock St., to find Joe there, as I had not expected him home until last night. He was feeling very seedy, as he had had a bad turn at sea sickness. However, he managed a Masonic Banquet last night and has gone to a Dance tonight. He does do it. I think he might have gone a bit quietly just lately, but no matter. I am glad we have got a nice eider down quilt, we shall be nice and warm, eh dearie? Won't it be a bit lively here this time tomorrow night, but don't worry about the furniture etc, for I shall see it is alright. There will be just twelve of us, and I have got the six chairs out of the Breakfast Room at Linwood Lodge, covered with red leather, so we shall be alright for a chair each. I will watch I don't knock myself up, and also the others as well for that matter. I must have them all in good form on Wednesday. I do so wish you were here now dearie, for the room here looks so nice and cosy and comfortable, and oh couldn't we enjoy our little selves. I picked up a book today about seaside resorts, and there was a page or two on Folkestone. A fine description of the Warren. We must go up there dearie, if it is fine enough, and I do hope it will be. I expect the folks back to Linwood Lodge on Monday. I shall sleep here tomorrow Sunday and Monday nights, and after then, if the servant has not arrived, I thought of asking Mrs. Sadler's husband to sleep here while we are away. I think he would do it. Well dearie, I must be off as I have to go to town to post this so for the present 'Au revoir'. All my love and a dear goodnight kiss.

Your own devoted Jack

The Masonic Record of Joe Hughes, Jack's brother, initiated in the Forward Lodge, No. 1180 in 1895. Joe continued a life of late nights and not so early mornings at the Works until he too was eventually married in 1901 to Mary Ann Homer, known as Polly. (V)

"Roselea", April 8th 1899

My darling Jack

You must really excuse a long letter this time, I have heaps to see to, I must race now to write this. So glad you are alright. I hope you will have a merry time tonight, I know you will so I need not wish it. I am writing to Proud's to order the chairs, thank you so much for letting me have them. I have had a letter from Caroline and she will be at Gravelly Hill about 3 o'clock on tuesday afternoon and I have told her to go to Mrs. Sadler's for instructions, so will you tell Mrs. Sadler all about it. I have lots more presents, too many to tell you, you must see them on tuesday. Ma has taken a double bedded room for you, Joe and Frank at Thrale Hall, as Nellie's children are both ill and she has no servant, Ma has arranged for breakfast of course. Well dearie au revoir lots of love

Yours ever Beatie

The altar at St. Alban's Church, Streatham Park where Jack and Beatrice were married on April 12th, 1899. It proved to be a beautiful day. (D)

It was recorded in the Streatham News *that all Streatham Park was "en fête" the day of Jack and Beatrice's wedding – a sunny, spring Wednesday afternoon. Many of the guests and family walked back to 'Roselea' from St. Alban's Church and caused a "flutter of excitement in Streatham". "Streatham could not have presented a more charming sight" wrote the* South London Press, *whose detailed account of the event is reproduced overleaf.*

Beatrice managed to "keep cool", and wore a dress of ivory satin with a brocade court train and Brussels lace. Mr. Mercer showed the most emotion being "so much affected" on rising to respond to the speeches that "he found it difficult to express his thanks to them". Although many guests "travelled expressly from Birmingham and other provincial centres", Jack's mother was noticeably absent.

Jack and Beatrice's marriage certificate. Joe was Jack's best man, and Aimée Tory the chief bridesmaid. Despite the absence of certain close members of Jack's family it was, in every other way, a happy event. (A)

No.	When Married.	Name and Surname.	Age.	Condition.	Rank or Profession.	Residence at the Time of Marriage.	Father's Name and Surname.	Rank or Profession of Father.
71	April 12th 1899	John Albert Hughes	28	Bachelor	Brassfounder	Elm Lodge Gravelly Hill Birmingham	Joseph Hughes (deceased)	Merchant
		Beatrice Catherine Mercer	28	Spinster	—	Streatham Park	David Dixon Mercer	Accountant

Married in the Church of S. Albans according to the Rites and Ceremonies of the Established Church by or after Banns By me, E. W. Bayly

This Marriage was solemnized between us, { John Albert Hughes / Beatrice Catherine Mercer } In the presence of us, { David Dixon Mercer / John Hughes. Aimée Tory }

The above is a true Copy of the Marriage Register of the S. Albans Church aforesaid.

Extracted this ___ day of April in the Year of our Lord One Thousand Eight Hundred and ninety nine

By me, E. W. Bayly.

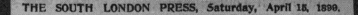

THE SOUTH LONDON PRESS, Saturday, April 15, 1899.

Wedding at Streatham.

HUGHES—MERCER.

Thrale-road, Streatham, recalls memories of Mrs. Thrale, bluff Dr. Johnson, and Oliver Goldsmith in his embroidered waistcoat and plum-coloured coat. Even in the picturesque days of the poet who "wrote like an angel" Streatham could not have presented a more charming sight than the wedding of Miss Beatrice C. Mercer, which took place at St. Alban's, Streatham, on Wednesday afternoon. The weather was delightful, and made the

THE BRIDEGROOM.

lovely costumes of the ladies look in perfect harmony with the semi-rural landscape, for Streatham Park has yet some lingering charms of the country

The bride at this charming wedding, which has caused quite a flutter of excitement in Streatham, was Miss Beatrice C. Mercer, only daughter of Mr. David Mercer, of Roslea, Streatham Park. The bridegroom was Mr. John A. Hughes, youngest son of the late Mr. Joseph Hughes, of Birmingham. Many ladies and gentlemen travelled expressly from Birmingham and other distant provincial centres to be present at this wedding. The wedding took

THE BRIDE.

place at St. Alban's Church, Streatham Park and this beautiful church, designed by Mr. Martineau, looked very beautiful in the spring sunshine, decorated as it was with flowers and filled with elegantly-dressed ladies, who nearly all carried lovely bouquets.

The officiating clergyman was the Rev. E. W. Bayly. Mr. Macpherson was at the organ, and he played a magnificent selection of organ music, including a minuet by Scotson-Clark, offertories by Batiste, and Mendelssohn's "Wedding March." Mr. Macpherson extemporised, too, with much skill.

The bride, who was given away by her father, wore a lovely bridal dress of ivory satin, with a brocaded court train; her veil was of old Brussels lace with orange blossoms, and her bouquet was of very choice flowers. The bridesmaids were Miss Tory, Miss L. Wallers, and Miss Nellie Morris, who were attired en suite in charming white muslin robes, with Valenciennes lace insertion, pink over pink, and carried bouquets of choice pink carnations. The bridegroom's gift to the bride was a beautiful diamond and sapphire ring, the bride's present to the bridegroom was a pair of elegant sleeve links, the bridesmaids also received elegant gifts from the bridegroom, whose brother, Mr. Joseph Hughes, acted as his "best man."

The brides's mother wore a beautiful costume of black brocaded silk, with petunia and silver design, and carried a bouquet of two shades of lilac.

After the ceremony, the guests were conveyed in many splendidly-appointed carriages to Roslea, Streatham Park, the home of the bride's father, where an elegant wedding breakfast was served in a spacious marquee specially erected in the lovely ground. Messrs. Paul and Collard, of Streatham presented this recherche menu:

Mayonnaise Salmon.
Oyster Patties.
Chaudfroid Quails. Chaudfroid Pigeons.
Roast Chicken. Ox Tongues.
York Ham. Raised Pigeon Pie.
Braized Beef. Galantine Veal.
Mayonnaise Lobster.
Russian and Italian Salads.
Chartreuse Bananas.
Maraschino Curacao. Noyeau Jellies.
Strawberry, Vanilla, and Chocolate Creams.
Trifles. Meringues. Eclairs.

DESSERT.

Pines. Grapes. Apples. Bananas.

The bridegroom and his charming bride sat at the head of the table, and among the guests were Mr. Joseph Hughes, Miss Tory, Mr. Flower, Miss H. Tory, Mr. T. Bayley, Mrs. Tory, Mr. Smith, sen., Mrs. Wallers, Mr. Lane, Mrs. Collins, Mrs. Hurst, Mr. Ibbetson, Mrs. Mottley, Mr. Woodward, Mrs. Woodward, Mr. E. Renard, Mrs. T. Bayley, Mr. R. Crafter, Miss Morris, Mr. E. A. Mercer, Miss L. Wallers, Mrs. Costello, Mr. Costello, Mrs. Vane, Mr. Ashwin, Mrs. White, Miss Renard, Mr. R. Mercer, Mrs. Renard, Mrs. Mann, Mr. Chalk, Mrs. Chalk, Mr. Watson, Mrs. Watson, Mrs. Wells, Mrs. Huxley, Mrs. Trigg, Mrs. King, Mr. Mottley, Miss Arkill, Mr. J. Collins, Mrs. Ibbetson, Mr. West, Mrs. Fleet, Mr. Fleet, Mr. A. Hawkes, Mrs. E. J. Mercer, Mr. Pattenden, Mrs. Lewcock, Mr. King, Mrs. Pattenden, Mr. Brettell, Miss West, Mrs. Hewlett, Mrs. E. Bally, Rev. E. Bayly, Mrs. Hawkes, Mr. Mercer, Miss Salter, Mr. F. Hughes, Mr. Ware, Mrs. Morris, Mr. Cawse, Mrs. Cawse, Mr. Rimmington, Mrs. Lymbery, Mr. Hurst, Mrs. Airey, Mrs. Smith, Mr. Wallers, Mrs. Ware, Mr. Limbry, Mrs. D. Mercer, Mr. J. Hughes, Mrs. Ashwin, Mr. Lewcock, Mr. Morris, Mrs. West, Mr. E. J. Mercer, Mrs. Rimmington, Mr. Airey, Mrs. E. Renard, Mr. Croft, Miss Woodward, Miss Sellers, Mr. Medlicott, Miss Lewcock, Mr. J. Harrop, Mrs. Honeysett, Mr. Burgess, Miss Vane, Mr. Smith, jun., Mr. Butcher, Miss Hogan, Mr. A. Salter, Miss M. Harrop, Miss Norris, Mr. Millard, Mrs. Lane, Mr. A. Beeson, and Miss K. Harrop.

Mr. A. C. Woodward gave the toast of the "Queen and Royal Family" in a neat speech.

Mr. E. Renard, F.S.A., was particularly happy in his speech in proposing the toast of the day, viz., "The health of the bride and bridegroom." He thought the toast only fell to his share because he happened to be the Methusilah of the family. (Laughter.) He had known the bride for many years, and well remembered when she was entrusted to his care on one occasion, and he was afraid of dropping her—(laughter)—but since that day he had learned a great deal as to how to handle infants. (Laughter.) He congratulated the bridegroom upon having obtained so good a wife, for he (Mr. Renard) had known the bride as a good daughter, an affectionate cousin, and one of the most domesticated girls he had ever had the pleasure of meeting in his life. (Applause.) His acquaintance with the bridegroom was of a more recent date, but he trusted that it would continue for many years. (Applause.)

The toast was received with many hearty cheers.

The bridegroom, in responding on behalf of his wife and himself, thanked the company for the unanimous way in which they had cheered the toast proposed in such happy terms. Although he had not had the honour of knowing his wife as many years as Mr. Renard, he could tell him that he was quite cognisant of the many good qualities spoken of by Mr. Renard. (Applause.)

Mr King gave the toast of "The Host and Hostess," and referred in eulogistic terms to the many good qualities of Mr. and Mrs. Mercer. That they had a very large circle of friends was proved by the large number present on that auspicious occasion. Mr. King assured Mr. and Mrs. Mercer that their names were still held in honour in Dulwich, the district in which they formerly lived.

The toast was accorded a most enthusiastic reception.

Mr. Mercer, who on rising to respond was much affected, said he found it difficult to express his thanks to them. He had been through many phases during his lifetime, but that day he had found himself in the most difficult position of his life. He felt overwhelmed by the kindness of his many friends. On behalf of his wife and himself, he could say that although they felt they were losing a most devoted daughter, they were gaining a son who would be worthy of the name. (Applause.) It had been his privilege to be acquainted with the family of the bridegroom for many years, and knowing Mr. Hughes, senior, as he did, he could only say that if the bridegroom would follow in his father's footsteps, he would prove a worthy man. (Applause.)

Mr. Medlicott gave the toast of "The Bridesmaids," and expressed a hope that their position that day would be the stepping-stone to becoming brides. (Laughter.)

Mr. Joseph Hughes responded, in an admirable little speech, on behalf of the bridesmaids.

The toast of "The Ladies", was proposed by Mr. Pattenden, who mentioned the gratifying fact that the bride's grandmother had been able to be present at the ceremony.

The Rev. E. W. Bayly responded in a humorous speech, remarking that his experience taught him that having more sisters than brothers made a man humble and modest. (Laughter.)

Mr. E. J. Mercer gave the toast of "The Visitors," responded to by Mr. Wallers (London) and Mr. Butcher for Birmingham and the provinces.

A very artistic souvenir of the occasion was presented to each guest, being the work of Mr. Renard, F.S.A. A large number of congratulatory telegrams were read from friends of the bride and bridegroom in many distant places. It was stated that illness prevented several friends from being present. The wedding party was photographed by Mr. Pym, of Streatham. The happy pair left in the afternoon, amid showers of rice and confetti, for Folkestone.

In the evening a charming musical party was given, the artistes being Mr. Scharten, Miss Jessie Hotine, Mr. Cawse, Mr. Ware, Mr. Chalk, and Mr. Smith. It was quite late at night when some of the guests departed for Birmingham, having spent a delightful time beneath a hospitable roof and amid most charming surroundings.

The presents were many, and testified to the popularity of the happy pair.

LIST OF PRESENTS.

From the bride's mother, table silver, complete, dozen silver fish-eaters and carvers in case; bride's father, trousseau and house linen; bride's grandmother, Mrs. Trigg, one pair of water-colour pictures; Captain and Mrs. David Mercer, silver teapot; Mr. and Mrs. E. J. Mercer, tea service; Mr. Ernest Mercer, silver table spoons; Master Reginald Mercer, silver egg-stand; Mr. Motley, handsome umbrella; Mrs. Motley; cushion and real lace square; Mr. and Mrs. King, satin eiderdown quilt; Mr. and Mrs. Morris, silver entree dishes; Mr. and Mrs. Euston, silver scent spray; Mr. and Mrs. Lane, silver fruit-dish; Mr. R. Crafter, three pictures (autotype); Mr. and Mrs. West, silver apostle spoons, tongs, and sifter; Mr. and Mrs. Hurst, silver trinity dish; Mr. and Daffarn, silver trinity dish; Miss West, hand-painted paper rack; Mr. and Mrs. Ware, coalport vase; Miss Arkill and Mr. Collins silver bread board and knife; Mr. and Mrs. Fleet, silver fruit-knives and forks; Mr. John Garland, silver fruit-spoons; Mrs. Wells, silver magnifying glass; Mr. and Mrs. Woodward, pedestal and pot; Mrs. Honeysett, silver and ivory bread fork; Mrs. Parker, dozen silver teaspoons; Mrs. Poanett, ivory and silver glove stretcher; Mr. and Mrs. Barclay, cut-glass and silver scent bottle; Miss Hogan, silver teapot; Mrs. Edward Renard, hand-painted plate, hearth-brush, and wooden spoons; Mr. and Mrs. Collins, cheque; Mrs. May, copper fern pot; Miss Sage, embroidered satin satchet; Miss Norris, real lace afternoon cloth; Miss Goldschmidt, Oriental satin table cloth; Mr., Mrs., and Miss Lewcock, cut-glass and silver claret jug; Mr. and Mrs. Hollingsworth, silver-spoon warmer; Miss Sellars, two oil paintings; Mrs. White, brass fern-stand; Miss Salter, real lace sideboard cloth; Miss Tory, silver toast-rack and silver sugar-tongs and sifter in case; Mr. and Mrs. Smith and Mr. E. Smith, silver saltcellars and spoons in case; Friend, bank notes (£100); Mr. and Mrs. Raby, silver crumb-scoop; Miss Collins, silver salt-spoons; Mr. and Mrs. Cawse, silver butter-dish; Mr. and Mrs. Lymbery, silver and ivory crumb-scoop; Miss Woodward, lace d'oyly; Mr. and Mrs. Rimmington, silver sugar-dredger; Mr. and Mrs. Ibbetson, scent-spray; Mr. and Mrs. Pattenden, silver cake-basket; Mr. and Mrs. Bullwinkle, one pair silver saltcellars and spoons in case; Mrs. Weston, table gong; Mr. Millard, fish-covers in case; Friend, bank-note (£50); Mr. and Mrs. Sutton, silver salver, Mr. and Mrs. Airey, handsome mirror; Mr. A. Salter, silver combination breakfast cruet; Mr. Frank Collins, inkstand; Mrs. Tory and Miss H. Tory, silver soup-ladle; Miss E. Renard, embroidered carving-cloth; servants, salad bowl and servers; Mr. and Mrs. Wallers, one pair Dresden plaques; Mr. Mr. and Mrs. Hewlett, porcelain dessert stands; Mr. and Mrs. Costello, silver hot-water jug; Mr. T. Rhys-Jones, jun., silver and glass preserve-jar; Rev. E. W. Bayly, Prayer Book; Mr. and Mrs. T. Bayly, diamond bracelet; Miss Moorcroft, Dresden flower-basket; Miss. F. Gill, Coalport sweet dish; Mrs. Huxley, table linen; Mrs. Innock, silk cushion; Mr. and Mrs. White, fern-stand; Mrs. Renard, furnished rosewood workbox; Mr. Adams, pair pictures; Mr. E. Renard, pair pictures; Mrs. and Mr. F. Watson, silver salts and serviette rings in case; Mr. Butcher, silver fish-carvers; Mr. Joseph Hughes, standard lamp; Mr. Frank Hughes, hall clock; Messrs. H.O. and T. Burgess, Ned Hands, A. O. Harrop, J. A. Harrop, S. S. Medlicott, and A. H. Beeson, brass fender and brasses; Mr. Brettell, oak and silver liquor-stand; Mr. J. H. Hawkes, Doulton vases; Mr. O. H. White, pair oil paintings; Mr. Franklin Davies, sepia drawing; Mr. and Mrs. Ashwin, tea service; employés of Messrs. J. and J. Hughes, timepiece; Mr. and Mrs. Huband, table ware; Miss Laura Wallers, hand-painted panels; Mr. W. Thornton, Gibraltar, one dozen Maltese lace d'oyleys; Mrs. Mann, satin veil-case; Masters Leo and Howard Mercer, Cupid sweet stand, china; and Dr. and Mrs. Gardner, silver sugar-basin; servants at Roslea, glass and silver salad-bowl, &c.

First Years Of Married Life

1900–1908

Wise words from Beatrice's mother following a first major tiff. Jack and Beatrice's only child is born at Eton Lodge and letters to grandparents tell of the great event. Beatrice in London for the funeral of her mother receives letters from home with news of domestic disaster. With the arrival of their telephone in 1907 the collection of letters ends . . .

For Beatrice, her marriage to Jack was a dramatic change in her lifestyle – not only from the point of view that, like most Victorian girls she embarked on marriage with relatively little knowledge of sexual matters, but also because it had meant a move from London to Birmingham. Their first year together, though idyllic in many ways now that they were at last in Eton Lodge together, did have its problems. Beatrice was having to manage a household by herself, with only one servant to help, and had left behind her a host of friends such as Aimée, the Morrises, and of course her beloved large family. The Birmingham theatres and art galleries did not offer such a glamorous choice of plays and exhibitions and she missed her shopping trips 'up west' to Derry and Tom's, and to her dressmaker. Jack, on the other hand, had re-established himself and his position within the family business and had slowly begun to improve relations with his mother. He devoted himself to his masonic duties and still enjoyed nights out occasionally with his Harrop friends. Beatrice missed her mother whose gentle wisdom was admired by all her family. Mrs. Mercer gave occasion for concern to all at 'Roselea' as her bad heart was causing a severe deterioration in her health. Jack and Beatrice visited 'Roselea' for Christmas and eventually spent alternate Christmases with Ernest and Laura.

"Roselea", Streatham Park. Nov 24th 1900

My dearest Chise

      I am indeed grieved to hear of the trouble you are in and know how much you would take it to heart. It is such a cruel eye opener when we discover a flaw in our idols, but then we must remember that we also have flaws, and have to come down from our pinnacle, when those with whom we live find out *our* little failings.

      I was only natural you should feel angry and hurt: that Jack should wish to go to a smoking concert next evening after a Masonic Meeting, and how difficult it would be to put a smiling face upon it: I can picture your feelings, but however hard it is we loose ground by letting our passions run loose.

      I know people with hasty tempers like you and I let our tongues run, and say what we don't mean, and wish we hadn't afterwards, we lessen our influence, do a lot of harm to ourselves.

Smoking concerts were very much the province of men, though smoking itself was indulged in by women, as this photograph of Beatrice shows. (A)

The first ten years of married life is always up hill work, we have to live with a person to know what they are, it applies to both.

Men are by nature, selfish more or less. We lessen our power by getting angry. He wants a change I know, it must be very trying working so many hours: if he imagines other society preferable to yours: I should let him try it. He will soon find out he has lost the substance, in grasping the shadow.

Men are so cruel: they would ask him to a Smoker: when he hesitated they would jeer: and say "he is afraid of his Missus" and to show that he is not he would against his better feelings go, and would be miserable as possible all the time.

The quiet life you lead is so different to what you have been used to and will take time to be accustomed to: a stranger in a strange land: we naturally expect our Husbands to take into consideration. Hitherto he has been good and thoughtful: and when this little storm has blown over he will be the same dear old Jack again and will mount his pinnacle once more. We must give and take.

You do need a change badly, you are unhinged and see through smoked glasses. Go out all you can: if Jack won't take you to the Theatre: do the next best thing go with a Friend, it isn't the same I know but it is better than not going at all and will help you to see things in a better light.

It won't be long to Christmas now.

The Woodmans send lots of kind messages we gave them a good supper which Ellen served beautifully.

I asked them for a late dinner: but they said they would come to tea, so tea it had to be with supper afterwards. She was charmed with "The Doyley". They talk about living at Brighton when Mr. W. retires.

I do hope you are feeling better: you are not equal to have this additional worry. When you want a change you have always a good home to come to and a welcome from those who love you, and appreciate your worth.

With our fondest love and fervent desire that matters may go smoothly in the future. Believe me

Ever Your Loving Mother
& Mercer

Beatrice with her daughter at the age of three months, named Margaret after her own mother. Aimée's letter to the new grandparents following the birth described her as "a fine girl, and as fat as butter, I was simply amazed at her size, fatness and the quantity of dark hair". (M)

Beatrice became pregnant at the age of thirty-one. Aimée, at Eton Lodge for the birth, wrote to the Mercers, "Jack had gone on an errand, and got back five minutes after, so I madly rushed round the Dining Room with joy and excitement". The doctor then "came rushing downstairs, saying, 'John, John, you have a fine girl, all is over'."

"Eton Lodge", Jaffray Road, Gravelly Hill. Nov 27th 1901

My dear Mr & Mrs Mercer.

At last we have been able to send you the good news.

I know how anxious you must all have felt: but please be assured that all is going on quite well.

Beat was a brick, and although she had a very sharp time, says she does not now mind what she went through a bit, and feels amply repaid. She says you need not trouble to send the prize from the sweepstake, as she reckons *she* has drawn the prize.

Our daughter is a champion: of course, you will say that is what they all say; but really both Doctor and Nurse agree that she *is* the finest child they have *ever* seen.

She is so bonny, with a wealth of dark hair, and dark blue eyes. At first sight of her I exclaimed.

"There's Air". (*sic*)

The news of her arrival has been telegraphed all over the country from Walmer to Glasgow. The Doctor arrived about 8 o'clock, and left about 12. It was a very sharp time, but although I felt so sorry for what Beat was going through I cannot say I was nervous, knowing she was in such capable hands. Beat speaks most highly of both Doctor and Nurse. I am sure Nurse will be a great comfort to her, she seems such a good character. We are so pleased our Doctor was able to take the case himself. I am sure we should have been nervous if his deputy had come, although he is highly spoken of.

Beat did not like the idea of Mr. Mercer coming before the event, but now the event has happened the sooner her Pa comes to see her and his youngest granddaughter the more pleased she will be. All is going well at the moment, and we shall let you know daily. Please give our united fondest love to Granny, Aunt, Laura and Ernie, and Reg and accept same for yourselves

Jack & Beatie.

A photograph of Margaret Hughes at the age of thirteen months. Her quantity of dark hair was still a striking feature. (T)

Prince wonders what is going on.

<><><><><>

For the next four years Beatrice was very much pre-occupied with bringing up her daughter. Joe, Jack's brother, had married, Alec and Jennie had two more children and Ernie and Laura, sweethearts for so long, had married also. Sadly, Frank died suddenly in 1903. Jack's mother, now Mrs. Phelps, had moved from Linwood Lodge and, with many of her own problems solved, found it in her heart to make her peace with Jack. Phelps began to mellow in the family's eyes to become an 'aimiable buffoon' with a taste for more than a drink or two, and was frequently banished to a separate bedroom to sober up. Jack meanwhile, continued to work hard and conscientously for the business, which had its ups and downs.

<><><><><>

"Eton Lodge", Jaffray Road, Gravelly Hill. May 8th 1905

My darling wife

You will be glad to know that I arrived here quite safely, after a comfortable journey, and found everything alright.

As I walked up this road, someone shouted "Daddie", and on looking round I found it was Margaret.

Fanny was wheeling her in the chair and they saw me turn into the road.

Jack and Beatrice's daughter as a young girl. She was a highly intelligent and capable girl who 'always won at everything'. Although spoilt in many respects she was brought up to conform very strictly to her mother's exacting demands and wishes. (P)

Mrs. Mercer's bad heart had caused her
almost to collapse outside 'Roselea' one
day where she had clung to the railings,
ignored by passers-by who thought she was
drunk. Mrs. Phelps and Mrs. Mercer,
again friends, took a holiday together in
May of 1905, during which Mrs. Mercer
collapsed and died.

Baby is very well, and after she had kissed me she said "Where is Mama" and I told her in London: she then said "Where is Grandma" and I told her she was a long way off.

I did not know whether she had been told anything of it, but Fanny since tells me that she had told Baby she would not see her Grandma again.

I think of calling in at Hammond's, then going on to Sutton for supper.

Fanny could not get anything from the butcher today.

I will send off the portmanteau tomorrow, and any further things you may want on hearing from you.

You will have a very trying time I know; but take things as calmly as you can, and don't worry on our account, for I think we shall be alright.

Please give my best love to your Pa, Grandma, Aunt, Reggie and all and accept heaps for yourself from

Your affectionate husband

Jack

This pen is more like a pin, Baby has been using it.

❖❖❖❖❖

"Eton Lodge", Jaffray Road. May 1905

Dear Madam

I received your kind letter and thank you very much for P.O. but I am sure you need not have sent me that for you have been very good indeed to me in more ways than one, I feel it is only right, that I should try and do my best which I am doing so. It pleases me very much to think I can do a little in return for you.

You ask me how it was Lizzie came to go I am afraid I cannot explain all but I will tell you what I can. The morning Lizzie went, the master rang the bell when he had finished his breakfast I thought it was for me to look after Baby, so I went in the dining room and then the master ask me why it was, that the porridge had not been cooked these two mornings, I told him I did not know, he then said tell Lizzie I want things done properly while the mistress is away. So I thought it best the master should tell Lizzie himself, I came in the kitchen and told Lizzie she had better go and hear what the master had to say, never thinking what was going to be the end of it. What was said I do not know, only I know Lizzie contradicted and argued with the master so the master told her to take a months notice several times and Lizzie said she should not take notice from him, that you engaged her and she would write to you. The master told her she should do no such thing, of course she said she should, and then the master told her to get her box packed and that she should go at a minute's notice. She said no she wouldn't as she had done nothing to be served like that, but the master was determined she should go, when the master had gone to business, Lizzie cried and howled something awful and said that someone had told him something, for him to turn on her so. She said she didn't care what anyone said there must be some underhanded work going on, that was to say, I had been saying something but I have not said a single thing about her to the master. He did say to me one night that a pie she made was like chewing wood. The master came home to lunch that day

Beatrice had gone back to 'Roselea' for the
funeral of her mother, leaving Jack to cope
alone at Eton Lodge with the help of
Fanny the maid and Lizzie the cook. Jack
had a bad time and the domestic problems
got the better of him. Fanny explained in
her letter how Jack came to fire the cook.

*A snapshot taken in 1914 at the home of
Ernie and Laura in Wallington, Surrey.
Jack looks elegant and assured in his
trilby hat. Beatrice sits in the centre with
Laura on her left. Ernie and Laura's
daughter, also called Margaret, was aged
six at this time. (A)*

The wedding of Jack and Beatrice's daughter, Margaret, to Alfred Millner in 1923. Between the bride and groom is seen Joe, who gave her away, and his wife Polly is next to the bridesmaid on the left of the picture, seated next to Laura. Behind Laura is Jenny. To the right of the groom in the picture is Doris, and standing far right, Ernest. Ernest and Laura's daughter, Margaret, known as Madge, is the bridesmaid seen on the right. Ernest and Laura had organized the wedding for Margeret who had been living on her own at The Chestnuts before her wedding. (M)

and brought Miss Ida with him, he then told Lizzie to be ready to go at 4 o'clock, and that he would wait and pay her what was due to her. Lizzie got herself ready and went just turned 4 o'clock. She came again on Saturday morning to fetch the remains of her clothes, and they came to fetch her box on Monday. She did not go home, she went to her friends down Aston, she said how her mother would go on to her but of course no one will stand cheek. You did not say if you were feeling better. I hope you are quite well by now; Baby is quite well and sends heaps of kisses to you

Yours Truly

Fanny

Ida was enlisted to help out at Eton Lodge following Lizzie's sudden departure. She wrote to Beatrice every day with news of Margaret who was allowed to "change the woollen petticoats for her flannel ones" due to the excessive heat. She also sent news of Jack who had just driven Joe's new car "and of course talked 'motor' for the rest of the evening".

"Eton Lodge", Jaffray Road, Gravelly Hill. May 11th 1905

My darling wife

    I thought you had quite forgotton my birthday, but was pleased to receive your card today and find it was not really so.

A black hat arrived here yesterday morning from the milliner at Herne Hill, and thinking it had been sent here by mistake, I sent it to you at "Roselea" by parcel post. No doubt you would receive it today.

Am glad the cards turned up yesterday, as promised, and hope they were as ordered.

Baby is very well and we are getting on quite alright.

I came home on the car last night with Joe, and we called round at Stonycroft first.

The only other birthday on which Jack had to write to Beatrice to thank her for her birthday greeting was six years earlier in May 1898 – the first letter in this story. This last letter was written in sadder circumstances, at the time of Mrs. Mercer's funeral.

Jack received a letter from Harry Phelps at this time with news of Jack's mother's health and the doctor's instructions, "That she must have extreme rest . . . as she is suffering from a quickened heart from shock", since returning from the fateful holiday with Mrs. Mercer.

My mother does not seem at all well, and she says she has been very poorly indeed since she got back home.

Monday, Tuesday and yesterday I had that nasty low feeling again, and decided yesterday to again become a teetotaller. I have stuck it for two whole days so far, and am certainly feeling better tonight.

I have made a proposal to the Alliance Co for an Assurance, and as I have to go to their physician next Tuesday for examination, I went to Donovan tonight and asked him to give me something to tune me up a bit, which he has done.

I shall come up on Saturday, leaving B'ham at 2.45, due Euston 4.45. I should return Monday 8.18 am from Streatham Common.

Please give my best love to all and especially your Pa and yourself from your *affectionate husband Jack.*

Probate of the Will

of

M John Albert Hughes

Will dated 27th February 1901
Testator died 4th February 1918
Grant dated 23rd Nov. 1918

The probate of Jack's will which he wrote in 1901, just prior to Beatrice becoming pregnant. When he did die, so suddenly, seventeen years later, he left an estate worth £32,650-14s-3d.

Some years later Jack and Beatrice moved house and it is evident that they acquired their first telephone, the number '64 Erdington' proudly printed on the letterhead. With the arrival of the telephone coincided the end of the letters. From these last letters in 1907, we know that Jack, Beatrice and Joe travelled to London to see Ida in a R.A.D.A. performance of As You Like It, after which they stayed for a nostalgic night at 'Roselea'. In 1918 Jack and Beatrice faced a cruel and unexpected blow. Jack was a victim of a pernicious 'flu epidemic and tragically died at the age of only forty-seven. In 1921, Jack's mother died – resplendent in bed in all her jewels, following which Ida re-married. That same year Beatrice died – as the palmist predicted – from a serious heart condition. Margaret, who married in 1923 and had one daughter, preserved these letters in the old shoe box and leather travelling bag in which Jack and Beatrice had kept them.

ACKNOWLEDGEMENTS

The compilers have endeavoured to trace all copyright owners but in the event of any omission apologize to those concerned.

Acknowledgements are due to the following:

*The United Grand Lodge of England
Miss P. Bratton and Mrs. R. Schmidt at the Lambeth Archives, the Minet Library, Clapham, London
The Folkestone Public Library Archives
The Local History Dept., London Borough of Greenwich
The Local Studies Dept., City of Birmingham Reference Library
The British Museum Newspaper Library*

Picture Credits: Anne Power, Jack and Beatrice's grand-daughter, loaned many items. (*A*) Anne Power; (*B*) Editor's collection (*Illustrated London News*); (*C*) Library and Museum of the United Grand Lodge of England; (*D*) Lambeth Archives Dept.; (*E*) Editor's collection; (*F*) City of Birmingham Public Library (CBPL) Local Studies Dept.; (*G*) Neil Barnes (*The Graphic*); (*H*) Peggy Mercer – Ernest and Laura's daughter-in-law; (*I*) CBPL (*The Birmingham Weekly Post*); (*J*) CBPL (*The Birmingham Post*); (*K*) Lambeth Archives Dept. (*The Brixtonian*); (*L*) The Museum of London; (*M*) Doris Monnington; (*N*) The Mary Evans Picture Library; (*O*) CBPL (*The Birmingham Daily Gazette*); (*P*) Bertie Todd – Ida's son-in-law; (*R*) Sarah Griggs; (*S*) Lambeth Archives Dept. (*Kelly's Directory*); (*T*) Peter Hughes – Ida's son; (*U*) Private Collection; (*V*) P. Lawley-Wakelin – grand-daughter of Joseph Hughes, Jack's brother; (*W*) Malcolm Lewis; (*X*) Lambeth Archives Dept., (*The South London Press*).